The Art of Technical Documentation

Second Edition

The Art of Technical Documentation
Second Edition

Katherine Haramundanis

Digital Press
Boston Oxford Johannesburg Melbourne New Delhi Singapore

Butterworth–Heinemann supports the efforts of American Forests and the Global ReLeaf program in its campaign for the betterment of trees, forests, and our environment.

Library of Congress Cataloging-in-Publication Data
Haramundanis, Katherine, 1937–
   The art of technical documentation / Katherine Haramundanis. — 2nd ed.
       p.   cm.
   Includes bibliographical references and index.
   ISBN 1-55558-182-X (alk. paper)
   1. Technical writing.   I. Title.
T11.H28   1998   97-39619
808'.0666 — DC21   CIP

British Library Cataloguing-in-Publication Data
A catalogue record for this book is available from the British Library.

The publisher offers special discounts on bulk orders of this book.
For information, please contact:
Manager of Special Sales
Butterworth–Heinemann
225 Wildwood Ave.
Woburn, MA 01801-2041
Tel: (781) 904-2500
Fax: (781) 904-2620

For information on all Digital Press publications available, contact our World Wide Web home page at: http://www.bh.com/digitalpress

Order number: EY–W908E–DP

10 9 8 7 6 5 4 3 2 1

Printed in the United States of America

Contents

---

3   *Precepts of Technical Documentation* 23

---

7 Tools   177

About This Book

Who Is the Audience of this Book?

If you are a novice or moderately experienced technical writer who works in the computer industry, or are considering such a position, this book is for you. If you work in other technical fields such as the medical, scientific, or engineering industries, you will also find this book useful. Read this book from start to finish; don't skip around. This book will help you become a better writer, and you'll find references and suggestions for further reading when you want to extend your knowledge.

To get the most from this book, you should have the following skills and experience:

- be well trained in writing English
- have had exposure to computer systems
- have taken at least one course or had experience in expository writing, such as doing investigative reporting or writing material based on fact
- have taken introductory courses in computer science and a science such as geology, biology, physics, or astronomy
- understand the logical flow of ideas

What Is the Thesis of this Book?

The thesis of this book is that the practice of technical writing is not the same as that of scientific writing, that it is closer to investigative reporting. When you create technical documentation, you need to gather information rapidly and identify audience; these are tasks the scientist need not perform. Scientists are thoroughly trained in their respective fields and know their audience well — their readership is primarily their colleagues, people trained in their field.

Further, technical documentation is as much an art as a science. Its practices can border on the intuitive, and require creative thought on your part. The work you do requires creativity and problem-solving skills, and you must use your imagination to write technical documentation, though what you write won't be fanciful — it's based on fact. You apply analytical thought to dissect and understand the information you gather, but there are few rules on how to gather information, or how to put that information together in a way that your reader will understand most readily.

When you gather information, you learn to work with your technical resources, and you learn from your reviewers. When you prepare your documents, your appreciation of your readers, what they know, and their reasons for using the documentation come into play. This is where new techniques are still being developed for the technical documentor.

Your art consists of the techniques you master to gather, understand, and distill your technical information; you show your craft in the effectiveness of your documentation and in your proficiency with your language and your tools.

The field of technical documentation is more than just its day-to-day practice. Its industrial practitioners are paralleled by a body of scholars in academia who help to explain and enhance professional practice. I cite academic references in text, at the end of each chapter, and in the Select Bibliography. You'll find short titles and (author, date) in the references in text or at the end of each chapter; the bibliography is alphabetical by author.

What Is the Structure of this Book?

This book is my view of what it takes to produce effective technical documentation. This is not a style guide that deals with all aspects of typography and copyediting, but presents for your use the distilled knowledge of my experience. After preliminaries, you'll find general precepts, then three chapters that address practice and techniques. The last chapter summarizes the issues you should consider when selecting and using software tools. Appendices gather reference material. In more detail:

- Chapter 1 defines technical documentation, and describes quality in technical documentation.
- Chapter 2 describes career paths and documentation management styles.
- Chapter 3 describes the precepts of technical documentation, and provides examples of applying those precepts. It includes sample document structures for several audiences and suggests how information can be developed in parallel with software.
- Chapter 4 describes the writer's workplan, the quality documentation process, planning, technical editing, indexing, practices for gathering information, understanding what you have gathered, and methods for testing documentation.
- Chapter 5 describes the use and preparation of graphics, important components of most technical documentation, and discusses the use of color, particularly for online presentation.
- Chapter 6 describes considerations of information representation, to provide insights on how different representations affect reader perception of your documents.
- Chapter 7 provides an overview of different types of software used in the technical writing world and for desktop publishing. It describes how to select tools

based on your requirements, including text processing and graphic tools, information structures, delivery formats, and file management.

- Appendix A lists and briefly describes professional societies, conferences, and journals relevant to the work you do, along with some internet resources.
- Appendix B contains lists and tables of relevant standards.
- Appendix C provides information about HTML, Hypertext Markup Language, a popular web page markup language.
- Appendix D contains information on SGML, the Standard Generalized Markup Language.
- The book ends with a glossary of terms, an annotated bibliography of books and papers, and an index. Each chapter ends with a list of classroom questions.

When you finish this book, or have at least skimmed it, keep it where you can pick it up while you are working. Use it for sample outlines; try out some of the information-gathering techniques and some of the presentation methods. Take opportunities to broaden your portfolio and extend the types of writing you do. If you write mostly user manuals, try to write a document for a programmer or system manager. If you write lots of highly technical manuals, try your hand at writing some marketing literature. Do some usability testing. Create a web page and get feedback on it. With additional experience, continued extension of the types and styles of writing you do, and an increase in the depth and breadth of your portfolio, you will be well on your way to mastering the art of technical documentation.

A Word about Style and Conventions

The writing style of this book is deliberately gender-neutral. The style favors non-gender-specific words such as author, writer, engineer, programmer, or developer, and avoids words like he or she.

You will also find a few professional tips, indicated by the word "TIP" and an arrow offset at the side of the page.

Acknowledgments

People and libraries have been essential to the success of this document. Those who have helped with technical information include Doug Borsum, Dave Eklund, Jim Flemming, John Francini, Marty Friedman, Richard Hansen, William A. Hunzeker, Susan Hunziker, Dick Howard, John Hughes, Scott Jeffery, Steve Jensen, Rob Limbert, Sarah Masella, Dan Murphy, Chuck Murray, Robert Pariseau, Carol Perlman-Ton, Holly Platnick, Andy Puchrik, Dick Rubinstein, Tara Scanlon, Ben Shneiderman of the University of Maryland, Nicole Yankelovich of Brown University, and Jan Walker of Digital's Cambridge Research Laboratory.

Reviewers who have spent long hours commenting on drafts of this book include John Herrmann, Dick Howard, Tara Scanlon, Dr. Peter Jordan of Tennessee State University, Dr. Robert Krull of Rensselaer Polytechnic Institute, Molly Miller of Ascend Communications, Inc., Linda Pesante of Carnegie Mellon University, Carole Yee of New Mexico Tech, and several anonymous reviewers (you know who you are!). To these dedicated professionals I owe my sincerest thanks.

I am also grateful to my management, Susan Porada, Kathy Richer, Susan Gault, and William Keating, for their support in this project, and to other colleagues who have helped in many ways to provide input.

The libraries of Digital Equipment Corporation, Northeastern University, J. V. Fletcher Library, Westford, Mass., Chelmsford Public Library, the Stevens Memorial Library, North Andover, Mass., and Boston College have been most generous in lending books.

I also acknowledge with sincere thanks the support and wise counsel of my editor, George Horesta.

Acknowledgments to the Second Edition

Leslie Barrett, William Gribbons, Barbara Mirel, Dave Sciuto, Nina Wishbow, Stephanie Rosenbaum, and many others too numerous to mention, have assisted in the creation of this new edition. I have been greatly supported by the librarians and libraries of Digital Equipment Corporation, Boston University, and the University of Massachusetts at Amherst. I also acknowledge with many thanks the advice and support of my editor, Elizabeth McCarthy.

The opinions expressed in this book are mine, and do not necessarily reflect the views of Digital Equipment Corporation. As always, I have benefited from the advice and comments of my technical resources, but any errors in this book remain mine.

Technical Documentation Defined 1

Things are always at their best in their beginning.
Blaise Pascal, *Pascal: The Provincial Letters*, No. 4, 1656/7

When you write technical documentation, you follow a discipline and create specialized types of material. The techniques you learn to use are generic; you will find that you can use these techniques whether you are developing documentation for computer hardware or computer software, and whether you are producing information to be printed or to be used online. You can also use these same techniques when you create technical documentation in other industries and for other business environments.

This chapter describes what technical documentation is and what constitutes technical documentation. Technical documentation is both the work you do when you prepare technical documents and the result of your work. This double meaning for the phrase is like the double meaning of the word "painting:" both the work the artist performs, painting, and the result of the artist's work, the painting.

Books are not going away anytime soon — people appreciate their handy size and their carefully crafted organization. In a book you can bring your reader at a measured pace through the learning process, building on what has gone before. And you can create cross-references for later examination so as not to impede the reader's train of thought. When a reader reads online chunks of information, the reader must develop a mental context with little assistance; sometimes this can impede understanding of new ideas or processes. A well-organized and thoughtfully designed book can greatly assist understanding.

People learn by induction. When you provide multiple, varied exemplars, you assist this learning mode. What readers see at initial contact on a printed page or on a web page is only data. Readers obtain information when they read to solve a problem, answer a question, or begin to assimilate a topic for comprehension. Each individual acquires knowledge only when reaching some level of understanding of the material read.

In the context of this book, *technical documentation* is any written material about computers that is based on fact, organized on scientific and logical principles, and written for a specific purpose. When you write technical documents about computers, the subject you write about has a technical nature and you write with a specific purpose. The scientific and logical principles you follow are:

- To substantiate, or be able to substantiate, the statements you write
- To develop your ideas logically

This is a narrower definition than that of technical writing, whose definition is still developing. Some suggest, for example, that technical writing is writing for a purpose, while others suggest that it is a language a social group has agreed is useful.

All technical documentation is nonfiction (though sometimes you may feel you are writing fiction!), and all technical documentation has technical content — whether the purpose of the piece is reportage, instruction, or persuasion.

According to *Webster's Ninth New Collegiate Dictionary,* the term nonfiction appeared only in 1909. Technical documentation is even newer. Newspaper articles, magazine articles, and biographies, for example, being based on fact, are all nonfiction, but such literature is not technical documentation. However, a newspaper article can be technical documentation if the article describes a technical subject related to computers, and if the writer handles the subject without exaggeration or gross inaccuracy.

In some engineering organizations, "documentation" includes the parts lists for a product, the engineering drawings, or the specifications prepared by engineers, but you won't usually work on this type of document, except perhaps as a technical editor. These should properly be called "engineering documentation." This book primarily addresses the writer creating original technical documents rather than the editor of documents written by someone else. However, sections of Chapter 3 provide details of how to edit your own documents or documents of your peers.

Types of Technical Documents

There are three types of technical documentation: marketing materials, materials that report, and instructional materials.

Marketing or sales pieces are intended to convince or persuade; pieces that report state the facts without a persuasive or instructional slant; and instructional pieces can both instruct and train. Pieces that instruct include traditional documents that describe a product for the user. Sometimes you may have opportunities to provide materials for use in presentations.

Table 1.1 shows the materials you may write in these three categories. This book primarily addresses writing instructional materials in the computer industry.

Table 1.1
Technical Documentation Types

Marketing	Reporting	Instructing
brochure	magazine article	customer manual
case study	newspaper article	user manual
sales pamphlet	journal article	instruction manual
press release	internal publication	site preparation manual
product handbook	technical paper	installation manual
product catalog	progress report	owner's manual
marketing script	internal report	reference manual
marketing talk	annual report	maintenance manual
sales presentation	blueprint	system manager's manual
advertising copy	web site	administrator's manual
technical summary		operator's manual
product brief		technical description
white paper		functional specification
"mock" paper		user interface specification
testimonial		glossary
data sheet		training manual
application guide		quick-start guide
online demonstration		presentations
		course materials
		online tutorial
		online procedure
		wizard text
		interactive procedure or process

Now that you have a view of what technical documentation is, you need a perspective of what makes high quality in technical documentation. This is the subject of the next section.

Quality in Technical Documentation

High-quality technical documentation is:

- Accurate
- Complete
- Usable
- Clearly written
- Readable

- Logically presented
- Concise
- Written with appropriate language
- Grammatical
- Appropriate in content and scope
- Presented in an appealing package

Accuracy

An accurate document contains neither errors of fact nor misstatements that will confuse the reader. For example, when you write that to perform a task the user should press the E key, and the user really needs to press the CONTROL and E keys simultaneously, you make an error. Or you might omit a step in a procedure or add an extra space in a command line. You can commit these errors if you write your document hurriedly or don't become familiar with your product. You should also verify, or have someone else verify, each procedure you write.

TIP ➤   *Take the time to verify your facts.*

A good way to verify a procedure is to draw a flowchart or a Nassi-Shneiderman diagram (see Chapter 4) of the procedure. This can often show missing steps or steps that lead nowhere. Another effective way to verify a procedure is to have someone who does not know the procedure follow your written text and perform the procedure. The tester can mark up your written text, or you can watch the tester follow the procedure and note any difficulties the tester has. (For more on these techniques, see Chapter 4.)

Completeness

A complete document does not leave out something that is important to the reader. For example, if you write a reference manual, be sure that it contains all the commands or statements of the product.

If you write a procedure, be sure there are no missing steps. Or if you write a manual to describe the error messages the user can see on a system, make sure it contains all the error messages. If you leave even one out, and the user sees that one on the system, confidence in the completeness and accuracy of your documentation will be eroded. So check your document carefully to be sure you have found and included all possible error messages. Your technical resources must help with this task by providing you with a complete list of error messages, but you are the one who must verify the completeness of your document.

Usability

A usable document is one your reader can use easily — it is not too bulky or designed in such a way that your reader must work extra hard to find the information. Usability applies both to printed books and online texts. The organization of your information is important too. If you don't organize your information so that your reader can grasp the information quickly, you will only frustrate your reader. Your reviewers can help you find out if your document or online text is usable (more on these topics in Chapter 4).

Usability tests help you determine if you have created a usable document and show you how to correct faults in documents that are less than usable. Usability tests also help you analyze the effectiveness of the information you provide.

When people began to write technical documentation, they practiced their art intuitively — the work was essentially a craft. As we have gained more experience, we have learned more about the effectiveness of technical communication and have developed analytical methods to examine and test documents. Usability tests, properly applied, can be extremely effective. If you conduct such tests and modify your information accordingly, you will find that your documents and information packages become more effective.

You can conduct your own usability tests — you don't need an elaborate laboratory setup to do this testing (more on this in Chapter 4).

Clarity

Write the text in your document clearly. Follow the rules of good writing, and trust your reviewers to help you find those muddy passages or that flawed logic. Even a reviewer who just puts a question mark in the margin of your draft helps you improve the clarity of your document. If that reviewer doesn't understand what you wrote, others won't either. Take the opportunity to discuss the information in the confusing paragraph or sentence with your reviewer. You will very likely find there is another way to present the information that is more clear.

The prize for ambiguity in writing belongs to the order issued by British headquarters at the battle of Balaclava (1854): "to advance rapidly to the front and try to prevent the enemy carrying away the guns." The intent of the order was for the Light Brigade cavalry unit to retake guns that had just been captured by the enemy; the result of the ambiguous order was that the Light Brigade charged an entrenched enemy position in the opposite direction and was slaughtered.

Most of what you write won't have such dire consequences, but if, for example, you are describing a software application that controls a nuclear power station, you might find that what you write is a critical piece of documentation. Consider in any text adding graphics to illuminate what you have written. While it is not always true that "a picture is worth a thousand words," there are many times when a graphic or illustration can greatly help clarify a concept or a procedure.

So when you are writing technical documentation, be aware of the ambiguity of what you write, and examine your work to eliminate ambiguity wherever possible.

Readability

Your text and document must be readable. What does this mean? If your document is readable, your reader will understand it. For example, if you are writing for experienced programmers, you can expect they will be familiar with the technical terms of the trade. But if you are writing for novices, you need to explain all your terms and be particularly careful in consistent use of those terms. Otherwise you will confuse your readers. Readers don't expect synonyms in technical documentation; in fact, they will be confused by an alternative word and may wonder if you are introducing a new concept.

If you like, you can use a readability test software program to help you determine if your prose is written at the level of education expected of your reader. Readability is not the same as legibility. You'll find more about readability in Chapters 6 and 7.

Logical Progression

Your text must flow in a logical progression, from simple to more complex or from start to finish of a procedure. To some extent, writing logically is part of writing clearly, but logical progression should be evident in your organization of information and in how you approach your subject. Clear logical presentation assists learnability, an attribute of high quality technical materials.

Conciseness

Avoid verbiage and keep your sentences and words as short as possible. Learn to discard ruthlessly words that add no information to your text. For example, avoid phrases such as "in order to" ("to" does the job). You can find these extraneous words by actively reading what you have written. Also read what you have written after an interval — some read their words aloud. Always use a short word rather than a long one if the two words have the same meaning. For example, don't use "utilize" when "use" will do. Many style books contain lists of such short substitutes for long and pompous words and phrases.

When you must get information across instantly, use the *one-page display*: distill critical information to a single page. You will need to put a lot of thought into a one-page summary of anything complex, but such a piece can be extremely effective. You will often need to use a diagram or a table to compress information onto a single page. Command lists, balance sheets, and reading paths are examples of one-page representations of critical information. For an example of a one-page display, see Figure 4.5.

Appropriateness of Language

Establish the language that is appropriate for your intended reader. When you write a sales brochure, for example, you have perhaps twenty seconds to catch the reader's interest: your text must be brief. So using the right words and the ideal turn of phrase is critical. The shorter your piece, the more important each word it contains. A sales piece will use at least one of the Great Attractors of technical documentation (for more on the Great Attractors, see Chapter 6).

Most technical documentation is written in a rather formal style. For example, when you write a computer manual, you will avoid slang and contractions. This book, although about technical documentation, is less formal than much technical documentation — it is not a computer manual, so I take some liberties with my writing style.

A good way to find out what language style is best for a specific piece is to read other pieces written for the same reader. That helps make you familiar with the terminology and phraseology of the subject about which you will write. Of course, if you are developing a piece for a wholly new readership, you have to rely on yourself and your reviewers to ensure that you use the right mix of words, tone, and phrases. You may be able to examine competitive literature for ideas about appropriate writing style.

You will find examples of several writing styles in this book.

Grammaticality

Be sure all your sentences and phrases are grammatical. Readers will give up if you make too many grammatical errors. These errors include errors in spelling and punctuation as well as errors in grammatical form.

For example, the sentence "The motor shut down when you press the disable key" is ungrammatical because the subject ("motor") and the verb ("shut") are not in agreement. (The verb should be "shuts.") Ask a copy editor or literary editor, or perhaps a writing peer, to review your work. Their constructive criticism can be invaluable in helping you find and correct such errors. Spell-checking software can find some spelling errors, but it won't warn you about grammatical errors. If you are not sure about your grammar, enlist the aid of another writer or an editor, or consult a grammar book. (You will find the names of some good grammar books at the end of Chapter 3.)

Appropriateness of Content and Scope

Your piece must have appropriate content and scope. For example, there is no point writing a piece for the novice that contains all the details only an expert could want to know, and there is no point writing a step-by-step user manual for an expert who will find the progression of thought and exposition much too slow.

You can verify your content and scope by checking your table of contents against the norms for your readers, by contact with your readers or potential readers, and from your technical resources.

Appeal of Package

The excellent book or online document you have written won't be read if the packaging that presents it to the reader is awkward, messy, or hard to use. If possible, work with those who guide the printing or online distribution process to ensure that your document resides in an attractive package when it reaches your customer.

Part of packaging for printed books is binding, which is discussed in Chapter 6. Consider the convenience of your reader, the lifetime of your book, and how frequently you will need to update your book when you think about packaging.

Further Reading

You can explore the quality elements of technical documentation by reading *The Elements of Style,* third edition (Strunk and White, 1979) and a good style guide (you will find several listed at the end of Chapter 3). You can also gain an appreciation for a variety of styles in English prose by reading *The Reader over Your Shoulder* (Graves and Hodge, 1964) or *Language in Action* or *Language in Thought and Action* (Hayakawa, 1941, 1978).

For More Ideas

Some popular books and articles on scientific or technical subjects can also help you understand the subtle elements of high-quality writing you can use in your work. Examples include *The New Physics* (Taylor, 1972), articles in *Science News* and *Scientific American,* and the works of Martin Gardner. *Popular Mechanics* is another good source for clearly written technical articles.

Exercises

1. List five of the 11 considerations that define high quality in technical documentation.

2. What is readablity?

3. What can you do to ensure that your document is readable?

4. How can you determine if your document is usable?

5. Name three kinds of marketing materials.

6. Name three types of instructional materials.

7. How do you ensure that the information you create is accurate?

8. What are the three types of technical informational materials?

9. What is the difference between data, information, and knowledge?

A scribe whose hand moves as fast as the mouth, that's a scribe for you!
Sumerian proverb, c. 2400 B.C., translated by Edmund Gordon, cited by S. N. Kramer in *The Sumerians.*

To give you an idea of what technical writers and information developers do, these next paragraphs provide scenes of the kind of day many writers have. The names and projects are purely fictitious.

Larry, the Documentation Project Leader

Larry Leader has been a writer at X Corporation for eight years. In that time, he has worked on four different software products and is now documentation project leader for the Xproduct, a software system that runs with the ABC operating system. Larry's job as project leader is to coordinate the work of the other writers, ensure that they keep up with software changes, and be a resource to them.

Larry starts his day at 8:05 A.M. when he drives into the large X facility along Route 495 in Littleton, Massachusetts. His well-lit office on the third floor contains color-coordinated office furniture, and a PC (personal computer). His neighbors include developers working on the Xproduct software as well as other writers working on the project.

Larry sits down and taps the mouse on his PC; the screen comes to life, displaying a password window. After entering his password, he opens a window to read his mail and then opens another to make changes (edits) to a document he needs for the writing team meeting he will run, scheduled for ten o'clock.

By 9:55 Larry has completed his strategy document and printed ten copies for his meeting. He picks up his project notebook and walks down the aisle to the conference room he has reserved. A writer is there already, and they chat amiably as the other writers enter the room in twos and threes.

Larry writes his agenda for the meeting on the whiteboard: current status of Version 1.0, plans for Version 1.1, documentation strategy for Version 1.1, and assignments. He ends his list with "other" to encourage discussion of topics not covered previously. By 10:05 he starts his meeting.

Jamie Junior, a novice writer who has been on the project for about eight months and who is new to X, asks when she needs to give her last book, the installer's guide, to production, the group that will prepare final copy. Because the software was not done when expected, the final software date has been delayed by two weeks. Jamie asks if she should keep her book open for the two-week period. After some discussion, and after hearing from several other writers on the project, Larry advises her to complete her document as planned but to check with him when she plans to hand her files to production.

Annie Able, writer of the programmer's reference manual and its online equivalent, also asks about the changed date. Will it affect her book? After more discussion, Annie agrees to complete her book on the date planned.

Larry passes out the new version of the documentation strategy, points out the changes he has made, and suggests tentative writing assignments. Jamie will update three small documents for the next version and agrees to write the Release Notes. This is a specially challenging assignment because she must work very closely with development during the last few weeks of the project and keep up with a steady stream of changes during field test.

Annie agrees to maintain the programmer's manual and to create a new reference card. The other writers agree to their assignments of administrator's manual, user's manual, help text, and troubleshooting manual. Larry assigns the installation guide to himself, in addition to a second book, the error message manual.

Larry concludes his meeting and returns to his office, where he makes his final edits to the documentation strategy and copies the completed file to the public area on the network system. (The public area contains files that others in the company can copy and print at their local sites by accessing the files over a network.)

He then sends electronic mail to the writers, the development team, the product manager, the customer services people, and those who have expressed an interest in seeing the documentation strategy, informing them that the strategy is available; he asks them to return comments within two weeks.

After lunch, Larry attends a development meeting. The room is already nearly full with developers, qualification engineers, testing people, and writers. Desultory discussions about equipment issues cease when the development project leader arrives, carrying a CD-ROM. He holds it up and asks: "I have this morning's software version here; is there any reason I should not make it available to our field test sites?"

This question prompts a lively discussion, with comments, questions, and sometimes complaints from both developers and testers. "There's too little time given to full testing," someone states. Yet there is agreement that they cannot test forever — somehow they must reach the moment when they can ship a reliable, tested product. Annie Able expresses a concern about the magnitude of the changes — they seem large. One command qualifier, for example, is totally new for this version of the software. Two developers agree to help her verify how the qualifier has changed the system response so she can change the manual that day.

The meeting concludes at 3:35. As Larry returns to his office, a developer stops by to ask when the Release Notes will be done. Someone from the training group arrives to ask for fifteen copies of the manuals for a training course to be given the following week. Larry tells her about the public area, where she can get a copy of any book at any time.

Larry gets several telephone calls, and more electronic mail arrives. Dealing with these interruptions occupies him until the end of the day.

By 5:15 Larry logs off his system for the day and leaves the building; the parking lot is still more than half full. At 8:30 P.M. Larry dials into his system from home to answer some mail he did not have time to answer at his office; by 9:15 he completes his work for the day, logging off the system one final time.

Jamie, a Junior Writer

Jamie Junior, less than a year with the company, is enthusiastic about her position with X. Her first job was to update the installation manual for the software, which had been written by another writer. She arrives at her cubicle at 7:30 A.M., greeting two nearby developers who have been in since midnight to use machines in the lab. She starts her system, checks her mail, and begins to edit a section of her manual. A couple of system prompts have changed, and she wants to improve a procedure that a couple of her reviewers found difficult to understand. The reviewers' comments helped her see that some steps in the procedure were not clear.

Soon the project consulting engineer stops by to ask her to come around to his office at nine to discuss his review comments. Before she can leave for this conference, the development project leader drops in to discuss how to get his last minute changes to her. By the time they have concluded their discussion, she needs to get ready to meet with the consulting engineer.

Gathering up her notebook and a clean draft of her manual, Jamie finds the consulting engineer in his office. They find a small conference room and go through his comments. He has made marks on nearly every page and for each mark provides a long, verbal explanation. Jamie takes notes and asks questions to clarify his points. Sometimes he draws diagrams on the board, sometimes he goes over completely new information, and occasionally he mentions information that belongs in another book in the set. (Jamie's book is only one of several books the customer receives with the product.) They conclude their discussion at 9:55 so Jamie can go to the documentation project meeting.

After the documentation meeting and a light lunch, she returns to her office at 12:50 and begins to rework her manual based on the morning's discussion. When she finds she cannot explain a new concept or procedure clearly, she seeks out the consulting engineer, but discovers he is in an all-afternoon meeting. She finds the development project leader, who clarifies several points for her. "You mean you have to put the tape in first, then put it in a second time?" she asks.

"Yes, that's the way we need to do it for now," he explains. "But we're fixing that. When we've changed the software, once will be enough."

Somewhat frustrated by this and similar exchanges, she returns to her cubicle and makes a note of the current status of the procedure and the probable changes. At four she goes to meet with the illustrator who is creating the diagrams she needs in her installation guide. They discuss the last-minute changes that have come up, and the illustrator agrees to have new drawings done electronically by the following Monday, when Jamie will need them for her final draft review. At 4:50 Jamie leaves the building after rather a trying day.

Example of a Project Team

Marta, the Documentation Supervisor

Marta Manager has been with the company almost ten years, after five years with another computer company. She was a writer and project leader before moving into management. Now she staffs projects and guides the writers who work on the projects that her group supports. She arrives at her office at 8:20 A.M. and answers electronic mail and phone messages until it is time to attend a morning project meeting. A writer stops by to ask about taking a course in C programming as she is leaving for the meeting. At the conference room, she notes the new faces in the project team. The only people she knows are the development supervisor and a development project leader.

The meeting opens with introductions, and Marta learns the names and functions of the people sitting around the spacious table: Mary is the product manager, who works closely with customers and the sales and sales support groups; Hank represents the service group who will support the product in the field; Terence is the hardware engineer who helped create the hardware part of the product; and Simon is the training contact. Arlene, the development project leader, mentions that the manufacturing person, Darlene, and the field test coordinator, Joan, could not be present for this meeting. After introductions, Arlene launches immediately into product scope and proposed schedule. Team members then provide status of plans and deliverables for the project.

They conclude the meeting at 11:25, and Arlene says that minutes will be sent to everyone in the next few days.

Returning to her office, Marta finds more electronic mail messages on her screen and two drafts of manuals on her chair. On her way to lunch, she takes a manual she had reviewed at home the previous evening to the writer. After a quick lunch, she answers her critical mail and then starts to draft a report on a customer visit from notes she made during the trip.

A few moments later, Arlene drops in to ask about documentation plans and requirements. "This seems like a product for the system manager," she says, and Marta agrees. "If that's the case, then we should try to do a system management documentation kit and online help," she suggests. Arlene responds, "We're not planning online help — there's no time in the schedule." "That doesn't sound like the right reason not to do it, when customers expect it nowadays," Marta protests. "It will mean more documentation, you realize," she continues. Arlene grins and says, "Maybe it's easier to do it that way."

Marta promises a rough estimate of the number of writers needed to do this work for the following week. She then returns to her report. A writer stops by to ask about taking a seminar. She describes the content and why it will be valuable to her, and Marta agrees that she can attend.

A little while later, Jamie, who reports to Marta, arrives, and they review the status of her project. Jamie describes where the development team is in implementing the software and getting to field test. She is anxious about her role on the project. The software is complex, and she is the sole author of the manual that describes the system installation. She wrote a fine plan for the document and an excellent outline, but now cannot get all the information she needs from the developers about software details. What does this command do? When should the user follow that procedure? The current draft is also weak on the basic concepts of the software.

As they discuss the problems Jamie is having, Marta suggests that it may be time for a documentation review meeting. The meeting will give Jamie the chance to obtain direct feedback from the developers as a group. Conflicting review comments can be resolved, and she can ask questions about the basic concepts to get views from several people. Marta recommends that Jamie add as many illustrations as possible to the draft she produces for the meeting, and they decide on a meeting date.

When Jamie has gone, Marta completes the draft of her report. She concludes her day in the office by updating her slides for a presentation she is scheduled to give the following morning.

By 6:05 P.M. she leaves her office, carrying her project notebook and transparencies for the following morning, and a draft manual to review.

Consuela, a Consulting Writer

The time is 10 P.M. The office on the second floor is dark. Suddenly the process lamp on the printer in the corner lights up and the printer starts to print pages. Consuela is printing her document that is due the next morning. When the printer has done its work, it shuts down. The draft remains in the printer until it is picked up the following morning at eight.

Consuela Consultant has worked as a writer for many years, often in a consulting capacity with different corporations. She recently developed several technical brochures for the company and has now written a specialty handbook for marketing a new product. While familiar with several authoring tools such as Microsoft Word and WordPerfect, she has agreed to use locally available tools to create copy for the marketing group. Once she has created her copy and it has been reviewed by the technical experts, someone else will take over preparing the final pages in both a printed brochure and as part of a web site.

When she arrives at the facility at ten the following morning, she goes directly to the cubicle of the contracting office where she had queued her file to print the night before. The contracting staff have already looked over her draft and discuss with her when she should return and any changes they see needed eventually. They agree on a date three weeks later, to give time for the draft to be circulated and reviewed. She offers to run a meeting where reviewers will get together to discuss the draft, view the online materials, and immediately resolve differences and conflicts. By 11:30 she leaves the building, off on another assignment at another company.

Career Opportunities

From the preceding fictitious examples, you can see that writers perform many tasks and are often full members of development teams. As a writer, your focus is different from the focus of your developers, who concentrate on designing and writing software. As a member of the development team you provide perspective and insight that help improve use of your product. You are the advocate for the user, customer, and reader.

Some writers specialize in scientific or medical writing; they follow the same basic precepts as the writer in the computing environment but have different background knowledge from that of the writer of computer documentation. They have training or experience in an area of science such as biology or physics, or in the medical field, and within these fields may specialize even more, for example in genetics.

Writers also often work with other specialists such as course developers and instructional designers who create courses and training on technical subjects, marketing writers who create brochures and other marketing or sales materials, and usability specialists who test the usability of products.

Career Growth in Technical Documentation

You may arrive at your new workplace armed with a degree in technical or professional writing, or you may be making a transition from another related field such as programming or science. Perhaps you studied humanities and then became interested in computers.

When you start on the first rung of a career in technical documentation, you can expect to work with other writers and perform fairly simple tasks. In some companies, you will write data sheets or information sheets. Sometimes you will update a document that has been written by another writer. When you have more writing tasks and experience behind you, you will begin to write your own documents — planning them from the beginning, creating drafts, working with your technical resources, fielding comments from your reviewers, and some-times negotiating with your technical resources to obtain substantive comments on your drafts.

Further along in your career, you will probably manage or coordinate the activities for a multiple-writer project. In some companies, this job is called lead writer or project leader. If you become successful at leading projects of moderate scope and technical complexity, in a corporation that is large enough to require a higher level of supervision, you may move into documentation management.

You may decide to move into documentation or writing management after you reach a plateau in your writing development, perhaps after you have writ-ten many different technical documents on a broad range of subjects.

Take opportunities to broaden the scope of your portfolio by writing mar-keting literature, traditional documentation, and online texts. As you continue to grow in your career, you will increase both the depth and breadth of your experience. To increase your depth, concentrate in a single area and explore all its aspects. For example, for one software product, write for every level of expertise, from novice to highly experienced programmer, system manager, or database administrator. To increase the breadth of your experience, increase the diversity of products you write about and expand the types of documents you write.

At your first job, with all the appropriate credentials, you will probably receive a starting salary in the mid-twenties, perhaps around $30,000 to $35,000 per year. After some years of experience, your salary will grow into the forties or fifties, and if you have been in the field for ten or more years, and have technical skills that are in demand, depending on those skills and market oppor-tunity, you can command a salary in the seventies or more. In a large corpora-tion, you can perhaps find positions that pay more, such as the highest levels of consulting writers and top management posts.

As a writer, information designer, information developer, instructional designer, or course developer you participate in a profession that continues to experience significant growth. Opportunities continue to expand, particularly into new areas and new technical specialties. The work today is different from the work of two decades ago primarily in the use of new tools and the need for sound approaches to new forms of rhetoric that are effective in a new technological envi-ronment, but the fundamentals of the work process have not changed. But new technologies, particularly the extensive user of computer-supported information (hypertext, online help, multimedia) impose new requirements on information deliverables. Organization and thorough indexing are more important than ever with the new technologies.

Documentation Management

Documentation management can mean several things: how the writers in a documentation group are managed, how documents in a corporation are dealt with, and how materials are archived. This section deals with the first two topics.

Managing an Information Development Group

There are five ways authors and course developers creating computer documentation are managed in most U.S. corporations: as a singleton operation, by collecting authors together in a separate group, by integrating writers into the engineering community, by using outside consultants, or by working with another corporation in a partnership. Additionally, the style of management where you work, whether formal or more laid back, depends on the personality or culture of the company where you work and on the company's management and business practices.

The Singleton Operation

In many small corporations, and sometimes in small, specialized divisions of larger companies, you may work in a singleton operation. You will be a lone writer working with a few others, your software or hardware technical expert, perhaps a company salesperson, and maybe even the vice president who takes a personal interest in all aspects of the corporate product.

In this situation, you must do everything: you will need to learn about your products, write about them, and use some text processing tool to create the sheets you send to the printer for copying in quantity. You may do other jobs as well. For some writers, this is an extremely satisfying environment — you do your own documentation management and report to someone who knows the documentation is needed but relies on you to get it done.

The Separate Writing Group

In some corporations, the writers are a separate group and sit in an area of the company that may be part of marketing or perhaps the data entry pool. They may be in a different building from the engineers or programmers. Documentation management is typically by a single manager or supervisor, who sees the writers employed by the company as tools to do specific pieces of work. Often a separate writing group reports to the marketing or sales department, because the writing activity is considered part of the customer support system.

When a document is needed for a product, whether a manual or a data sheet, a request is made directly to the supervisor of the writing pool, who chooses a writer to carry out the assignment. Projects tend to be short, and a writer typically does not get involved in developing product documentation until the product is well under way. In this environment, it is difficult for a writer to help improve the product itself.

You may have your own desk and access to a PC but some writers will have their own equipment at home that they use.

Part of Engineering

In corporations where writers are part of the engineering or product team, they tend to have desks or cubicles within the engineering organization. The philosophy is that writers need to be close to their engineering resources, to talk with them on a daily basis and keep up with changes. The documentation managers or supervisors have offices or cubicles near their writers, but sometimes writers are dispersed over a wide geographical area.

The Partnership

In many corporations, software or hardware is created today in cooperation with external partners, other corporations who supply a significant component of the product. Often this external supplier or partner will provide documentation files to describe their component. Your corporation may be able to use this material as is, without revision, simply adding it to the set of documents you supply to your customers, but frequently you must revise the information to make it meet your corporation's standards (for presentation, use of logos, and so on), or to correct it, if it is too generic to apply to your product, or contains statements that do not apply to your product. If you are faced with a significant amount of material supplied by external partners, you will very likely need, at minimum, a project leader, and a strong technical editor to deal with such documents. Depending on your corporate policies, and the arrangement your corporation has with the partner, you may need to alter the covers and all references to the software or component in the materials you receive, before you can distribute them to customers. This is more editorial than writing work, but is essential to how your product will be received by your customers.

To deal with such material effectively, you must have an agreement in writing from the supplying partner that they will clarify or correct problems with the information they supply, to your satisfaction. Without such an agreement, you can be faced with making major revisions to documents at the last minute, without adequate information.

The Outside Documentation Consultant

If you act as an independent contractor, you obtain assignments from different companies and work on each independently. You will probably travel more than the writer who works for a single company and experience a wider variety of projects. You may restrict your travel to local distances, but depending on your expertise, you may have to travel more extensively. You may have your own hardware and software tools, or you may use the facilities of the company that holds your contract.

The work of the singleton operation, the integrated environment, and the outside consultant tends to be quite unstructured, unlike the work of a separate writing group. If you work in any of these unstructured environments, you will make many of your own decisions, though you will always need to keep someone informed of what you are doing. Depending on your preferences, you may feel uncomfortable because of this lack of structure, or you may thrive on it.

In a more structured environment, you will be given assignments and deadlines, and will need to meet those deadlines. In this environment, deadlines tend to be short, and there is rarely time to plan a document or a documentation set. You may be asked to develop an outline before you begin to write a manual, but for most assignments, an outline won't be expected. Sometimes this can lead to difficulties if the book you write is not what the customer needs.

Managing Documentation Projects

Management of any writing group involves assigning writers and possibly contractors to engineering projects, working with the writers to ensure that project needs are met and books prepared on time, evaluating the work of the writers who report to you, and managing the resources the writers need to do their work — for example, equipment, office space, or training. Sometimes documentation management must negotiate with engineering to ensure that appropriate funds are available to support the requests for documentation. This will depend on the internal organization of the corporation and how it runs its business.

Often a project is managed by a project leader who has responsibility to ensure that documents and online files are delivered on schedule. The project leader has many responsibilities, and will typically attend many meetings and work closely with individual writers to ensure the quality of their work and the scheduling of their deliverables. The project leader must heed the requirements of marketing and engineering yet support the needs of writers to have adequate development, testing and review time. A project leader must refrain from micromanaging every detail yet be close enough to the project to know what is going on. It is a delicate balancing act.

Managing Documents

For any group, a systematic and well organized means of dealing with the mass of material you create is essential. In the ideal system, each author can create all pieces of the documents, tutorials, multimedia presentations, online demos, or any informational materials, directly on the system they use daily. This includes text, graphics, including animation or video, sound files, and so on. Authors can manage their own files while they reside on their own system, but once the project is complete, all files, including all source files, should be archived systematically, using a consistent and uniform system. How to do such archiving could be the subject of an entire book, but at minimum each document and document set should have its files saved together, and clearly labeled. A list of all products and the documents that describe them should be maintained. Electronic archiving systems exist, and many are a great assistance in actually doing the archiving. If you still send camera-ready copy to your printers, you will probably need to retain those pages, and store them so they can easily be found.

At the outset of creating sets of product documentation, you will save yourself a lot of problems if you establish a way to record each product and the documents that support it, and keep such a list up to date. Whether you save your archive on diskettes, on a hard disk, or just as your camera-ready copy, having the archive will greatly assist you when you need to create a new set of product documentation, or update an existing document set. To find tips for authors in dealing with many drafts and types of files, see the section Know Your Tools, in Chapter 3.

This chapter has given you some vignettes of what a career in technical documentation can be like. The next chapters describe techniques that can help you be successful in your career. The computer industry, which employs many writers, instructional designers, course developers, information designers, marketing writers, and usability testers, is still growing. The potential for considerable growth in the career of technical documentation parallels the growth of the industry.

Further Reading

ACM SIGDOC's *Asterisk, The Journal of Technical Writing and Communication* is an excellent source for topics of interest to writers, managers of writers, and teachers of writing. The *Proceedings* of the International Technical Communication Conference (ITCC) are another good source of information on activities in the field. IEEE publishes the *Transactions on Professional Communication* that also contains articles from practitioners in the field. Surveys of salaries for writers in the field are published periodically by the Society for Technical Communication; some include information on documentation management. For suggestions on writing career opportunities, see *English for Careers* (Smith, 1985). "Documentation Project Management" (Haramundanis, 1995) provides definitions and examples of a variety of writing projects, with tools and methods for managing them. *Managing Your Documentation Projects* (Hackos, 1994) provides an excellent overview of documentation management based on many years experience on a broad variety of projects. Unique features include a dependency calculator for estimating time to complete a project, and heuristics to assist in rough estimates such as five hours per page of completed material.

Exercises

1. What is a likely starting salary for an undergraduate with a technical writing degree?
2. What is a documentation team?
3. What is a development team?
4. Do writers create their own graphics?
5. Can writers create or work with material other than text?
6. List examples of items you might include in your portfolio.
7. How can you increase the depth of your experience?
8. What can you do to increase the breadth of your experience?
9. Describe two types of documentation management.

Precepts of Technical Documentation 3

But yet I run before my horse to market.
William Shakespeare, *Richard III,* act 1, scene 1, c. 1594

This chapter describes basic precepts that will become second nature to you, the more technical documentation you create.

You will find that your work is both linear and iterative. As a writer, you must keep in mind the overall process from research and planning to final result, and you must also have the flexibility to deal with reviewer and editor comments, make changes, and proceed through the overall process with a number of iterations. Knowing the overall process helps you focus on your work, while the iterative process helps you improve the material you prepare.

Following certain basic principles can help you ensure that your material is accurate, appropriate, complete, and timely. These include:

- Following a specific work methodology
- Researching and understanding technical concepts
- Interviewing and discussing material with technical experts
- Performing audience or reader analysis
- Designing the complete information set
- Designing courseware or training
- Evaluating and developing appropriate screen or book design
- Organizing your material
- Establishing and adhering to schedule
- Using the forms of writing appropriate to your subject and reader
- Reexamining and testing material
- Performing required editorial tasks

The sections that follow describe these activities in more detail, and Chapter 4 expands on the techniques you can use.

When you write technical documentation, you act as a bridge between the designer of the hardware or software product and the user, typically a customer who obtains the product. As a writer, you create part of this product — the information component. You may present information to the customer in printed or online form, or both.

You cannot take the design of the hardware or software component of the product and map that design into your information component. You must create the design of the structure, tone, and content of your information package, and use your own methods to address your reader. Developing the right information structures, writing with the right tone, and providing the relevant content constitute a large part of your work.

For example, you cannot expect to read a functional or implementation specification and follow the structure of the specification to create a manual. You will have to develop your own information design. You will also find that your design can change in some measure as you progress in the project, so keep in mind that your process in developing an information design is iterative.

When you follow the basic principles and work methodology of technical communication, you can help a documentation project avoid common errors, such as late participation of technical documentors in a project, incorrect assumptions made about your reader, and lack of an iterative process to design, develop, refine, and finalize informational materials.

Work Methodology

Part of your *work methodology* is the development and internalization, through training and experience, of four precepts. The work methodology is a process you learn that gives structure to what you do and how you go about gathering information, finding ways to use that information, and verifying that what you do works. The four precepts, set in rhyme to help you recall them and in the order in which you will use them, are:

- Know your subject
- Know your reader
- Know the rules
- Know your tools

"Know your subject" means that you must be knowledgeable in your subject before you can write about it, although you don't have to be an expert.

"Know your reader" means you must have a fair idea of the reader for whom you are writing.

"Know the rules" means that you need to be experienced in the rhetorical and grammatical aspects of English, including spelling, punctuation, and all other mechanical aspects of writing skill.

"Know your tools" means you must become proficient in the use of the editing and text processing tools you will use to create text and graphics.

When you learn and put into practice each of these precepts, you will always be successful in documenting even the most complex products, and you will provide just the right amount of information in the most effective form to your reader. As a writer, you make many decisions about what to convey to readers and how to convey it; how you present information can significantly affect reader comprehension.

Know Your Subject

Because you must understand your subject before you can write about it, the first precept requires that you do your homework. Knowing the subject gives you the basis for what you write and makes it possible for you to ask relevant questions of your technical resources and understand their responses. Most technical resources won't want to answer your questions if you haven't made an effort to understand the subject.

Sometimes you may have very little time to get to know your subject, but most writers of technical documentation love to learn about new products and new tools and so learn rapidly.

Technical Concepts

Under the precept "know your subject," you must learn the basic concepts of the technical field in which you work. You can only develop accurate and appropriate material if your level of expertise is close to that of your readers. In some cases, you must know more than your projected readers to develop effective materials for them.

If your level of knowledge is too far above that of your readers, you might create material that is incomprehensible to them because you make too many assumptions about what they know. If your level of knowledge is too far below that of your readers, you may make errors of omission, leaving out important concepts or describing concepts insufficiently.

In the computer industry, there are several levels of expertise in both software and hardware concepts and methodologies. You need not be an engineer, programmer, or software developer to write material that is accurate and targeted correctly to your readers, but you must have sufficient knowledge to clearly understand the training level of both the engineer or software developer and of your readers. You must at least understand the basic vocabulary of the field and the general principles of hardware or software operation.

Use of Technical Experts

Much of what you do is dealing with, interviewing, interrogating, and working with experts who are knowledgeable in a specific area. Only by experience will you develop the techniques to learn your subject at the appropriate level of detail, to ask the right questions, and to immediately comprehend the answers given by the experts with whom you work.

You may be readily accepted by the development or engineering community and thus gain quick access to technical experts, or you may face significant frustrations in obtaining the experts' time and attention. Earning the respect of your team peers requires study, dedication, good interpersonal skills, sincere interest in the subject about which you are writing, and respect for those with whom you work.

Writers develop many strategies to obtain information. The most effective writers are generally those who can meet with their technical resources as peers and who can suggest improvements to the hardware or software as well as accept comments and recommendations on the drafts they present to the experts for review.

Sometimes you will have to be creative in finding people who can provide technical information. At other times, you will be flooded with information you must digest before you can produce the needed document. You will find that your technical experts are most receptive when you are consistent about meeting your schedules, meticulous with technical details they provide, and diligent in trying to understand the information they convey. When you and your expert work together as a team to create a document, your reader will always benefit.

Know Your Reader

Under the precept "know your reader," you must identify the readers to whom you are writing, evaluate what they require of the documentation, and determine why they will use the documentation. Audience or reader analysis is an area still undergoing considerable research, and no absolute rules are yet established that enable you to unequivocally identify and define the readers to whom you write.

You can classify readers by three main characteristics:

- Education
- Experience
- Expectations and needs

In the list below, levels within these three characteristics map into specific reader categories. For example, the novice has no computer experience and needs to perform only a few tasks, but the system programmer has both traditional and technical education, significant experience with computers, and stringent requirements for plentiful, accurate information.

As the computer industry changes, product readership also changes, and while the lists below are appropriate today, the increased availability of inexpensive systems and personal computers can sometimes blur these distinctions. For example, with some systems, the user is novice, operator, and system manager all at the same time. If you are documenting this kind of system, you won't have three different readers but only one.

For computer software, typical reader levels (in order of increasing complexity) are:

- Novice
- Experienced user
- Operator (in computer room)
- System manager
- Information systems manager
- Language programmer
- System programmer
- Applications programmer
- Diagnostics programmer
- Software designer
- Software implementor/developer
- Sales representative
- Sales support representative
- Technical service or support representative
- Software consultant
- Database consultant

You may never write documents for all these readers, but you are likely to write for the novice, the experienced user, the system manager or administrator, and the programmer.

In the hardware engineering realm, levels of expertise include:

- Owner
- Technician/board swapper
- Experienced technician
- Hardware engineer
- Mechanical design engineer
- Logic design engineer
- Board layout engineer

- Diagnostics engineer
- Microcode engineer
- Manufacturing engineer

You are most likely to write manuals for the owner and the technician.

Your product and the market where the product is sold help dictate your projected readership. Depending on your work environment, you may have direct access to existing customers or you may work through another person or another group to establish a customer profile. Understanding the customers and what they do with the product is an important aspect of your customer analysis.

If you work in a corporation that creates a specific type of product, for example, a spreadsheet application, the experience of your company with its existing customers and what they expect of the product will be invaluable in understanding your customers. You can use the documentation of your existing products as a model.

If you are working on a wholly new product, with no previous models to follow, first determine approximate reader levels based on the intended market, then refine those estimates by asking potential customers why they would use the product. That will help you decide what must go into the documentation. If there is insufficient time to do this, you must rely on the recommendations of those who understand the business need the product is intended to meet.

The following paragraphs provide guidelines on writing for typical readers. These are restricted to instructional types of technical documentation and don't address promotional literature written for marketing purposes or material written only as reports. You'll find descriptions of reader types first, with information on what kind of material they want. In the next major section of this chapter ("Know the Rules"), you will find sample outlines of books written for these readers.

Writing for the Novice

When you write for the *novice,* develop ideas simply, write in a tutorial fashion, and provide clear instructions. Try not to assume that your readers have any experience with the system. This can be surprisingly difficult to do. Your tone must not intimidate your readers, and even the look of your document should be friendly. Don't write a 500-page book for your novice — this will seem so intimidating that your reader may not even open it. Keep your books for the novice as short and clear as possible. Once a novice has completed your book or tutorial, the next instructional manual won't seem so daunting. By all means encourage your novice readers as much as possible.

Tip ➤ *Try to make no assumptions.*

Tip ➤ *Keep your examples short.*

Provide working examples, but keep them exceptionally short, and be absolutely sure they all work. There is nothing more frustrating to the novice, and more demoralizing, than to use an example from a book and find that it doesn't work. An expert may be able to realize that the example itself was wrong, but a novice won't and may lose a lot of time. Keep your topics short, and be very selective in the topics you cover. Don't try to give too much information. In writing for the novice, "less is more" works best.

Writing for the Experienced User

An experienced user needs less tutorial information for usual tasks and often needs more detail for some common tasks than the novice does. *Experienced users* may want a "getting started" document that brings them quickly up to speed in the concepts and use of a product. Such a document is more common for computer software than for hardware.

Often experienced users will be familiar with a similar product; thus what they need is not a tutorial for a novice but a conceptual and easily used document that can get them usefully working with at least the most prominent features of the software within half a day. A document of this type can be quite a challenge to write.

Tip ➤ *Your examples must work.*

The experienced user always wants working examples, but sometimes it is quite difficult to develop a set of working examples that illustrate the features of the product. Depending on the complexity of the product, you may be able to develop your own examples or you may be able to have good, short examples provided by the programmers or developers who are creating the software product.

When you ask programmers to provide working examples or sample applications, however, be aware that they may not always realize the need to keep examples in documentation short and explanatory. The examples you provide must not only show how the software works but also be short enough to be easily understood. If, for instance, you have a working example that requires 50 pages of software code, it will be much too complicated for you to explain to your readers in any reasonable amount of time, and it will probably take your readers weeks of study to comprehend. So even for a complex product, keep your examples simple.

You can expect your experienced user to understand computer concepts and similar products, but you still need to describe your own product clearly and in logical order. How you structure your document for an experienced user depends somewhat on the product, but in general you will provide introductory or concept information and a "getting started" section, and then go directly into commands and perhaps customizing information. You will rely quite a bit on the knowledge your reader has already.

Writing for the Computer Operator

When you write for an *operator,* you may address readers who are either novices or experienced. If your readers are novices, provide remedial or tutorial information. If they are experienced, provide more detail for specific operator tasks than for novices.

For example, an operator in a computer room may need to know how to run certain applications or system utilities such as a batch process or disk-to-tape backup. Or the operator may need to know how to change paper in several printers or the recovery procedure for when an application fails. You must determine the typical tasks the operator performs to establish the content of any operator document.

Writing for the System Manager/Administrator

A *system manager,* also called a system administrator, requires broad concept information and modifiable task lists and procedures, and can typically use reference information directly, without intermediate, explanatory documents. The system manager has usually received more technical instruction than the operator and may even write procedures the operator carries out.

A document written for the system manager typically contains information on system security, processor operations, disk, tape, printer and terminal management, performance, system accounting, user account setup, and networking. The topics you address depend on the product you are documenting. When you document an operating system such as UNIX, Windows NT, you need to provide information on all such topics that apply to your system. Sometimes you will find ways to combine both hardware and software information in *system documentation.*

Tip ➤   *Try to take the wide view.*

When you write documentation for an application that runs on one or several operating systems, you typically need to describe how to install the product on the operating system and anything special the system manager must do once the product is installed. For example, for a spreadsheet application used by several people who can communicate over a network, you may need to explain how the spreadsheet files can be shared or used together.

Writing for the Information Systems Manager

An *information systems manager* requires a broader view of a system, will be quite familiar with the available reference material, and will often be generating procedures for others. You provide different information for a system manager, a system administrator, a database administrator, and an information systems manager, because the training background for these readers is similar in level but not in specific content.

The database administrator, for example, knows the details of establishing and maintaining a database, working with database users, and so on. The information systems manager knows what the products on the system are, how they are maintained, how they are installed, what the security and backup procedures are, and so on. Thus structure your documentation for technical managers according to the tasks they perform.

Writing for the Programmer

A *programmer,* software developer, or software engineer can use reference information without a great deal of tutorial or explanatory information. All different programmer types, from system programmer to designer, have considerable expertise in a specific area and can use reference material at any level of difficulty. When writing for these readers, provide basic concepts of the product and go directly to the technical information with little preamble.

Tip ➤ *Don't digress when you write for experts.*

For experts, organize commands or utilities in alphabetical order, with no task-oriented procedures, and sometimes prepare documents like encyclopedias, with topics in alphabetical order. What programmers want is technical content directly presented. They won't object to passive voice, for example, but will be very unhappy with any technical errors (for which they will look with an eagle eye!).

For some programmer documentation — for example, computer language documentation — you may write user manuals or reference manuals or perhaps both. A user manual introduces the language concepts and explains how to use the language, how to compile, link, and execute programs in that language, perhaps how to debug programs you have written, and how to perform input and output operations with the language. Depending on the complexity of the language, you may need to create a debugger manual.

A reference manual for most languages contains descriptions of the language elements such as assignment statements or control statements, how to create subprograms or subroutines, components of statements (variables, constants, whatever is appropriate for the language), and syntax for all the statements you can write with the language. You must also cover any special aspects of the language such as recursion, and special characters.

Tip ➤ *Show variants from standards.*

A reference manual must be a complete description of the language. If the language is supported by an ANSI standard, specify somehow (with color or boldface type or shading) those statements in your local variant of the language that are different from the standard. (See Chapter 6 on the effective use of color.) Every computer language has slightly different attributes; your reference documentation must reflect the language you document accurately. If the user can customize the software in any way, you must supply an explanation of how to perform the customization.

For your internal programmers or developers, the ultimate documentation is the software code itself, a type of material you generally won't write, although sometimes you may help to add to or improve comments in software code or to improve error messages. Often the feedback you give to a programmer who has written error messages can be invaluable, because with your understanding of the reader, you are a good advocate for the user. You may supply working programming examples and help debug software under development.

Writing for Other Industries

In industries other than computer hardware and software, similar reader categories apply, though detailed descriptions of these categories are well beyond the scope of this book. In the automobile industry, for example, the novice reader corresponds to the prospective customer; the owner corresponds to the experienced user (someone who already knows how to drive); the owner/repair person corresponds to the computer operator (in terms of functions performed, such as adding windshield washer fluid, battery water, engine oil; changing tires; and perhaps running automated inspection or diagnostic stations); and the shop repair person corresponds to the maintenance programmer, performing the standard shop repair functions (shop repair information usually includes specialized subdivisions for electrical system, fuel system, power train, and so on).

An automobile manufacturer needs information that goes beyond what is required by the customer or shop. During automobile design, information on details of design and technologies is required to develop new concepts that can ultimately be implemented in a component or automobile. Once detailed design is done, implementation begins. This stage in the development process requires additional and different levels of implementation detail — for example, accurate layout of autobody parts and functional components. Table 3.1 compares the computer and automobile industries.

Table 3.1
Readers from Two Industries

Computer Industry	Auto Industry: Deliverable
novice	prospective customer: brochure
experienced user	experienced driver: owner's manual
computer operator	service attendant: owner's manual, folklore
programmer	shop expert: shop repair, maintenance manuals
designer	auto manufacturer: design specifications, engineering drawings, plans, tooling specifications, and so on

Every industry similarly separates information by its areas of expertise.

Literature developed for one reader can be used by another, but to develop the most effective literature, target a fairly narrow readership. With customer software documentation, for example, your target reader for a product that runs on a personal computer can be a novice, a user with some experience, and an experienced user. Sometimes you can combine more than one reader level because the system or application you are writing about makes it easy for you to do so without flooding your novice with too many details. But in general be careful about combining your target readership.

Writing Technical Reports and Marketing Literature

Depending on where you work, you may have opportunities to write internal technical reports, marketing literature, or copy for sales brochures, advertisements, or other promotional documents. Sometimes this is the major work you do. Writing marketing literature can be very demanding because such documentation requires both an understanding of the technical features and benefits of the product and a feel for writing in a sparkling, engaging tone that attracts the reader but does not mislead. If you write a great deal of technical material for the system manager, for example, you may find it quite a challenge to shift gears and write marketing literature.

Your Technical Training

You may need technical training to understand the subject about which you are to write. Your training can be either informal or formal, and the amount of your training makes a difference when you write for different reading levels.

The best time for you to write for the novice, for example, is when you first become acquainted with a system, before you forget your initial questions and frustrations. This may also be true if you are writing a "getting started" document for a complex application such as a database system. However, if you are documenting a complex system, you may need to have quite a lot of experience to be successful in writing a "getting started" or "quick-start" guide.

Once you attain user-level proficiency, you will need additional training to increase your proficiency level to write for the operator, system manager, or programmer. And when you have enough background to write for the experienced programmer, it will be much harder for you to write for the novice. In some situations, on-the-job training suffices, but in others, you must attend classes or seminars, take labs, study documentation, and work with others to gain the next level of skill and knowledge. When you write specialized material for the applications programmer, for example, you must be very familiar with the applications development environment.

At higher levels of expertise, writers often have many years of training and writing experience behind them. Sometimes a programmer-turned-writer may have excellent writing skills and be a key addition to a writing team; at other times, a programmer with an interest in writing may require coaching, training in writing fundamentals, or a good editor to produce high-quality documentation.

There are two separate camps on this question: do you get better documentation if you give technical training to someone who knows how to write or if you give writing training to someone who knows the technical material? My experience is that you can always provide the technical training; a person who creates technical documentation must start in the job knowing how to write. Naturally, there are always exceptions to any rule. Sometimes you find a programmer or engineer who writes beautifully, but this is rare.

The most successful technical writers have both writing skills and technical interests: they love to write and are intensely curious about computers. This combination seems to provide just the right balance in writing, interpersonal skills, and understanding technical details well enough to describe them clearly to others. Writers who lack sufficient interest in technical details may never write for the most demanding readers. As a writer, decide for yourself how much technical training you want.

Know the Rules

The next precept, "know the rules," refers to aspects of your work that are closer to guidelines than to rigid rules. These guidelines relate to:

- Organization
- Terminology
- Style

Organization of Material

An important part of your work is the organization you impose on the information you create. The organization of a document or set of documents must be appropriate for your readers, for the information the document contains, and for how you expect your readers to access the information. Organization is the single most important aspect of information delivery you consider in planning. An organization appropriate for a tutorial, for example, fails for a reference document.

Designing the Complete Information Set

In designing a complete information set that anticipates what is needed at each step in the analysis, design, implementation, deployment, and maintenance phases of product development, take the opportunity to design all aspects of the information, even if there is neither time nor resources to create all components. With a complete information design, you will be able to select the critical ones to create within your budget and resources.

Most software development is both linear and iterative. Some describe this in a spiral form. Development of a typical software product begins with a concept of what the product is to be, for example a spreadsheet program or a network server. Often a product definition begins with requirements analysis, that is, what is required of the product? Or perhaps contextual inquiry sessions at a customer site help to establish how the customer will use the product. Other questions that may be asked during requirements analysis include: How will the product assist customers in their work? Who is the customer? What do they need to do their job, and so on.

With requirements and preliminary product descriptions written down, preliminary user interface design can be started, and some of the sales brochures and marketing literature can be developed. This is also a good moment to create a description that can be placed at the company web site so that salesmen, partners, or others who can view early information about new products can see it.

With the product now being fleshed out, a system designer will develop the high level system design identifying components and their attributes such as user interfaces or other specifics. From this a full system specification will be developed, and implementation, module by module. A test plan will be developed, defining which modules will be tested in what order (unit testing), and then, after integration of each module with the others, full system test will be done. UI (user interface) testing can sometimes be done at the unit test stage, but is frequently only done when the system is undergoing full system test.

As the top level design is done and individual modules are started, it is often possible and desirable to begin any needed user planning and system installation documents. These will be only in preliminary form at this stage, but they can assist in providing the needed information in an appropriately structured format. Planning documents often need worksheets which can also usefully be scoped out at this stage.

Once system testing begins, the main body of informational text can be written. This should include the user manuals, online help for the user, the system manager or system administrator's manual, any reference documents such as commands manuals. This is also the moment to begin supplementary release notes that can be very useful in capturing rapidly changing information during internal and alpha or beta testing.

When the software goes into external or beta testing, it is a good time to develop maintenance information, or put information on a web site for technical support, including technical training such as technical courses. The correspondence of developed information in synchronization with the software development process is shown in the Information Design and Software Development Timeline.

Table 3.2
Information Design and Software Development Timeline

Software Development	Information Development
Requirements analysis	
	Preliminary information set design
Contextual inquiry	
Top-level system design	Sales brochures
	Marketing literature
	Internal web site
User interface design	
System specification	System planning document
	Preliminary installation document
Implementation of modules	User manual
	System manager manual
Unit test	Reference manual
System integration test	Online information
User interface testing	Release notes
Field test or beta testing	Technical support web site
Deployment	Maintenance information

Every project will not use or need all these items, but a complete information set is likely to need most of them.

Organizing Information

In English major organizational devices are:

- Topical
- Temporal
- Alphabetical
- Chunked

Topical and temporal organization can be thought of as hierarchical; when your readers understand the hierarchy you impose on your information, they can deduce where new information is likely to reside. Alphabetical and chunked information is nonhierarchical. When you produce these types of information, you must be particularly careful to provide a conceptual framework to avoid having your readers become lost in the information or frustrated because they are unable to find a piece of information.

In technical documentation, information is usually organized by topic. For example, this book addresses a single general topic, and its chapters each address groups of related topics. A good topical organization leads the reader from introductory material to topics of increasing scope and complexity.

Whether you write a system manager's manual or a programmer's manual, you must identify significant topics for your readers, then develop each to an equivalent level of detail. The significant topics for system managers are the tasks they must learn to manage the hardware and software on the system. The level of detail you provide for adding a new account should be the same as the level of detail you provide for setting up a secure system. For the programmer, keep your discussion of the language statements and attributes the same throughout an entire reference document.

Design for Online

You may need to design online information to:

- Present information using an authoring tool that prepares online information, for example, RoboHelp
- Create a new user interface design

Each of these requires a different approach, different methods, and will achieve different results.

If you are working with a tool such as Microsoft Word that can prepare online information with little change, you won't have much control over the look of your online information. However, knowing what your online information will look like frees you from spending time on the look of the information, and lets you focus on exploiting this information form to develop your content and present it effectively.

With a tool such as Doc-To-Help, for example, that you use to process Microsoft Word files for online presentation, you can include several different heading levels as hypertext links, and you can create pop-ups, for example, for glossary terms. When coded with the Doc-To-Help tool, a glossary term is shown in green to the reader; the reader can click on the green term to obtain a pop-up box that contains the term definition. This feature is of course not available in a printed book. You can also have margin notes in your book converted to pop-ups, or conditionalize text in your printed book that is not to appear in the online form. Learn the attributes of your tool, and develop your writing material accordingly. For example, with Doc-To-Help, any material that starts with a fourth-level head appears online as a procedure box by default.

If you are involved in a project where you can contribute to the user interface design, become current in user interface design. Universities teach such design, and there are many books available that you can use for guidance. UI design is a topic that deservedly should be studied on its own, and a few paragraphs summarizing it cannot do it justice. However, a few basic principles can be useful. See the bibliography for additional resources.

- Screen resolution, about 75 dpi (dots per inch), is far lower than the resolution of the printed page (300 to over 2000 dpi).
- Because of low screen resolution, use san serif fonts. They break up less that serif fonts on screen.
- Use bold and uppercase text sparingly. They are harder to read on screen than normal text.
- Use white space, not ruled lines, to separate information on screen.
- Provide information in screen-size chunks; avoid long bodies of text that run over several screens.
- Type sizes on screen should be 10 to 12 points. Smaller type forces people to finger-read on screen, increases fatigue and errors.
- Select a font with a relatively high x-height and thick line weight, Helvetica, for example, rather than Times Roman. In making this selection, use regular characters, not a bold font.
- Use color carefully. Human visual perception is finely tuned to changes in color, and the human eye can notice amazingly tiny variations. When screen resolution improves, we will be able to exploit these attributes more fully.
- The hierarchy of what is noticed on screen is:
  - Motion — anything that moves or blinks is looked at first
  - Size — larger items are looked at before smaller ones
  - Brightness — a brighter word or object is looked at before a darker one
  - Position — location on screen can be important, just as it is in newspapers and advertising. But most positional research has been based on print media, not on screen displays, so more research is needed in this area. In the English-speaking world where we read from left to right, people typically look at the

top left of the screen first, then scan down the left side of the screen. But on some screens they skip quickly to the right side of the screen. The mix of text and graphics can have a profound impact on reading sequence.

- Color or hue attracts attention if there is only one color on an achromatic background such as a white or gray screen. But many colors on a screen may contribute little to readability, or aid in navigation. There is no standard hierarchy for colors because colors are rarely used consistently within a culture.
- Shapes, except for a few such as triangles and the red hexagon, standardized for traffic and in international airports, are low on the information delivery hierarchy. Use them rarely and only if you have a way to define them for your users.

For more information on colors and their terminology, see Chapter 5, Graphics in Technical Documentation, and the glossary for definitions of terms relating to color.

Tip ➤ *Follow the programmer learning path.*

Organize a computer language manual to follow the order in which a programmer uses the language statements. For example, in a FORTRAN manual, explain the overall structure of the program first, then the first line of the program containing its name, then how to set up language variables, how to work with COMMON, and so on. In a Structured Query Language (SQL) manual, follow a structure suggested by SQL language statements. Let the structure of a program written in the language help you to decide on the structure of such documentation. This is how a programmer will want to learn about the language.

If you write a reference manual for the programmer who already knows the language and needs only to verify the syntax of that language on your system, alphabetical order of statements is the most common and the most useful. For a reference manual that provides language statements, put the statements in alphabetical order. Similarly, if you are documenting an operating system with a large number of commands, such as UNIX, organize the system commands in alphabetical order. With a large system containing more than about forty or fifty commands, also supply more than one way to find the command to do a task — for example, special indexes or cross-reference tables. Just because you have documented a command doesn't mean your readers will remember the command's name.

Tip ➤ *Find a common order for reference books.*

If you write procedures, place the steps in the procedure in the order in which readers perform them, and assign numbers to your steps to indicate their order. This is a temporal organization, which is common in operator manuals, installation manuals, and sometimes in system management manuals, where you describe specific tasks. In hardware, use temporal organization for hardware installation or site preparation books, owner's manuals, and user manuals.

Another method to organize information suitable for the special case, which is not topical, alphabetical, or temporal, is *chunking*, useful for online systems. When you create material as chunks of information, you decompose broad topics into small, useful pieces of information. Menu-driven systems can sometimes be described in no other way. Some document authoring systems, such as Hyperties and the classic Symbolics Concordia writer system, assist the writer in creating this type of documentation.

Tip ➤ *Menu systems are hard to document.*

In chunking you omit transition phrases and supply links or hooks between the chunks. Because you cannot know the order in which your reader will access the information, you cannot provide all the possible transition material, so with this style of writing you leave out any transitional phrases or sentences and make each chunk of information self-contained.

Course Development and Tutorials

When you need to organize material for training or the development of courses, the content will not be significantly different from what is in the corresponding technical documents, but your approach to the material and its presentation will. Courses or training are most effectively presented to students by a person with knowledge of the subject, using slides and handouts and any supplementary, supporting information. Hands-on workshops or demonstrations on a computer system are very helpful to encourage learning. Good training builds carefully from the basics to more complex information, and provides clear road maps to go from one part of the training to the next. For more details on course development methods, see the readings at the end of this chapter and the bibliography.

Format Considerations

Much technical material is created for reference only; it is not intended to be read through from start to finish. When you create such material, keep its reference nature in mind, and clearly distinguish it from tutorial information. Format any reference material for easy reader access, and consider your reader when you design your document.

For example, establish a common format for commands in a commands reference manual and adhere to it throughout. For a language manual, establish a format for syntax and follow it consistently. Use the command or statement as a main head, set in a larger type size than your normal text to aid reader access. Spell out your syntax conventions in the first few pages of your manual, and follow those conventions throughout. It is a good plan to include worked-out examples for each command and statement, but many reference documents do not include this level of detail. If you omit examples from your reference manual, place them in a companion user manual.

Tip ➤ *Use large, bold heads for command formats.*

The Military Standard

The U.S. Department of Defense (DOD) issued a Military Specification Standard (June 4, 1985) that defines the format and content of a variety of specifications. Called MIL-STD-490A, the standard addresses both general specifications and documents for specific types of information.

If you create military specifications that must conform to this standard, you will need to become familiar with the requirements of the standard and how to recognize and use the specialized Data Item Descriptions (DID) described in DOD-STD-2167. Data Item Descriptions include specifications for plans and documents such as a Software Test Plan (DI-MCCR-80014, AMSC No. N3590), a Software User's Manual (DI-MCCR-80019, AMSC No. N3595), an Interface Design Manual (DI-MCCR-80027, AMSC No. N3603), and a Data Base Design Document (DI-MCCR-80028, AMSC No. N3604). For more information on the content and format of these specifications, see the Military Standard, which should be available in a large public library, if not at the company where you work.

Tip ➤ *Use CALS where required.*

Computer-aided Acquisition and Logistic Support (CALS) is a U.S. Department of Defense and industry strategy to move from a paper-intensive system to an automated and integrated computer-based operation. In a world where the technical documentation to describe a jet aircraft weighs more than the plane, and where the amount of paper required to describe a battleship weighs as much as the ship's entire load of ballast, a move from paper to electrons is inevitable.

The primary focus of CALS is improving the integration of systems that support technical information transfer for weapons systems. The goal is to have a system that can include product definitions, engineering drawings, logistic support analysis data, technical manuals, training materials, technical plans and reports, and operational data. Standards are placed between the contractor and the government to ensure that information transfer is accurate and timely, and to minimize the flow of paper.

MIL-M-28001A, developed for CALS, addresses the automated publication of technical manuals. This specification recommends use of standards for

- SGML (Standard Generalized Markup Language), the industry standard for documentation representation
- Graphics
- Data interchange

The development of other technical and data standards is coordinated by the National Institute of Standards and Technology (NIST), which works with the American National Standards Institute (ANSI). The two organizations work together to avoid overlap and use existing standards as much as possible.

If you write CALS-compliant documents using military standards, you will need to become familiar with SGML and use it when you write. Readers of your documents will most likely read them online, not on paper. Consider how you present information and how your readers will use it.

Categories of Technical Documents

The most common types of document are:

- Primers
- User guides, user manuals
- Reference manuals
- Concept or introductory documents
- Quick-start guides

Less common types of documentation include:

- Reference cards
- Wall charts or posters
- Wordless documents

The Primer

A *primer* is tutorial; it begins with simple product concepts, then leads the reader on to more complex concepts and gives a few hands-on examples. For example, a primer for the BASIC language might have the organization shown in Table 3.2.

Table 3.2
Sample Primer Outline

Chapter	Content	Rough Size
	introduction	2 pages
1	the BASIC Language	2 pages
2	functions and function evaluation	10 pages
3	more BASIC	15 pages
4	data processing	20 pages
5	solving equations	20 pages
6	extra exercises	15 pages
	glossary	6 pages
	answers	15 pages

The User Manual

What you place in a *user manual* depends on the product you are documenting. A user guide for an operating system may have the structure shown in Table 3.3.

Table 3.3
Sample User Manual Outline

Chapter	Content	Rough Size
1	system overview	10 pages
2	basics for system users	20 pages
3	description of system tutorials, if any	20 pages
4	using an electronic editor	10 pages
5	using the mail system	10 pages
6	summary of system commands	5 pages
7	information about the file system	10 pages

Include in your user manual information about the documentation that comes with the system, so that once done reading the user manual, readers know what to read next. A *documentation map* or *reading path diagram* that shows in what order to read books in a large set is helpful to your readers. For an example of a documentation map, see Figure 4.5. What you select to put in your user guide depends on the features of the system the first-time user must know, and those things every user must know to use the system.

Tip ➤   ***Create documentation maps for your readers.***

The Application Guide

If you are writing a user guide for an application that runs on some operating system, you may have an organization like the sample application guide outline shown in Table 3.4.

The User Guide

You may write user guides for many hardware or software components. If, for example, you are writing a user guide for a computer terminal, you may follow the organization shown in Table 3.5.

Because every application is different, has a different purpose, and may address different readers, the organization of a user manual must be flexible. Sometimes you need to avoid writing a manual altogether: for example, software that performs short tasks like running a calendar or giving you

Table 3.4
Sample Application Guide Outline

Chapter	Content	Rough Size
1	introduction/concepts	10 pages
2	describe what the application does	10 pages
3	describe special files or features a first-time user needs to know about	5 pages
4	provide a brief summary of frequently used menus or commands	20 pages
5	describe how to perform a task for which the application is intended	20 pages
6	provide a working example the reader can follow to obtain results	10 pages
7	describe other typical tasks and give working examples	10 pages

Table 3.5
Sample Hardware User Guide Outline

Chapter	Content	Rough Size
1	introduction	1 page
2	commonly used terms	1 page
3	controls and indicators	8 pages
4	setup mode	16 pages
5	editing	4 pages
6	self-testing the xyz terminal	2 pages
7	what to do in the event of a problem	4 pages
8	installation, interface information, and specifications	9 pages
9	programmer information	37 pages
10	xyz terminal options	2 pages
Appendices:		
A	ANSI definitions and notation, glossary	3 pages
B	ASCII code chart	1 page
C	fill character requirements	1 page

money at an electronic teller must be self-documenting. The user should never need to use any documentation other than what is seen on the terminal display. Even a reference card should not be needed for these short task applications.

But as an application becomes more complex and performs more complicated tasks, you need to provide more documentation. For example, a user guide for a sort/merge utility could contain the topics shown in Table 3.6.

Table 3.6
Sample Utility Manual Outline

Chapter	Content	Rough Size
	preface/new and changed features	2 pages
1	sort/merge description:	2 pages
	sorting records	5 pages
2	merging files	5 pages
	collating sequence	5 pages
	sort/merge specification file	4 pages
	optimization	8 pages
	summary of commands	4 pages
2	sort/merge usage summary	10 pages
3	sort/merge qualifiers:	1 page
	sequence qualifiers	4 pages
	input file qualifiers	4 pages
	output file qualifiers	5 pages
	specification file qualifiers	5 pages
	index	6 pages

For a database product, your user guide might contain different headings, as shown in Table 3.7.

Some hardware and software products may need programmer manuals. Your computer terminal or system may have a programmer manual that lets you define how your screen displays information or accepts data from a computer, telephone, or modem. A software product may have a programmer manual that describes how to change the software or add new features to your package. The organization for these documents will be similar in intent to other user manuals: describe the product briefly, then provide enough information so the user can perform typical user tasks.

Tip ➤ *Create reference cards.*

Cards, Wall Charts, and Posters

You can create *reference cards* (which are very popular) to summarize information — for example, for menus, commands or setup information, or for language documentation to provide a quick reference to the language syntax. For complex syntax, you may decide to provide wall charts or posters that summarize the syntax at a glance. Syntax posters can be very useful for languages with many statements or for database systems. For a reference card, you can usually place commands or statements in alphabetical order, but sometimes your readers demand organization by task.

Table 3.7
Sample Database User Guide Outline

Chapter	Content	Rough Size
1	an overview of the product	10 pages
2	what does the product require?	2 pages
	application files	5 pages
	sources of data	5 pages
	runtime system	5 pages
3	how to create a database application:	2 pages
	databases	4 pages
	connections to data sources	4 pages
	forms and reports	5 pages
	menus	2 pages
	help and error messages	2 pages
4	features of database applications:	6 pages
	menus	
	forms/reports	
	user assistance messages	
	windows and tasks	
	security features	
	database commands	
	macros	
5	working with a database application:	20 pages
	invoking the database systems	5 pages
	choosing a set of key definitions	2 pages
	running a database application	2 pages
6	using building tools to define an application:	
	building an application file	5 pages
	building the database	10 pages
	building a form/report	2 pages
	testing your application	4 pages
	creating a help message	2 pages
	creating a macro	10 pages
	making future changes	2 pages
7	keypad designs	2 pages
	glossary	10 pages
	index	5 pages

Create wall charts or posters.

A novice benefits from summaries, repetition, illustrations, examples, and succinct definitions of terms, but not from the details that only the more experienced reader will want. Organize reference material for skimming or quick reference with bold heads, horizontal lines, bulleted lists, notes, and tables. A reference manual typically contains introductory information about the product and then goes immediately to the detailed reference information, which is alphabetically arranged.

Concept and Introductory Documents

For a *concept* document, treat your material as though you are writing a primer, leading from the simple to the complex. A concept document might have the organization shown in Table 3.8.

Tip ➤ **In a concept document, develop ideas from simple to complex.**

Table 3.8
Sample Concept Document Outline

Chapter	Content	Rough Size
	preface	3 pages
1	overview	12 pages
2	users and applications	27 pages
3	data management	24 pages
4	hardware	15 pages
5	networks	9 pages
6	services	6 pages
7	future considerations	2 pages
	glossary	7 pages
	index	5 pages

An *introductory* document may have more detail than a concept document. Table 3.9 shows that an introductory document for a programming language might go into quite a lot of detail.

The Quick-Start Guide

A *quick-start guide* brings your readers quickly up to speed on the features and use of a product. Intended for new users of an application, not necessarily novices, it shows how to begin to use the application. A quick-start guide typically contains working examples and leads readers through a set of exercises. Once readers have completed the exercises, they should be well along in understanding what the

Table 3.9
Sample Introductory Language Manual Outline

Chapter	Content	Rough Size
1	introduction and basics	15 pages
2	types and variables	40 pages
3	operators and expressions	14 pages
4	control flow	15 pages
5	functions and complete programs	50 pages
6	independent compilation and data abstraction	22 pages
7	exceptions	16 pages
8	concurrent programming	17 pages
9	the C processor	10 pages
10	a database query example	7 pages
Appendices:		
A	library functions	50 pages
B	C tools	5 pages
C	ANSI standard C	1 page
D	ASCII table	1 page
E	implementation-dependent characteristics	1 page

Table 3.10
Sample Quick-Start Guide Outline

Chapter	Content	Rough Size
1	getting started	5 pages
2	starting to write	10 pages
3	creating lists and tables	15 pages
4	resolving cross-references	5 pages
5	creating a table of contents	5 pages
6	building a book	4 pages
	index	3 pages

product does and how it can be used. A quick-start guide for a text-processing system might contain the topics shown in Table 3.10.

The Documentation Set

When dealing with a *multiple manual documentation set,* you provide cross-referencing and a master index. (A *master index* is a combined alphabetical list of all index entries from all books in the set.) The term "master index" can also mean an index like that in a large encyclopedia, such as the *Encyclopedia Britannica,* that provides extensive cross-referencing for article topics and topics within articles. Such an index is rare in computer documentation; however, it will become more common with increasing use of online methods.

A master index is particularly valuable in a large documentation set, because readers use it to select the book in the set that contains what they seek. In general, software documentation is used much more for reference than for instruction.

The menu-driven system, for example, is very difficult to document using traditional chapter organization because a person using a menu-driven system can navigate through the system by many routes. It is impossible to represent all these routes with a traditional organization. The solution is to document the material in chunks and to ensure that the software provides *context-sensitive help.* With context-sensitive help, when the user encounters a problem and receives an error message on the screen, the user can press a special key, perhaps the PF2 or HELP key, and the software responds with appropriate instructions to correct the problem. With a software system that provides good explanatory messages in response to a user request for help, you won't need a manual to explain recovery procedures; the procedures become part of the software.

This is an area where writers can contribute succinct messages and recovery procedures. If the software system does not offer context-sensitive help, you will have to provide your reader with lots of documentation: explicit procedures, maps of menus, and perhaps mapping of all tasks into tables with quick look-up facilities.

A special style of presenting technical information is *structured documentation,* in which you prepare information displays across the two open pages of your book. One page contains a diagram, the other contains your supporting text. This method has been very successful in hardware maintenance guides, where you show the physical component in your picture and provide the maintenance procedure in your text. The following illustration shows the page layout you use for structured documentation.

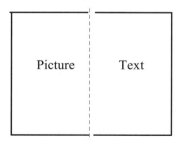

Another style of documentation is *wordless* documentation, a style of developing information that relies on pictures rather than words. Pictures can be used to illustrate procedures — for example, how to install a piece of hardware — but they have serious limitations for detailed instructions and reference information. However, as more graphics capabilities become available, you are sure to find ways to exploit this area further.

Whatever system you use for the overall organization of the information you write, you must also know and follow the usual organization of sentences and paragraphs. Sometimes online systems impose special requirements, for example, requiring you to reorganize a paragraph or section so that information critical to the readers' understanding appears early in the text. Screen displays are much shorter than printed pages, and their use can force changes of paragraph structure to accommodate your readers' needs.

Organizational Elements of Technical Documents

Technical documents must virtually always contain certain organizational elements:

- Title
- Copyright and trademarks
- Table of contents
- Chapters
- Index

On rare occasions — for example, when you prepare a reference card or a syntax poster — you don't need an index or a table of contents.

Optional elements include:

- Abstract
- Glossary
- Lists of illustrations, figures, tables, examples
- Appendices
- Bibliography
- Footnotes
- Notes (explanatory or cautionary)

Your *title* describes in a brief way the content of your document, and since it is a name, it should convey a complete thought. A title is usually a noun phrase, rarely a sentence. Create a title that reflects the subject of your document accurately. For example, the title *Write Right!* is a sentence, but *The Art of Technical Documentation* is not.

The *copyright* specifies who holds the rights to copy the document. When you work for a company, large or small, the copyright of your documents is owned by that company. If you work as a contractor for hire, the company that hires you typically owns the copyright. If you work in a freelance capacity, you may be able to negotiate for some of the copyrights to your work. Books in the public domain, for example, publications of the U.S. Government, are not copyrighted because they were paid for with taxpayer money.

The page that contains the copyright statement typically contains the names of any *trademarks* you have mentioned in your document. Sometimes a long list of trademarks is placed on a separate page. To protect your company against litigation by others, and to protect your company's trademarks, you must state not only what names are trademarked but also which company owns that trademark and whether or not the trademark is registered. For an example of trademark use, see how trademarks are handled in this book.

The *table of contents* shows all the major organizational elements of your document. If you write a book divided into chapters and sections and subsections, your table of contents shows the headings you have supplied for each of these elements.

The *chapters* or paragraphs of your document form the bulk of its informational content.

An *index* provides a way for your readers to access specific topics without having to read the entire document. Based on the number of lines in a document, an index can be from 1 to 15 percent of the document's size. So for a document containing 100 pages, each of 38 lines, or 3800 lines, a reasonable index would contain from 38 to 570 lines. Since an index is usually printed in two columns and set in a smaller type size than the rest of the book, this suggests an index of from 1 to 8 pages. The more technical the material, the larger the index.

An *abstract,* typically placed on the title page of a book-length document and at the beginning of a shorter document, briefly summarizes the document's content. When you write technical documentation, the abstract usually contains a statement about the intended reader — for example, that the manual is written for the system manager or the applications programmer. In a book, a subtitle may substitute for the abstract. The following is a typical abstract for a manual:

ABSTRACT

This manual describes the concepts, commands, and features of the C++ Language-Sensitive Editor for the advanced programmer.

A *glossary* contains definitions of all the salient terms you have used in your document. It should not contain familiar words, but only those used in your document and those not generally known to your readers. For example, in this book my glossary won't contain an entry for "computer" because the word is commonly understood, but you will find an entry for "bitmap" because not many people yet know what this word means.

The *lists of illustrations, figures, tables,* and *examples* you supply are normally placed at the end of the table of contents. They are not necessary for some documents, such as brochures or perhaps some very short tutorials. However, supply them if you have more than four or five entries for such lists. Often your readers will remember a table or diagram rather than the section where you described something; the list will help the readers find the table or diagram again.

Place reference and supplementary material in *appendices.* What you decide to place in an appendix is up to your judgment of how you expect your reader to use your document. Try to design your document so that readers do not need to flip back and forth to understand a piece of information, but don't try to put everything at the front of the book either. You will find that some things, like a list of commands, keypad diagrams, and long lists of details such as hardware addresses, fit best in appendices. Sometimes these will fit well in short tables in the body of your text, but when the tables become too long and get in the way of smooth reading, that is the time to put the lengthy lists at the end of your book.

Tip ➤ ***In design, consider how your reader will use your book.***

You may supply a *bibliography* in some documents to show which materials you used to support your information or to provide your readers with other places to go for information. Often in technical documentation, you supply a list of associated documents in the preface rather than in a separate bibliography. But if you provide a bibliography, it generally belongs at the end of your book. In a primer or tutorial, you can place bibliographies at the end of each chapter. In documentation plans or strategies, you can include an informal list of *sources of information,* which can be less formal than a book bibliography. For example, you may cite internal reports or specifications only by author, title, and date, if appropriate.

A bibliography must use a uniform format, so before embarking on a long bibliography, determine what format you will use and what pieces of information you need for each entry.

Use *footnotes* when you need to provide a short piece of peripheral information important enough to be on the same page as the information it goes with but not important enough to include in the main body of your text. A footnote may explain with a few extra words a concept you describe in your text with broad brush strokes.

You can also use footnotes at the bottom of your pages for cross-reference information or to point your reader to another information source, but this is not a typical use of footnotes in technical documentation. The most common reason to use a footnote in technical documentation is to clarify something or introduce a caveat. This use is very much the "fine print" of hardware or software descriptions.

Use *notes* to warn users not to do something or to tell them what is at risk if a procedure is not followed correctly. A note needs to stand out clearly from the surrounding text, so whatever document processing system you use, you must find ways to make your notes SHOUT at your reader.

You can also use either a *caution* or a *warning,* depending on the severity of the result if the reader ignores the note or the importance of the statements you write. Your company may have conventions regarding the meaning of these elements. For example, a note may simply provide information you need to set off from other text, such as an exception; a caution may tell readers that care and due consideration are indicated; and a warning may indicate that if readers do not heed the warning, physical injury may result. If you need to use a note — and be sparing in the use of these devices — you should ensure that your readers see it first so as to take the right action. Don't describe a procedure and follow it with a note readers needed to read before beginning the procedure. You also need to adhere to ethical standards when supplying these notes; never omit information the customer must know to use the product safely.

Endnotes, notes placed at the end of chapters, are not common in technical documentation.

Tip ➤   ***Use notes sparingly.***

Balance of all elements helps you determine if the organization you have planned for your book is correct. For example, a document with three chapters and one appendix seems reasonably well balanced, but a document with three chapters and ten appendices seems out of balance and should probably be reorganized. You may find that you still need all those appendices, but it is a good plan to take another look at your organization when you find that your appendices hold most of your information. There is no single rule that can cover all cases, and balance is up to your own judgment. When in doubt, ask someone else. You'll probably get some unsolicited opinions from your reviewers.

Tip ➤   ***Scan your table of contents to check organization.***

Your table of contents reflects the organization of your document, so scanning it on its own can help you improve your organization.

Information Structures

Like the data structures of computer science (stacks, tables, ports, linked lists, and queues, for example), you use information structures appropriate to the material you create and to your reader. Just as the data structures of a computer system dictate the algorithm the software developer uses to work with the system, so the information structures you select dictate how your reader will locate and use information.

The traditional information structures of writing are those of the printed book. These structures have evolved over many centuries, and people are familiar with what books are and how to use them. A book typically has major divisions, called parts or chapters, and minor divisions, called sections, subsections, and paragraphs. Finer subdivisions include tables, lists (numbered if order is important), and perhaps illustrations. Whether an illustration is a subdivision or part of the text depends on its nature. Examples are another information structure you will use a lot.

Another type of information structure is the *chunk,* which can be either text or text with an illustration that conveys information on a specific, narrowly defined topic. The chunk is the most common information structure used in hypertext documents. A chunk is sometimes called an information block in the terminology of Information Mapping. With Information Mapping, a group of information blocks together make up an information map.

When you use Information Mapping, you learn to classify information into seven types: procedure, process, structure, concept, principle, fact, or classification. You then use specific ways to present this information to your reader for each of these types: a procedure table, an IF-THEN table, a procedure diagram, a stage table, a WHEN-THEN table, a process diagram, and so on. For more information on these techniques, contact the company that provides this training. Their method is copyrighted, so I cannot describe it in detail.

Information Mapping techniques are particularly useful for task-oriented or procedural information. If you use Information Mapping, you will find that it causes you to look at what you write from a new perspective.

For example, let's say you have been asked to describe how to start your car. You might write the following paragraph:

> When you want to start your car, go to your car, open the door on the driver's side, get into the car and sit behind the wheel. Then check that the gear is set at PARK or, if you are in a car with a manual transmission, press down the clutch with your left foot. Next, put the key in the ignition, and turn the key. The car engine should turn over. To move away from your stopped position, put the car in gear, disengage the brake, if it is on, and then press the accelerator with your right foot.

This is a fairly long paragraph that is better represented with a procedure table as shown in Table 3.11. The next example, Table 3.12, shows an Information Mapping IF-THEN procedure that describes how to edit a file.

Table 3.11
Basic Procedure Table

Step	To Start Your Car
1	Have your car in PARK or depress the clutch.
2	Put your key in the ignition.
3	Turn the key in the ignition.
4	Put the car in gear.
5	Step on the gas.

Table 3.12
IF-THEN Procedure Table

IF You Want To:	THEN	AND
Edit a file	Enter EDT *filename* and press RETURN. Press c RETURN at the * prompt.	Enter text and other elements such as HTML tags.
Stop editing and save your edits	Press CTRL/Z.	Enter ex RETURN at the * prompt.
		Your file has been saved when you see the system $ prompt.

Tip ➤ *Provide easy access to your information structures.*

Supply a way to find each information structure. For example, the table of contents of a document shows where to find major divisions and may show where to find subdivisions including sections, subsections, and perhaps tables, illustrations, and examples. You can also show the reader where to find a small piece of information by effective indexing. And you can help to catch your reader's eye with graphics, icons, and perhaps colors.

In a hypertext document, careful structuring and thorough indexing greatly assist access for your readers. Be careful to avoid too many levels that can frustrate your reader. With many authoring tools, chapter titles and section heads become hypertext links, and chapters become a hierarchy of links that reflect the original organization of the manual. For example, the chapter titles in the quick-start guide, outlined in Table 3.10, Sample Quick Start Guide Outline, would each become a hypertext link when the document is viewed online.

Theorists and those experienced with human factors often decry the process of "dumping books online," suggesting that it is better to rewrite for online. Unfortunately on most projects this would nearly double the cost, so it is rarely done. Reality suggests that with careful use of conditionalized text, technical material can be successfully single sourced for both hardcopy and online deliverables without loss of comprehension on the part of the reader. Single sourcing means only that information is collected in a single file and used, with appropriate procedures, to create both the printed book and online deliverables. Online material in many situations may be the only information available to most users, so there is no conflict with delivering all available information in both the online and the hardcopy information.

The greatest problem with this is that at the present state of technology, online screen resolution is much poorer than the resolution of the printed page. Details can be lost online, characters must be larger on screen, and fewer characters per line or lines per page are visible at a glance. However, online forms can exploit color much more than printed forms, and animation becomes possible, though as yet rarely seen in technical reference materials. The reader skimming hypertext, however, traverses information differently from the reader skimming a book. A person reading a book often checks the table of contents to view chapter titles, and then goes to a likely chapter, checks the index for the piece of information wanted, or drops into the middle of the book and flips back and forth looking for a topic, a table, a diagram, an example, or a heading that appears to address the question. In an online world, the reader is most likely to drill down headings to a likely one, or check entries in the index. But it is more difficult to flip back and forth as in a book, and there is a greater need to rely on short-term memory than when using a book. We have yet to develop fully effective and robust methods for dealing with the online medium.

When working with a software development team to develop online text and error messages that are part of the software, keep the text separate from the software code. The best way to do this is to have the development team prepare the software so that it calls in the online text and error messages from a separate file or files. That way you can edit the separate file without changing the software files. Also, separate text files are helpful if you work in a multinational corporation that expects to translate such text.

Terminology

For skill in the language in which you write (English, for example), you need to understand its basic morphology, grammar, syntax, and orthography, and you should adhere to the technical communication active writing style. The terminology you use to convey technical information must be specific to your subject discipline and industry sector.

As a writer or member of a writing team, you must develop the unique terminology of your subject and find ways to convey the meaning of that terminology. The most common way to do this is to develop a comprehensive *glos-*

sary of terms. When you work with a team of writers, you may also decide to develop a *style sheet.*

Tip ➤   *Compile and use a style sheet.*

You use a style sheet or style guide to ensure consistency of use and a glossary to ensure consistency of meaning. On a project with several writers, or even if you are on a project as a singleton writer, it is useful to have a style sheet or style guide. Often your project editor can prepare such a style sheet and keep it up to date. If you are the only person on your project, you will be the one to create and maintain it.

The style sheet can contain:

- The list of all books in the documentation set, with accurate and complete titles
- Perhaps the list of all other documentation components such as online help files, reference cards, and so on.
- The list of typographical conventions to be used throughout the information set. For example, use of italics for the titles of referenced manuals, use of bold for terms defined in the glossary, use of monospaced font for examples of code in your text, how to show keyboard keys (Return or <RET>, for example), the conventions for notes that are informational or warn about damage or safety (Note, Caution, Warning), conventions regarding use of horizontal and vertical ellipses, and for command syntax ({ } = at least one required, [ ]= all optional), use of BNF for command syntax, and so on.
- A style guide can also contain information about what goes on your title page, what belongs in each preface, what goes in the headers and footers of each document, how to deal with figure, table, and example captions, and a glossary.
- The glossary for a multi-volume document with several writers is the key to making the definitions and spelling of technical terms consistent. The glossary can be a separate document, or it can be included in a single document of your set. If you have an extremely large glossary, make it a separate document. Sometimes there is a main glossary for a document set, with a few terms specific to only a particular document defined in that document, but it is often simpler to just collect all terms in one place. Your glossary contains definitions of the unique words that describe the product, and you use these words consistently throughout the documentation for hardware, software, and user interface. Establish the terminology early in a project to ensure that everyone on the team uses the same terms in the same way.

Often a team of writers develops the glossary, and one individual may take charge of keeping it up to date. Sometimes new terms are considered jargon, but there is a fair body of evidence that suggests jargon is an essential ingredient of all types of technical writing. Include in your glossary or define in your text when first encountered any acronyms you use; spell them out. It is also helpful to index acronyms. Don't let jargon get out of hand; sometimes words used internally in a company are not understood elsewhere.

A layman will have great difficulty understanding the technical jargon of the physician, but by virtue of their training, physicians have become familiar with a wide variety of very specific technical terms. These terms were developed to ensure that when physicians communicated with each other, they knew they were talking about the same thing. The same is true in every discipline.

For example, botanical nomenclature is very detailed and specific so that the identification of a specific plant can be made with great accuracy and confidence. But over-specialization can cause redundancy. To ensure clarity, avoid using redundant terms and minimize or eliminate synonyms.

Tip ➤ *Avoid synonyms.*

Naming and Classification

To communicate with your technical resources and to help your readers, establish *naming conventions* early, and when you must use acronyms, try to make them speakable. That helps make them writable. For example, don't adopt an acronym like CHIOUR (Channel Input-Output Unit Record Utility) because you may construct sentences like "keep the CHIOUR on a disk that is accessible to all users." Use a well-thought-out acronym.

BASIC is a well-thought-out acronym, both speakable as an acronym and meaningful. The word itself helps you remember what BASIC is: Beginner's All-purpose Symbolic Instruction Code, a computer language for novices. When you construct an acronym, it is easiest to recall if it is a real word, and easiest to translate into its expanded meaning if each letter in the acronym corresponds to the first letter of a word in the expanded meaning; however, this is not required. Sometimes you can create a superior acronym that is easy to recall by using some other letters from the expanded meaning. A better acronym for CHIOUR might be CHIP, which takes some letters from the beginning of words and some from the middle: CHannel InPut-Output Record Utility. A familiar acronym that does not rely only on initial letters is TV (TeleVision).

Tip ➤ *Create speakable acronyms.*

When you use an acronym, always spell it out the first time your reader will see it. Use one representation convention and always follow it: either give the acronym first followed by its explanation in parentheses or give the spelled-out version first followed by the acronym. For example, BASIC (Beginner's All-purpose Symbolic Instruction Code) or Beginner's All-purpose Symbolic Instruction Code (BASIC). In less formal documents such as concept documents or brochures, you can use commas rather than parentheses.

When you gather information, you often must classify it into workable groups. For example, when you document a utility, you need to describe all its commands, any qualifiers or subcommands, information about what the utility works with (files, directories, devices, and so on), and the tasks the utility performs. If you learn the utility well, you will have little difficulty classifying your information appropriately. And when it comes time to develop your plan and write your document, you will find it is much easier to deal with the mass of information you have accumulated.

Classification is an abstraction process. When you invent a classification, you help make discussion possible. The ability to develop and understand abstract concepts is a crucial part of the technical documentor's skill set. Like the math student who can understand algebra but not calculus, technical documentors who cannot develop abstract concepts will be limited in the types of problems they can solve. There is no perfect way to classify information; once you find one that works for you, continue to use it until you develop a better one.

Tip ➤ *Classify your own way.*

The Active Writing Style

There are many excellent texts that describe the craft of technical writing. Some are for the novice writer, others for the engineer or scientist, and others for those writing reports or memos. See the end of this and the next chapter for a selection. Choose one that is appropriate for your needs and keep it on your reference bookshelf.

In this book, I stress the *active style* of writing. This style is particularly successful in conveying technical information because it emphasizes:

- Active voice
- Present tense
- Consistent use of terms
- Parallel construction
- Short rather than long words
- Second person
- Clear and well-defined organization of information
- Defining acronyms
- Repetition of key concepts (for some forms)

The active writing style avoids:

- Dangling prepositions
- Duplication or redundancy
- Extraneous words or phrases
- Misuse of words (*affect* for *effect,* for example)
- Foreign terms (*viz., via,* for example)
- Making verbs into nouns or nouns into verbs
- Making poor cross-references
- Overuse or incorrect use of the word "it"
- Contractions of words
- Contractions of thought

For additional specifics on grammar and punctuation, see Chapter 6.

Your style of writing affects not only your work but also the work of your readers. Using the active style enhances clarity of exposition and helps minimize the number of words necessary to convey a thought or concept. Even in this definition of the active writing style, some attributes are in conflict. For example, how can you avoid duplication yet repeat key concepts? The specific attributes you use in your writing style depend on the document you are writing.

When you work as a member of a writing team, your writing style and the style of the other team writers must match. You may often share files containing paragraphs or definitions. Sometimes one writer begins a document and another completes it. Within the copyright domain of a single company, such sharing of written text freely among collaborating writers is not plagiarism. In fact, such sharing can enhance clarity and productivity.

Tip ➤   *Craft your words to use a single source for both hardcopy and online information.*

You will often encounter the need to produce material that is suitable as both hardcopy and online text. With an authoring tool that lets you conditionalize your material, and care with your writing style, this is achievable. Simply write your text with both in mind, and conditionalize as appropriate.

For example, the following text is written for a printed manual; its reference is to a chapter title.

"For more information on setting up your configuration, see Chapter 7, Managing Your Configuration, in this manual."

To change the text so that it also reads correctly as part of a hypertext online document, you can rewrite it as follows, with the *underlined* words conditionalized to be presented only in the printed document, not visible online.

"For more information on setting up your configuration, see *Chapter 7, Managing Your Configuration, in this manual.*"

You could also change "in this manual" to "in this text," wording that applies to both hardcopy and online deliverables.

Active Voice   The active writing style is more than just using the active voice. You'll need to get familiar with all its attributes to improve what you write. Even in technical documentation you may need to use the passive voice on occasion, but your readers will usually prefer you to use active voice.

The active and passive voices qualify the verbs you use. When you write in the active voice, the subject of your sentence acts; in the passive voice, the subject is acted upon. For example, the following sentence is in active voice:

> The utility compares two files.

The subject is "the utility" and the active verb is "compares." The object of the sentence is "two files." You could convey the same idea by a sentence in the passive voice:

> Two files are compared by the utility.

The sentence in the passive voice is longer, less direct, and harder to understand. You can usually recognize a verb in passive voice when you see a verb ending in "ed" preceded by the verb "to be" (is, are, was, were, will be, and so on). But sometimes a verb ending in "ed" is in the past tense. If you are not clear on the distinction, see a grammar book.

Present Tense   Present tense is the verb form you use to indicate that something happens now. For example, the following sentence is in present tense:

> The programmer writes a utility program.

For technical documentation, write in the present tense. You may find yourself writing about a product that is still being developed in the future tense. After all, what you are describing isn't available yet. But your future tense will seem wrong to your reader when the product ships and your text goes along with it. The following sentences taken from a hardware manual show how such writing reads:

> When you press the Restart button, the system will run a self-test. If the system fails self-test, the processor will not reboot the operating system.

Here are these sentences recast in present tense:

> When you press Restart, the system runs self-test. If the system fails self-test, the processor does not reboot the operating system.

This shortens your text by two words and makes the meaning more clear.

When you write a report describing something that has been done, however, you can write in the past tense, reporting on the results.

Consistent Use of Terms   Be consistent in how you use the terms at your command. Consistency builds confidence in your readers — they feel they have understood the information and can begin to use it. For example, don't call a utility a "file formatter" in one sentence and a "reformatter" two sentences later. This only confuses your readers.

Parallel Construction   When you develop a set of related items, use parallel grammatical construction and parallel formats. Parallel constructs and formats help make your ideas more coherent to your readers. Parallel your nouns with nouns, your active verbs with active verbs, your gerunds with gerunds, and so on. For example:

> *Incorrect:* Consider the origin of computing and how computing has changed over the years.

> *Correct:* Consider the origin of and change in computing over the years.

If you are preparing a language, commands, or utility manual, establish a standard format and stick with it. A parallel and consistent format makes access for your readers easiest. Don't have a table of contents with the following entries:

Laying Out Pages

Design of Your Book

Preparing a Screen Layout

Your reader is encouraged by consistent phrasing, so a better table of contents would contain:

Page Layout

Book Design

Screen Layout

Short Rather Than Long Words   English is a language rich in synonyms, words that mean the same thing, but in technical documentation, you must not only use the same term for the same concept but choose the shorter word or a single word instead of a phrase whenever you can. Don't, for example, write "utilize" when "use" will do or "central processing unit" when "processor" will do. As you gain experience you will add more of these shorteners to your repertoire.

Table 3.13 lists my least favorite long words and my preferred alternatives. You can find others in style guides and books on good writing.

Table 3.13
Short Words

For This Long Word	Use This Short One
approximately	about
accordingly	so
activate	start
assistance	help
facilitate	help
functionality	function
initiate	start
interrelated	related
irregardless	regardless
issue	give
modification	change
orientate	orient
preventative	preventive
utilize	use

Second Person   When you write in the second person, you make your readers feel more comfortable by introducing a personal touch to your text. Your readers feel that you speak directly to them and can thus relate more easily to the information you provide. In the third person, your writing is more abstract and thus harder to understand. Help your reader by writing in second person when you write instructional materials. Here's a sentence written in third person (abstract):

> Online access capabilities make it easier for the user to browse through the catalog by author or title, than by using a card catalog.

Here it is rewritten in second person (more direct):

> Online access capabilities make it easier for you to browse through the catalog by author or title, than by using a card catalog.

Notice that this sentence is still unclear and poorly constructed. Here it is improved by rewriting to clarify the concept and eliminate extraneous words and thoughts:

> You can browse through an online catalog more easily than through a card catalog.

Clear and Well-Defined Organization of Information   Present your information in a clear and well-defined organization to help your readers find facts quickly. Use your Table of Contents to show the organization of your document, and subordinate your topics in an understandable hierarchy. For examples of some well-constructed documents, see the sample outlines earlier in this chapter.

Defining Acronyms   Always spell out any acronym the first time your reader will see it, and repeat the spelled-out version if you present the acronym many pages or chapters later. You can either give the acronym first, followed by its explanation, or give the explanation first, followed by the acronym. Separate the second element either by commas (less formal) or parentheses. The following lines show an acronym treated both ways:

Process Identifier, PID

PID (Process Identifier)

Whichever conventions you adopt, stick to them throughout your document.

Repetition of Key Concepts   For tutorial texts or material for novices, you may sometimes need to repeat key concepts, although in general avoid repetition in technical documentation. In a primer, for example, you probably will repeat some key concepts in different contexts to help your reader learn the new material. You can start by giving a general description of the product, then, in later chapters, expand each of the key features you mentioned. For examples, see the sample outlines earlier in this chapter.

The active writing style deliberately avoids several writing styles and faults described in the next few paragraphs.

Dangling Prepositions   Don't end a sentence with a preposition such as "of" or "with." Rewrite the sentence.

Incorrect: A program that crashes is something I won't put up with.

Correct: I won't put up with a program that crashes.

Better: I won't tolerate a program that crashes.

Duplication or Redundancy   When you write a reference document, eliminate duplicate information. This is more for practical than for pedagogical reasons: if you repeat information, you have to keep two parts of your document up to date, and with short schedules and things changing up to the last minute, this will lead to difficulty. There is nothing more frustrating to your readers than to be given two conflicting pieces of information for the same product — there is no way they can tell which piece is correct. So avoid duplication whenever possible.

Tip ➤ **Don't duplicate information.**

Extraneous Words or Phrases   Constantly reexamine your work to find and eliminate extraneous words and phrases. My least favorite extraneous expressions are shown in Table 3.14.

Table 3.14
Extraneous Expressions

For This Construct	Use
allow x to	let x
and/or	or
in a way that	so that
in order to	to
in use of	to use
in which	where
is equipped with	has
it is often the case that	often
need to	must
refer to	see, call
take into consideration	consider
with regard to	considering

There are thousands of such constructs in English. Become familiar with those you write most frequently and rewrite to omit them. But be careful not to remove words that assist the reader. For example, the following sentence is made ambiguous if the words "enables…to" are changed to "lets."

Onboard memory enables a card to buffer frames going to and from the network.

Also see Brogan's *Clear Technical Writing* for more examples.

Misuse of Words   Many style guides provide excellent lists of words you must know well and perhaps avoid. Table 3.15 lists words and phrases I frequently find used incorrectly in the work of novice writers.

Foreign Terms   To avoid ambiguity, use English, not foreign, terms. The most common foreign terms to avoid are those in Table 6.2, on page 145.

Making Verbs into Nouns or Nouns into Verbs   To avoid misunderstanding, use verbs as verbs and nouns as nouns.

Table 3.15
Words That Are Often Misused

Word/Phrase	Meaning	Example
affect	to influence	Running this program affects system performance.
effect	a result (as noun) or to bring about (as verb)	This program has an effect on system performance.
compared to	to represent dissimilar entities as similar	Compare a brain to a computer to show how different and how similar they are.
compared with	to examine similar entities to note similarities or differences	Compared with C++, Java programming is easy.
can	the ability to do something	The program can capture data.
may	permission to do something	You may go to the lab.
different from	compares two similar entities directly	His programming style is different from Jake's.
different than	makes a comparative statement	Programming today is different than it was a decade ago.
flammable	can burn	Gasoline is highly flammable.
inflammable	can burn (do not use this word because a reader can confuse it with "non-flammable," its opposite)	
like	use only as a preposition, not as a conjunction. When you need a conjunction, use "as."	*Correct:* She writes like an expert. *Incorrect:* The machine runs like a machine should. *Correct:* The machine runs as a machine should.
principal	as a noun, a head or chief, or capital that earns interest; as an adjective, main	The principal asset of the company is its writing team.
principle	a rule or standard	On principle, she avoids late drafts.
that	use to introduce a restrictive clause you must have in your sentence	The draft that needed retyping is ready.
which	use to introduce a clause you can omit without altering the sentence meaning	The draft, which Tom wrote yesterday, needs retyping.

Incorrect use of verb as noun: He submitted the run to the computer.

Correct: He submitted the program to run in the computer.

Better (as instruction): Give the submit command to run the program.

Incorrect use of noun as verb: The CPU faults when it encounters an error.

Correct: When an error occurs, the CPU suspends normal processing and captures data about the error in a file.

Making Poor Cross-References   A poor cross-reference does not help your readers find information. Don't suggest that your readers look "above" or "below" for information or "to a previous chapter." Be as explicit as you can by providing a section number and title. As much as possible, avoid forward references, which can frustrate some readers. But don't over-reference. Adding cross-references to every paragraph impedes and tires your reader. However, when writing for online delivery, frequent cross-references are the norm.

Using the Word "It"   The worst offender for ambiguity in English is "it," because this word has many meanings. When you find you have used "it," rewrite your sentence, substituting for "it" the word you intend "it" to mean. You will often find that your sentence changes meaning. This is an example of an ambiguous sentence with "it":

A control character is received, and it generates a core dump.

Better:

The program receives a control character and stops; the program then generates a core dump.

Contractions of Words   In more formal technical documentation such as reference manuals, avoid contractions. In less formal documents such as brochures, contractions are more acceptable. Your company may have a house style to guide you.

Formal, without contractions:

Do not exit from the program with CTRL/C; use CTRL/Z instead.

Less formal, with contractions:

Don't exit from the program with CTRL/C; use CTRL/Z instead.

"Cannot" is not a contraction and you can use it even in formal documents.

Contractions of Thought   Sometimes, particularly when you write rapidly, you may inadvertently try to compress more than one thought into a single sentence.

The cure for this is to step away from your writing for at least a day or so and then reexamine your words and sentences. Asking another writing peer or editor to review your text can also help you find these compressed thoughts.

The following sentence compresses two thoughts:

> An OpenVMS cluster system connects many large Alpha processors and Digital Storage Architecture (DSA) storage devices to form a single system, one that enhances the performance and storage capacity of any single processor with the OpenVMS cluster system and increases the availability of processing.

This sentence is more clear separated into two:

> An OpenVMS cluster system connects many large Alpha processors and Digital Storage Architecture (DSA) storage devices to form a single system. Such an OpenVMS cluster system enhances the performance and storage capacity of any single processor and increases processing availability.

Tip ➤   *Try this experiment.*

Even the most inexperienced writer can begin to develop an active style of writing with a simple experiment: write out a rough paragraph describing an object or task, such as a room you are familiar with or the steps in tying a shoe. Your paragraph should contain at least six sentences so that as you write, you let the words flow to create the thought you are trying to convey.

Once you have written the paragraph, set it aside for a while — a day or at least an hour or two. Then pick it up again and examine it for the attributes avoided by the active style of writing. Search out passive voice and eliminate it; make future tense present; find extraneous words and delete them. Examine sentences for appropriate parallel construction, and rewrite sentences to make them parallel. This rewriting usually shortens the written material and always makes it more clear, easier to read, and more accessible to your readers.

The next example is taken from a technical document, but the method works equally well with other types of material.

> The CMEXEC privilege allows the user's process to execute the Change Mode to Executive ($CMEXEC) system service. This system service lets a process change its access mode to executive, execute a specified routine, and then return to the access mode that was in effect before the system service was called. While in executive mode, the process is allowed to execute the Change Mode to Kernel ($CMKRNL) system service. You should grant this privilege only to users who need to gain access to protected and sensitive data structures and internal functions of the operating system. If unqualified users have unrestricted access to sensitive data structures and

functions, the operating system and service to other users can easily be disrupted. Such disruptions can include failure of the system, destruction of the database, and exposure of confidential information to unauthorized persons. (138 words)

Eliminating passive voice and extraneous words provides the following paragraph:

The CMEXEC privilege lets a user process execute the Change Mode to Executive ($CMEXEC) system service. This system service lets a process change its access mode to executive, execute a specified routine, and then return to its prior access mode. While in executive mode, the process can execute the Change Mode to Kernel ($CMKRNL) system service.

Grant this privilege only to users who must access protected and sensitive operating system data structures and internal functions. Unqualified users with unrestricted access to these data structures and functions can easily disrupt the operating system and service to other users, causing system failure, destruction of the database, and exposure of confidential information to unauthorized persons. (112 words)

The shorter text represents a 19 percent reduction in the number of words, yet presents the same amount of information, strengthens the concept for the reader and makes the information more accessible.

Of course, removing the passive voice is not a panacea and will not alone correct poor writing, but you must understand its benefits and use passive voice only where appropriate.

Internationalization   If you work for a multinational corporation, you may also need to consider *internationalization.* Many internationalization considerations are simply good technical documentation practices. These include:

- Defining your terms in a glossary
- Eliminating duplicate information
- Making your documentation set as modular as possible, separating the information into useful pieces
- Using the active writing style
- Using automatic cross-referencing
- Avoiding cultural bias as much as possible (use universal units of time and length in examples; keep country-specific information such as telephone numbers and addresses in a separate section; don't mention seasons — some countries have four seasons, others have only two)

Localization   Localization is the translation or otherwise making a technical document accessible to a local population. This can include:

- translation of text into another language
- changing software to accept another language
- changing diagrams and figures to conform to local standards or customs
- changing placement of front and back matter to conform to local requirements
- changing date, time, and currency formats

When you initially design your information set, you may need to consider and plan for localization. This may mean ensuring that localization groups have access to files, including graphics files, you use to create your documents.

Modularization   Keeping your documentation modular means not developing large, monolithic files, but separating documentation sets into books and perhaps books into chapters, each of which can reside in a separate file. If you deliver your documents to others as files rather than as hardcopy, keeping your material modular can simplify the translation process, if translation is done.

Elements of English Words   As you create documentation, you will need to coin new words and phrases. When you do so, reflect on the elements of English words, the subject of the next section.

When you redefine or create new terms, it helps your readers if you pay attention to the terms' *morphology* (word structure), *etymology* (word history), and *semantics* (word meaning). Whenever your material requires a new word or term, make every effort to define the term clearly and use it consistently throughout the document. Sometimes you create a new word most easily and understandably from two existing words. Sometimes you give an old word a new meaning, and sometimes you invent a totally new word.

When you use two existing words to form a new one, you typically place them side by side in several contexts. Then, through usage, the two words become hyphenated. Finally they become concatenated and merge into one. For example, from the two words "data" and "base," some writers formed the noun or adjective "data-base." After some time and as readers became increasingly familiar with the hyphenated version, the hyphen was dropped and the result was "database." When you work with technical material you will find that words evolve rather straightforwardly this way.

The morphology of words depends on your *natural* language, the language of normal speech. English, an inflected language, has words composed of *morphemes,* to which prefixes and suffixes are added to change the words' parts of speech or to add grammatical meaning. For example, to make a plural from a singular noun, you add the letter *s*. However, there are exceptions to this rule, and you must be reasonably fluent in English to recognize them. Similarly, to present the negative of a word in English, you add to the word the prefixes *un-, non-, in-, im-,* or *il- (unable, nonfunctioning, inflammable, immoral, illogical)*. A reputable, recent-edition dictionary is a good tool to use for guidance on these topics.

As new objects appear for naming, and as new environments need description, you will be constantly challenged to create terminology that is clear, accurate, and consistent with the norms of English. You will need to work closely with software developers to ensure that commands they create are consistent with good usage. And as terms are translated and used in the international market, their meaning will be subject to additional interpretation. Clear early definitions can help maintain clarity and retain the individual meaning of new terms needed by new technologies.

The *etymology* of a word is important in its construction. While you don't need to know the etymology of all English words, be aware of common roots so you can form suitable new words when necessary. Sometimes common usage is sufficient. For example, the computer term *path,* a route over which data passes, uses the meaning of a *path* along which creatures pass.

An example of an error in word creation is the word "fugoid," coined to describe a mathematical function that represents wing flutter in aerodynamics. The inventor of this term mistook the Latin *fugere,* to flee, as the root for the new word, when correct etymology requires the Latin *volare,* to fly. Thus fugoids should really be voloids.

Another example demonstrates poor use of an English word for a computer concept: the word "crash," as in "The system crashed!" In English "crash" means "to break violently and noisily, or marked by a concerted effort and achieved in the shortest possible time."

The evasive action a computer system takes to prevent damage to itself *is* marked by concerted action and achieved in the shortest possible time. The original use of "crash" was as an adjective (as in "a crash program"), but the adjective has now become an awkward verb. To say the system crashed seems as though it ran into a wall — perhaps not so farfetched when you consider the little bomb icon the Apple Macintosh shows when it crashes! But the term "crash" is likely to remain part of computer terminology.

Experiment with new words, and when you have full mastery of all your linguistic tools and rules, you can start to break the rules, or at least bend them a bit.

Know Your Tools

Under the precept "know your tools," you must be proficient in the tools you use on a daily basis for creating, analyzing, and producing technical documentation. As a technical writer, you perform many tasks daily. These include research and communication, interviewing knowledgeable people, organizing and codifying technical material, reviewing the material, and using the feedback that is normally the fruit of a review. Your efforts reduce information chaos to order.

To do your work, you use computerized tools such as editors, graphics systems, text processing, electronic mail, and code management systems. Your proficiency in these tools and the quickness with which you learn new tools are important components of your productivity. Some strategies for dealing with tools are described in Chapter 7.

Further Reading

If you want to start with a short style guide, try:
Write Right! (Venolia, 1988). The best workbook for eliminating wordiness is *Clear Technical Writing* (Brogan, 1973). My choice in a grammar book is *Harbrace College Handbook* (Hodges, Whitten, 1990), though there are many others available. To help answer questions on usage, read *Webster's New Collegiate Dictionary* (1987) or the *American Heritage Dictionary* (1976). An outstanding dictionary for computer terms is the *Dictionary of Computing* (1982); considering its small size, its coverage and definitions are amazingly complete and accurate. If you need a real beginner's dictionary, try *The Illustrated Computer Dictionary* (Spencer, 1980).

You may also want to use a thesaurus such as:
Roget's International Thesaurus (1962) or *Webster's Collegiate Thesaurus* (1976) to find alternative words or to find a word in a dictionary when you cannot recall the spelling. A department or group of writers needs to select one general dictionary and perhaps several specialized dictionaries that everyone uses for primary definitions and spelling. This helps maintain consistency of terms throughout all materials the group creates. You may need to develop your own dictionary for local terms. To develop a neutral, nonsexist writing style, see *The Nonsexist Word Finder* (Maggio, 1987) or *The Handbook of Nonsexist Writing* (Miller, Swift, 1988).

For more details on course development techniques, instructional design, and electronic support systems, see:
Handbook of Task Analysis Procedures (Jonassen, Hannum, Tessmer, 1989), *Principles of Instructional Design* (Gagné, Briggs, Wager, 1988), a standard text, *Electronic Performance Support Systems* (Gery, 1991), or *Developing Instructional Design* (McArdle, 1991). There is an entire discipline in instructional design and course development which you can learn about through local universities, colleges, and libraries.

For More Ideas

Other excellent books on the nonfiction writing style include:
The Careful Writer (Bernstein, 1965) and Zinsser's *Writing with a Word Processor* (1983), *On Writing Well* (1990), and *Writing to Learn* (1989). *ANSI Z39.16*-1979 gives good advice on how to organize and construct a paper or scientific article.

If you need another grammar book, try one of the following:
The Harper Handbook of College Composition (Shaw, 1981) or *Practical English Handbook* (Watkins, 1986). If you need a more formal style guide for copyediting, try one of these: *The Chicago Manual of Style* (1982), *Words into Type* (Skillen, Gay, 1974), the *Chicago Guide to Preparing Electronic Manuscripts* (1987), the *U.S. Government Printing Office Style Manual* (1973), or the *ACS Style Guide* (Dodd, 1986). The last two specialize in styles for government documents, such as the *Congressional Record,* and books and articles on chemistry, respectively.

For English alone, there are hundreds of available dictionaries:
The magnificent (and enormous) multivolume *Oxford English Dictionary* and its supplement provide, in addition to definitions, the history of many words. The best of the unabridged dictionaries is *Webster's Third New International Dictionary Unabridged* (1966); others include *Webster's New Twentieth Century Dictionary Unabridged* (1970) and the *Random House Dictionary of the English Language* (1987). Be aware, however, that unabridged may not mean complete. *A Dictionary of Modern English Usage* (Fowler, 1987) is a classic.

Specialist dictionaries, such as computer, scientific, and medical dictionaries, are becoming increasingly common. Consult your dictionary frequently — occasionally read it for pleasure.

Dictionaries that contain computer terms include:
The Digital Dictionary (1986), *Computer Dictionary* (Sippl, 1982), *The Computer Glossary* (Freedman, 1991), the *Concise Science Dictionary* (1980), and the *Dictionary of Technical Terms* (Crispin, 1970).

Mencken's *The American Language,* 4th ed. (1978) is interesting reading and gives the derivations of many words that have become common in American speech.

Dictionaries for other specialties include:
The Merck Index: (1983), an encyclopedia of chemicals, drugs, and biologicals, and *The American Medical Association Encyclopedia* (1989).

To increase your technical knowledge, take courses in computer science or technical subjects. Find current encyclopedias in your company or local public libraries.

Several encyclopedias are devoted to technical subjects: *McGraw-Hill Encyclopedia of Science and Technology* (1987), the shorter *McGraw-Hill Dictionary of Science and Engineering* (1984), *McGraw-Hill Concise Encyclopedia of Science and Technology* (1984) — in one volume, *Prentice-Hall Encyclopedia of Information Technology* (1987), and *McGraw-Hill Personal Computer Programming Encyclopedia* (1989). An excellent book from which to learn programming is *An Introduction to Programming* (Conway, Gries, 1979), and there are many others in the bookstores.

Exercises

1. What are the four major precepts of technical documentation?
2. What are five different reader levels or audiences who use computer documents?
3. What are three different audiences for hardware documents?
4. What is the best time when you are learning about a product to write for a novice user?
5. What are three major organizational devices for information design?
6. When writing for a programmer or software developer, how should you organize instructional material?
7. What are five types of technical documents?
8. What is a documentation map?
9. Prepare two organizations for a user guide and show why each is preferred.
10. When might you use a poster or wall chart of technical information?
11. Why should you avoid duplicating information in a technical documentation set?

Development Techniques   4

Words like winter snowflakes.
Homer, The *Iliad,* Book III, Line 222, c. 700 b.c.

This chapter describes techniques you will find useful as you gather information and decide how to present that information to your reader.

When you work for a company, you help create part of the company's product, and you work with other people who also create parts of the product. The group of you working together are a product team. Depending on where you work, on the management philosophy of your company, and on the type of product your company produces, you will find that product teams are different. When you write documentation for computer software, for example, you are a member of a team that contains writers, software programmers or developers, people who test the product, people who represent the service organization that services the product after it reaches the customer, perhaps people who will help train customers to use the product, and people who deal with new customers or prospects for the product.

On a daily basis, you perform different tasks depending on the stage of the project. Figure 4.1 shows the steps of the writing process from inception of an assignment to its completion.

While in the information gathering or research phase, you attend meetings, read specifications or other literature, and communicate with knowledgeable people on the telephone, in person, or by electronic mail. You will also devise some system for understanding and categorizing your information. Often during the research phase, you simply accumulate information and find ways to ensure that you have looked into all areas to a sufficient level of detail.

Once you have accumulated a sufficient body of material, you spend a good part of your work day studying and evaluating the information and discussing difficult points with technical resources. You must assimilate and understand the new information to plan and execute documentation that describes the product. Sometimes in the research phase of a project, you may take classes or seminars to increase your expertise in a subject. Getting training in your subject can help ensure your success in developing the documentation.

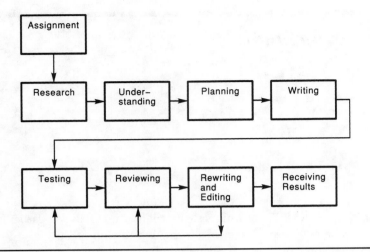

Figure 4.1
The Writing Process

A Typical Writer's Workplan

Once you have gathered and understood a critical mass of information, you begin planning. Your written plans must be reviewed and agreed to by the other members of the product team. When you create a formal plan that other members of the project team review, you ensure that everyone knows what you intend to do, and you avoid developing a document that is not needed or leaving out one that is essential. Your documentation plan should contain the following elements:

- Sources of information
- Identification of target readership
- Writing staff
- Reviewers
- Outline of document
- Schedule
- Risks

Sometimes a plan contains other elements:

- Documentation requirements you place on other groups (resources, time, technical information another group must provide)
- Assumptions used in creating the plan, risks associated with timely execution of the plan

- Issues that must be resolved
- Support for several forms of documentation in the software
- Internationalization guidelines
- Usability testing plans
- Identification of unanswered questions
- Identification of unresolved issues

The level of detail for these additional items depends largely on the project and product for which you are planning documentation. You can also include in your documentation plan a *workplan* that specifies the tasks you will perform and their order.

Sample Writer's Workplan

You can include the following tasks in your workplan:

1. Research topics, seek out individuals to act as resources, and identify principal reviewers.
2. Create a documentation plan giving milestones and an outline or design of the document.
3. Have the plan reviewed and agreed to.
4. Accumulate technical information.
5. Determine needs for illustrations.
6. Establish a first feature-freeze date.
7. Write a first draft.
8. Have the draft reviewed, perhaps chapter by chapter.
9. Incorporate comments from the review, resolving conflicts between reviewers.
10. Establish a second feature-freeze date.
11. Prepare a second draft.
12. Conduct a second review.
13. Incorporate comments from the review.
14. Establish a final feature-freeze date.
15. Prepare a final verification draft.
16. Have the final draft verified.
17. Incorporate comments from the final verification.
18. Prepare the document for production (preparation of camera-ready copy) and printing.
19. Send the document to the printer.
20. Recommend follow-up procedures to determine reader reaction to the document.

Most of the terms in this list are self-explanatory; for example, a first draft is your first reasonably complete and reviewable draft of the entire document. A first draft of a chapter is not a first draft of the entire document.

The *feature-freeze* date is a date you establish on which to observe the state of the software or hardware. You then document the software or hardware as it appears on that date. If changes occur later, and they will in virtually all projects, you ignore them until you are ready to establish your feature-freeze date for your next draft. Using a feature-freeze date for early drafts helps you convince your development peers of the importance you attach to specific features of the product that are visible in the documentation. Establishing a feature-freeze date does not require that development stop making changes to the hardware or software product; it only requires them to avoid making changes that must be reflected in the documentation. Development can still make changes that are not visible to the user.

Tip ➤   *Use a feature-freeze date.*

When you approach the end of your project, development must freeze all features visible to the user when you complete your final draft. No new commands, switches, screen displays, or error messages are possible. If some seem needed, they must be delayed until the next software release. The same is true of hardware. Mockups and prototypes must be as close to the final product as possible. If possible, they should be identical. That helps to keep discrepancies between the product and the documentation to a minimum and builds confidence in your readers.

There are few things more demoralizing to customers than to read product documentation and find some details that do not coincide with the product they have received. To keep this under control (and to avoid writing a work of fiction), work with your development team to establish your feature-freeze dates, and keep them. This work process is illustrated in Figure 4.2.

Some modifications of the work process are possible. For example, you may decide to have two, not three, drafts. But you need to go through each of these steps for all projects. Sometimes the time you spend in one phase, for example, research, may be shorter than in other projects, but all projects go through all the major steps. You may be able to shorten your research time because of your earlier experience or prior knowledge of the topic. If you participate in developing documents for a product obtained partially complete from somewhere else, you will probably have almost no time to understand the product, but you still must understand it to do anything useful with the documentation.

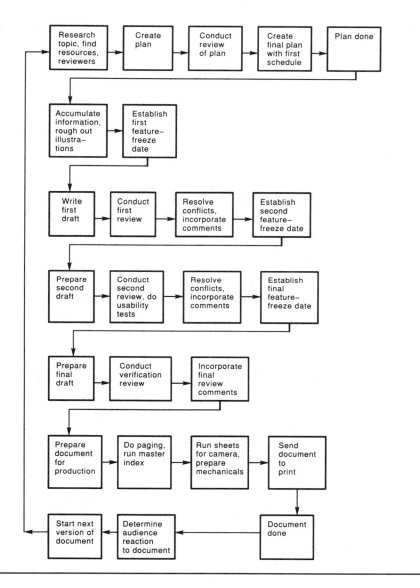

Figure 4.2
Documentation Workplan and Process

The Quality Documentation Process

The process that has been demonstrably successful in producing high-quality documentation contains several major task categories:

- Researching
- Understanding
- Planning
- Writing
- Reworking
- Receiving the results

Research

The *research* in which you engage begins with exposure to the project and continues through reading you do to examine functional specifications, design information, library materials, and any written information that is available. Research also includes discussions you hold with knowledgeable people who understand the product and meetings you attend that are pertinent to the project. You do research throughout most of the development process, but you always start a project devoting most of your time to gathering information. If you shortchange yourself at this stage, you will be unable to complete your documents well.

Tip ➤   ***Don't overlook research time.***

Your research usually includes some study of your potential readers. Sometimes you can talk to actual customers and use their recommendations in developing your documents; sometimes you will only have a rough idea of your readers. Your company reviewers are *proxies* for your true readers, and you need to understand your true readers as well as possible and remain an advocate for them — the product customers — in what you write. With your appreciation for the work customers do with your product, you may be in a better position to judge what they need than are your software developers or hardware engineers.

Using the product and experimenting with different ways to develop the material and make it accessible to your readers are also part of the research phase of your project. The techniques you develop for doing your research remain applicable to any project on which you may work. One basic technique that is invaluable during the research phase is to *write down* the words you have just heard from technical experts or other people you are interviewing. Write the words in a computer file, on a scrap of paper, or in a notebook dedicated to the project. Writing down a piece of information aids recall (even if you lose the scrap of paper) and preserves a record of the event or utterance.

Tip ➤   ***Write it down.***

I like to dedicate a spiral-bound 8 $1/2$-by-11-inch notebook or a spiral-bound steno-notebook to each project. With a dedicated notebook, you collect all your notes for a single project in one place and don't need to hunt through individual sheets of paper. When there are papers that go with the project, I keep the current ones in a slash folder that is the same color as my notebook and label both with the project name. That helps me keep the right things together when I must work on several projects and eliminates hunting for the right papers. I never use white folders or binders because they are too easily lost in a sea of white papers. On my computer system, I use the same names in my electronic folders, though I don't yet have a way to color-code computer folders as I color-code my paper documents.

Tip ➤ *Color-code your folders and notebooks.*

When working with other writers and distributing files to reviewers, you can save yourself a great deal of time and confusion if you or your project leader establishes a common disk area to hold files for general distribution or access.

Tip ➤ *Use common directories.*

This can be a disk area accessible over the network containing your files for distribution, or a web site with pointers to the files for common access. Establishing common areas can also help your group obtain or maintain ISO certification, if that is a goal of your organization.

Tip ➤ *Use electronic mail.*

Electronic mail is an effective way to help keep in contact with your reviewers, get answers to questions from developers, reach people at distant locations, and record questions you ask and responses you obtain. Many mail systems let you file messages by category, for example by project, for later retrieval. Use the folders capability of a mail system to help you separate mail into appropriate categories.

Understanding

Once you have done a sufficient amount of research and have assimilated most of what you have gathered, you progress to the *understanding* phase. With a fairly complete picture of the project, the product, and the needs of the market, you can understand the needs of your readers; this understanding, or internalization, of product, market, and reader is essential to success in the next phase in the process.

Your *project* is the collection of activities directed at achieving a specific goal. You may work on a project that is to build a model airplane, or you may work on a project that is to build a new aircraft simulator, or you may work on a project that is to design a new automobile. A project will have specific goals, items that must be created to meet those goals, and some time interval during which the project must be done.

For example, when you build your model airplane, your goal may be to build a World War I biplane from scratch. You'll probably set your own schedule, but you might need to have it done by the date of some exhibit or contest. A project to design a new automobile might have design goals of miles per gallon (say, 100), passenger capacity (4), and 0 to 60 performance (2 minutes). In the computer industry, a project can have a goal of building a piece of hardware — say, a new processor, a new printer, or some interconnect device — or of building software to fill a specific need. Each piece of software, for example, Microsoft Word, or AT&T's Writer's Workbench, is a product, and each is created with a project focused on creating that product.

The *product* is the result of the work of the project. It is an entity your company sells to your customers. In the computer industry, there are three major categories of products:

- Hardware
- Software
- Firmware

Products on which you work have one of these forms.

Hardware is any physical item, such as a terminal, processor cabinet, disk drive, mouse, and so on — in other words, something you can touch. *Software* has a physical existence, but you can't touch it. The physical aspect of software is its electrons stored as bits and bytes on your computer hardware, in files, for example. But you don't touch those bits and bytes; you manipulate them with the functions supplied by the software. When you edit a file, for example, you rearrange the bits and bytes on your system.

Firmware is between hardware and software. It is software stored permanently in ROM (Read-Only Memory). You can't change it, though the manufacturer can perhaps supply you with new ROMs, and you can't touch it either.

You may work with a project team (those who work together to create the product) that has marketing representation — a person from the marketing organization who knows the market and can inform you and others about it. A marketing expert can be invaluable in directing your attention to what the market, your customers, must have.

For example, you think you need to provide a document for novice users, but your marketing representative shows you that because the product on which you are working is intended only for experienced programmers (a CASE tool, for example), a document for a novice is very low on the list of priorities. Because there are never enough resources to do everything that everyone might suggest, the project team must always work together to set priorities and be sure that all the essentials are delivered.

When you are collecting materials and determining market needs, you may need to have outside training. This is particularly true if the technical knowledge you need to understand and use the product is more than what you have. It is part of the task of management to ensure that you obtain adequate training for all your projects. Your schedule must allow time for training when training is mandated.

Tip ➤ *Keep a notebook handy.*

To help you keep track of action items from meetings, information obtained from interviewing developers and others, and other project related information, keep a notebook that is dedicated to the project on which you are working. Some writers find that they can keep track of all they need in a daytimer, but I find that there is not enough room on those pages to hold the notes I may take. This is, of course, a matter of personal work style. I find the dedicated notebook handy because I use it to keep a running record of all major items that I collect, and it's also a record of all meetings I attend, and what I bring back from the meeting. The main thing is to have a consistent record of what you need to know, including dates that are decided at a meeting, changes in the project, new people who come onto the project, and so on. Thus it becomes a record to which you can refer, either as a reminder of what you need to do next, or a reference to determine when an event occurred.

Conceptual Techniques

Experienced writers develop techniques to understand and explain particularly difficult, complex, or intractable problems or products, and they find ways to organize material even when there are still many unknowns. These techniques include brainstorming, decomposition, metaphor, mapping, and modeling.

Brainstorming   If you have begun to gather information but sense that what you have so far is incomplete, you may resort to *brainstorming*. With this technique, you call a meeting of a number of knowledgeable people (ten or fifteen is ideal), give them the brainstorming rules, and encourage all participants to come up with ideas. As participants give the ideas, record them on a board for all to see and ask for more. To do brainstorming:

- Start with the topic of interest and write it on the board. For example, your topic might be paper clips: are there new ways they might be used? This is a way to explore potential new markets.
- Strive for quantity; encourage your participants to give lots of ideas, even if some seem foolish or long shots.
- Don't judge a suggestion by saying "We've already tried that" or "No one will ever let us do that" because that will discourage people from making more suggestions.

- Strive for far-out ideas and far-flung concepts, because these are often the most fruitful. Even if you don't decide to build that model airplane with four wings and seven ailerons, thinking about it might produce a model that does work better than the current ones.
- Build on a concept by expanding or contracting the view of it: for example, if you are thinking about paper clips and what you might do with them, think about how they might be used if they were really tiny (in medical procedures?) or really big (base for a couch?).

For software products, you might want to explore new ways to deliver information to your customers; for hardware products, new ways to develop wordless documentation.

Brainstorming cannot last more than a couple of hours because of its intense nature, but it can be extremely effective in gathering new ideas and filling out important gaps in information. You need to be a good facilitator for the most effective brainstorming.

Decomposition   *Decomposition* is a method to use when you are attempting to solve a problem and it remains amorphous and elusive — you cannot get a good handle on it. In many technical subjects, decomposition of the material can yield useful ideas.

To decompose a subject, identify its component parts, and then work exclusively on each part independently of the others. When you write down what you learn about the specific component, you have completed the work on that component. This frees you to proceed to the next part. In this technique, attention to detail and persistence in extracting the maximum amount of information from each part are essential to success. Once you have finished all your components, you can tie them all together.

For example, say you need to document a software system with three different user interfaces or environments, and each user interface contains fifty or so commands. Make a list of all the interface names and lists of all the interface commands. Then begin by preparing your description of one command from one interface. Once you are done with that one, go on to the second command, and so on.

Do each one independently, then proceed to the ones that are not yet done. Eventually you will have described every command for every interface. In most projects, you won't have the luxury of creating your descriptions only once, because changes occur in the software. But if you take an organized and methodical approach, you'll keep track of each piece and keep the entire documentation effort under control.

Metaphor   *Metaphor* or analogy is a good technique to use when you need to convey an unfamiliar concept. Metaphor gives your readers a familiar idea on which to build.

A metaphor helps to show relationships, but don't use it to map details: a metaphor that works at a high level may break down when you introduce details. You must also be careful about metaphors in an international environment: a metaphor understood by your U.S. readers may not be understood when your document is translated into Japanese.

Even translation from the U.S. to the British environment can cause problems. For example, to describe something that goes counterclockwise, you may use as your metaphor a highway rotary: "The red spot on the dial advances like a car traveling around a rotary." In countries where cars travel on the left, however, rotaries run clockwise, not counterclockwise, so you will not give the right information if you use a metaphor like this.

Another example: building software can be compared with building a house. The architect of the house is like the architect of the computer system. Both design the entity at a high level and create design documents: the blueprints of the house architect and the design documents of the software architect.

The house architect provides specific layouts for every floor and room of the house and materials lists for everything needed to build the house. However, most architects are not builders; usually they will not work with the contractors to dig and pour the foundation, buy the lumber, or contract with the plumbers and electricians and carpenters to do the work.

It is here where the metaphor breaks down, because the software design architect, unlike the house architect, may work on the implementation, at least to verify the functions that are implemented by others, and will probably follow through to see that the design is correctly implemented and tested. However, this varies a lot from place to place.

Many software terms start as metaphors: electronic mail is like mail in the post office in concept but not in form; software helps you collect things in files and folders that are all electronic but these collectors are only named files and folders because they function like the files and folders in your desk; an electronic bulletin board is not something where you pin things up, except electronically, and so on. Thus the software world is one of virtual realities and metaphors.

For example, consider this transportation analogy for operating systems (concept after Hunzeker):

> IBM's MVS is like the Queen Mary, elegant, expensive, and a bit passé — it's too big to go to most ports, carries mostly wealthy passengers, and needs lots of highly trained people to keep it running. Lots of people love it, however.

> OpenVMS is like a fleet of sturdy cargo ships, some small enough to go to tiny ports carrying only a few goods and people, some large enough

to be cost effective at carrying many large containers to the biggest and busiest trade centers. None of these ships is very elegant but each gets its job done.

Apple's Macintosh operating system is a bit like a private yacht, spectacular in its way, but mostly for fun, though sometimes people try to use it for serious business.

UNIX is like a fishing trawler — it goes to any port, but offers no protection from the weather.

MS-DOS is like a tugboat, sturdy and strong, but can't do very many jobs.

The Sun operating system is like a new catamaran, a bit flashy, though useful for those who know how to use it. It may not work better than any other ship, and sometimes one of those flashy features doesn't work at all.

The HP operating system is like a naval vessel, well maintained but just basic. No glitz or glamour, but popular for some work.

Each operating system has its devotees, and sometimes it's just what you are used to that you like.

Mapping   *Mapping* is another technique you can use to understand and describe information. You will often use it with metaphor to illuminate concepts. With mapping, you draw up lists of concepts or blocks of information and map them into familiar information structures such as lists, outlines, or paragraphs.

Sometimes the first attempt to map information into a logical structure is unsuccessful in conveying the information desired. With electronic tools, you can experiment with several mappings until you find an optimum organization.

As an example of a map, consider this sample path diagram that shows a process to follow in developing complex systems:

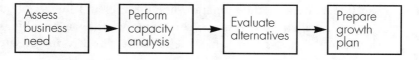

You can develop even more elaborate and extensive maps, using similar diagrams.

Modeling   *Modeling* is a technique you can use to organize information. You develop a model of the information flow, then present the information in accordance with that model, following the order it dictates. If the information fails to flow in a logical manner, you know that either the information still lacks important segments or the model needs revision. In either case, you have a strategy to improve the written material.

Design of Information Forms   When designing an information set that contains multiple components, for example hardcopy books, online material, and perhaps CDROM deliverables and web site deliverables, it helps your audience identify product parts easily if you can adopt some unifying tokens so that each separate component is clearly distinguishable as part of the information set. This can be a graphic, a border, an icon, or a distinguishing mark. You can further unify your product components by adopting font and layout standards and styles that give a common look and feel to them all.

Planning

Once you understand the basics of the product itself, and have worked with others to establish the readership for the product documentation, you can begin *planning*. Planning, at least at the structural level, is essential to accurate scheduling and for establishing the direction that leads to project deliverables being produced on time.

In the planning phase of a project, the writer or project leader typically creates a *documentation plan* or *documentation strategy*. Sometimes you may produce a *master documentation plan* that describes the books in a large set.

A *project leader* helps to coordinate the work of all the writers on a documentation team. Often the project leader writes the top-level document, and individual writers create individual documentation plans for their books. The terminology and to some extent the content of these documents can differ between different corporations or parts of corporations, but in general, every plan contains information on items to be written and the schedule against which the writing will be done. If the project is large and requires the scheduling of several documents, sometimes the strategy or master plan contains only a list of the document titles with a rough schedule for all documents and common elements. The individual documentation plans contain the detailed outlines for each book and the dates when drafts and final copy will be available.

A strategy document has broader scope than a master documentation plan; it provides information beyond the documentation kit details, covering all readers who need information on a specific product or set of products, competitive information, and perhaps both internal and external readers. For example, a documentation strategy for a new product might address the following:

1. Summary of recommendations
2. Competitive information
3. Requirements for success

4. Proposed documents
   - For customers
   - For presales and prospects
   - For company presidents
   - For technical decision makers
   - For corporation service providers
   - In online forms
   - In error messages
   - In user interfaces
   - Proposed funding
5. Sources of information used in creating the strategy

This is an example of the contents of a documentation strategy for an information kit to ship with your product:

1. Overview
2. Revision history
3. Sources
4. Key assumptions
5. Risks
6. Documentation requirements
7. Project summary
8. Reader categories
9. Proposed information kit
10. Staffing and reviewers
11. Documentation schedule
12. Internationalization
13. Online documentation support for development
14. Documentation usability testing

A master documentation plan might contain the following items:

1. Overview
2. Plan for the future
3. Support for the next software release
4. Implementation of online strategy
5. Complete revision of certain books
6. Revision of other books
7. Development of Release Notes

8. Risks and contingency plans

9. Draft schedule

10. Review and distribution

11. Packaging and production

12. Contents of documentation kit for Version x.y

13. Camera-ready copy schedule

The documentation plan for an individual manual might contain:

1. Overview

2. Staffing and reviewing

3. Sources of information

4. Milestones

5. Internationalization

6. Online help

7. Online documentation support

8. Manual outline

9. Production information

The plan for a hypertext document might include the following:

1. Overview

2. Staffing and reviewing

3. Sources of information

4. Milestones

5. Internationalization

6. Online documentation support

7. Document topics

8. Document-linking strategy

9. Production information

The two most critical components of your documentation plan are the *outline* and the *schedule.* While both are liable to change, defining them lets you write your document or documents within a needed time. With any plan, you establish the framework within which you will work as well as frameworks in time (your schedule) and conceptual space (the topics you cover).

Your outline provides a structure for collecting information in chunks or modules and placing it in the document. Even when you can't fill in all the blanks, you are not halted and can progress by skipping the missing section or chapter temporarily. The outline remains as a reminder of the totality of your document.

Some call the outline a documentation plan and the schedule a workplan, but these are inexact uses of the terms. As you can see from the examples above, a documentation plan is more than just your outline, and a schedule is the implementation of your workplan. (More about schedules later.)

Outlines sometimes change as you work through a book. As more information appears and is assimilated, you often realize that there is a better way to organize or present it. Two sections may be combined, for example, or a new topic introduced. Sections or paragraphs may flow more smoothly when their order is reversed. You often won't see these needs until after you begin writing. This is the nature of technical documentation and how technical information is transferred from one person to another. If you find that you need lots of reorganizations, you may need to recast your outline as a more up-to-date structure.

Scheduling specific dates when each draft (and each illustration, perhaps) is to go to review is critical to the success of technical documents. Always put your schedule in your documentation plan; you may also need to keep your schedules updated in reports (weekly or monthly). But don't keep returning to your documentation plan to keep it up to date once it is done.

Tip ➤ ***Don't iterate your plan repeatedly.***

Creating a book always takes longer without a defined schedule than with one. A defined schedule lets you pace yourself against its milestones and helps to guarantee that you can deliver your document at the required moment. Whether this is due to a human tendency to procrastinate or because a written schedule creates a sense of urgency and accountability is not clear.

As an example, the schedule in Table 4.1 shows the milestones for a seven-month documentation project.

Often a project leader is responsible for helping a team of writers schedule books through review and production cycles with a minimum of conflicts and bottlenecks. In a large set of documents, critical-path activities where bottlenecks are likely to occur include the creation of illustrations and the preparation of final reprographic masters. The project leader who plans for these activities in the project schedule provides the members of the writing team with a more smoothly running environment than does the project leader who leaves these important details to the last minute.

A good way to ensure that you don't shortchange yourself in time is to draw a graph of your schedule by weeks. Use large, squared graph paper and label the weeks across the top. Don't schedule due dates on weekends or holidays, even if you might work on those days to meet your schedule. Use the entire interval over which

Table 4.1
Sample Documentation Schedule

Milestone	Date
Preliminary doc plan available	Nov 23, 1998
Final doc plan approved (signoff)	Dec 14, 1998
Feature-freeze for first draft	Dec 21, 1998
First draft to review	Jan 4, 1999
Deadline for first draft comments	Jan 15, 1999
Feature-freeze for second draft	Jan 29, 1999
Field test begins	Feb 8, 1999
Distribute second draft to review	Feb 8, 1999
Deadline for review comments	Feb 19, 1999
Feature-freeze for verification draft	Feb 26, 1999
Distribute final draft to verify	Mar 8, 1999
Documentation field test ends	Mar 12, 1999
End final review	Mar 19, 1999
Final edits	Mar 22, 1999
Prepare camera-ready copy	Apr 19, 1999
Documentation to printer	May 3, 1999

you expect to work on the document. I like to use Mondays, but some use Fridays. Then black in the squares when you are doing work on the book. For example, when your document is in review, you may be able to work on another document, so leave those days or weeks blank.

Tip ➤ *Graph your schedule.*

If you work on more than one book at a time, using graph paper can help you avoid a snafu like scheduling that you will send both those books to review on the same day. Once you have set or agreed to a schedule, your reviewers and others will expect your book when promised. A graph of the schedule in Table 4.1 might look like Figure 4.3.

Tip ➤ *Shorten your schedule.*

Examination of typical schedule milestones can show you ways to reduce the time it takes to create a document: you can shorten your review times by a day or so, you can have only two reviews, not three, or you can shorten the time between drafts.

Depending on your environment, you may be able to reduce the time from start to finish significantly. But no matter how you reduce the time in your

Month	Nov		Dec				Jan				Feb				Mar					Apr				May
	23	30	7	14	21	28	4	11	18	25	1	8	15	22	1	8	15	22	29	5	12	19	26	3
Doc. plan to review		PR																						
Final plan				FP																				
Feature-freeze 1					Fr1																			
First draft to review							R1	R1																
Feature-freeze 2										Fr2														
Start doc. field test												FT												
Second draft to review												R2	R2											
Final feature-freeze														FF										
Verification of final draft																	V							
End doc. field test																		Ftend						
Make final edits																		Fedits						
Prepare production copy																							Prod	
Send book to print																								TP

Figure 4.3
Schedule Graph

schedule, remember that your goal is to document the real product, not some-one's idea of what the product is. So be sure to include sufficient time to check your examples with the product itself.

Writing Your Documentation

Once you have written your detailed plan, and the plan has been reviewed and agreed to, you can begin *creation* of your documents. During the creation of text, you use the research materials previously gathered and continue to converse and work with the technical members of your project team. You also use the software or hardware as much as possible to understand not only theoretically but also practically how it works.

In some cases, you may create the working examples for the documentation and find bugs (errors) in the software. Examples are your responsibility, but you may need the assistance of a programmer or developer to create them for complex software. There are two rules for examples:

- Examples must work.
- Examples must be short.

Your readers will try to use any example you put in your book, so be sure the examples you present work. Try them out yourself, or, even better, write them yourself. Whether you are writing about commands for a utility or a procedure for a system manager, or preparing a programmer's manual, your examples will be used, so be sure they work by testing them. An example must instruct, not just show a fancy way of coding with the language or a special, unusual syntax possibility for a command. Decide where to put your examples, and work with your technical resources to develop examples that are short and meaningful. An example that is too long won't be used.

Tip ➤ *Keep your examples short.*

Sometimes development may show you that for their software, the only correct, working example requires 50 pages of dense code. Instead of printing this long example, have your developers provide it in softcopy (on the software medium) with the software, and just describe it in your document. Such a long example is sometimes called a *sample application.*

To create technical material, you must have proficiency with the tools available; this is so their use does not inhibit your work. You also need an understanding of ancillary tools your illustrators may use. For example, you may not be an artist or an illustrator, but if you understand what is needed to create diagrams with a graphics tool, you can describe to the illustrator just what you want. Sometimes you may become proficient in using several tools and can therefore be nearly a one-person publications department. However, while it is of great value to be conversant with several tools, usually you will feel most comfortable relying on no more than half a dozen to get your job done.

When you work with word processing or text processing tools, you soon find that your daily work contains significant time spent using an electronic editor to enter text into files, move information around (sometimes called "cut and paste" operations), and perhaps process files to verify what the final format looks like. Some tools enable you to exert considerable control over the output format; other tools make virtually all formatting decisions once you have made a fundamental determination of the look desired in the final document.

No matter which electronic editor you use, however, you must develop a repertoire of commands or control sequences with which to instruct the electronic editor. Entering actual text can represent up to 60 or 80 percent of writer activity with the editor. The rest of the time you will be entering or deciding on command sequences, selecting menu items, and processing files to produce final output.

In this regard, many writers are like software developers who design software and implement it by entering statements into computer files in the language of choice. While the developer uses a computer language such as C++ or Java, you use a computer language of control characters or tags/labels, combined with the natural language text of the document being written. Both "compile" their code or have it processed by a computer. The developer's result is executable code; the writer's, readable text "executable" in the mind of the reader.

Of course, if you write straight text into a file, you perform fewer of these steps, but to produce a table of contents or to print your file, you process your file in some way. If not, you must do many tasks that other software tools could do for you. The characters you see on your screen are not the same characters that get printed on your printer: they are transformed by the magic of electronics from one medium to the other through the memory of your computer.

The major advantage of the electronic editor and its companion text processing system is the ability they give you to make changes and rewrite, recast, or correct information. This is a capability not available to the writer pecking out a draft on a manual typewriter. Even word processing systems have limited reorganizing capabilities and can be restrictive in the amount of room they require for storage of text and graphics.

As demand has increased for information exchange between groups such as writers and publishers, efforts have been initiated to standardize both the language of writing tools and the file formats in which documents are stored. One standard, supported by the U.S. government and the publishing industry, is the Standard Generalized Markup Language (SGML). The popular HyperText Markup Language (HTML) began as a subset of this standard.

Departments or large groups often evolve their own style guides that writers must follow, as do publishing houses who develop their own "house" style. You will need to become familiar with the local style to meet local requirements.

To produce large technical documents, you need tools with internal cross-referencing and extensive indexing capabilities. An internal cross-reference is a reference you place in one part of your book that refers the reader to another part. For example, in Chapter 4, you may need to refer the reader back to a table in Chapter 2. You make this internal cross-reference so that you don't have to repeat the table.

Following the *guideline of no duplication,* you make the reference and don't repeat the table. If you repeat information, keeping its every occurrence up to date and consistent will become a maintenance nightmare. Even if you don't have a text processing tool that makes it easy for you to make internal cross-references, keep such cross-references to a minimum.

Some text processing tools let you introduce *symbol, symbolic,* or *logical names* (these are all synonyms) that the document processing system uses to prepare accurate cross-references for chapters, sections, figures, tables, examples, and so on. Such systems also prepare correct tables of contents and indexes as needed, saving much labor on your part and on that of any editor or proofreading staff. You must still create your index entries, however, and develop appropriate symbol names for elements throughout your document.

A *symbol name* is a word or abbreviation you place as an argument to a title of a chapter, section, figure, and so on. At processing time, the text processing system replaces the symbol name with the actual title.

For example, the symbol name for the schedule table in this chapter could be SCHED. You can't use the actual table title as a symbolic name because it may be too long or have spaces or other characters that your text processing system won't let you use.

You would not see this symbol name in the table title, but it would be in my source file and let me refer to Table 4.1 without having to worry about table number changes if I move parts of my document around. Symbol names simplify your work because you don't have to remember to check all your internal cross-references even when you move whole paragraphs, sections, or tables; the text processing system does it for you. Some authoring tools still require that you explicitly enter cross-references, a method that is always prone to error.

Tip ➤ ***Have all your graphics in place for your final draft.***

Because you want your reviewers to have a chance to see your entire document intact, have all your diagrams in place when you send your final draft out for review. You often cannot get final diagrams before this stage, but at least for your last verification of content, have any diagrams in place.

Reworking Your Documentation

Once you have created a draft, your document enters its testing phase. This is the time for review by members of the technical team, perhaps peer writers who have experience in similar documentation, perhaps your management (this varies from company to company), perhaps a representative of a translation team, and sometimes an editor. This is also the time for procedural or usability testing of the document. Usability testing can be done by a writer trained in this specialty or perhaps by a human factors or testing group, if your company has one. You must allow time in your document schedule for testing or it will not be done.

Reviewing

Each reviewer brings a different perspective and viewpoint to the examination of your manuscript. Your technical reviewers must examine the document from the perspective of the technical information it contains: is it complete, accurate, and appropriate? On many projects, no single technical reviewer understands the entire product. Then you must rely on several individuals, each of whom contributes a particular expertise to the document review. Sometimes you can separate technical expertise by chapter, so that you rely on one individual for one chapter, on another individual for the technical details of another chapter, and so on.

Tip ➤ ***All reviewers won't review everything.***

You also need to help your reviewers understand that you need their substantive comments, not just question marks. For example, if a reviewer hands back your draft with the comment "Huh?" in the margin, you will have to go back to that reviewer and ask what "Huh" means. That is not a very helpful comment. Or a reviewer may concentrate entirely on typographical errors; that's also not very helpful because it means the reviewer will probably miss errors of fact or incorrect descriptions. When you deal with reviewer comments, never take them personally, and find ways to distinguish between fact and opinion.

For example, the following sentence was prepared for a draft of this book:

MIL-M-28001 addresses the automated publication of technical manuals and recommends use of the SGML industry standard for markup languages.

A reviewer annotated the sentence and added new information, shown in italics, as follows:

MIL-M-28001A (updated) addresses the automated publication of technical manuals: It recommends use of SGML (Standard Generalized Markup Language), the industry standard for documentation representation, and additional standards for graphics and data interchange.

As a result of these comments, the final text became:

MIL-M-28001A, developed for CALS, addresses the automated publication of technical manuals. This specification recommends use of standards for:

- SGML (Standard Generalized Markup Language), the industry standard for documentation representation
- Graphics
- Data interchange

The reviewer provided technical and literary comments, and the final text shows that both were taken into account. The technical comments included the statement that the standard had been updated (and this reviewer kindly supplied the new number, which is not always done) and that it applied to more than the markup language. The literary comments included dividing the sentence into two and changing some of the wording. Writing peers are often extremely valuable reviewers. They bring to their reviews a wealth of experience and a variety of perspectives. Many times an experienced writer can recall a similarly difficult information transfer process and suggest improvements in your structure or writing. Translation or training coordinators can help you identify potential trouble spots for different national or cultural environments.

Tip ➢   *Use peer reviews.*

Experienced writers have learned effective ways to convey information to certain readers and a variety of methods of presentation. Because technical communication is the work they do, they often have many suggestions for you, the new writer just beginning a career in technical communication.

Technical Editing

A good technical editor is a must for all projects which produce informational materials. The editor should be armed with or create a style sheet or style guide that details the conventions used throughout the information set. For example, a style guide should contain instructions for writers on:

- title page (what's on it, and its format)
- copyright page (what goes on it, in what order, perhaps font size)
- table of contents (how many header levels, chapter numbering and heading format)
- headers and footers throughout the document (what they contain, and in what format)
- index (conventions for creating index entries)
- conventions used in the information set (for example, use of bold for glossary terms, italics for manual references, monospace for code examples, all conventions that are to be maintained across the document set)
- graphics conventions (size and font of words, any standard icons)
- glossary

The editor should religiously follow the style guide when reviewing a writer's draft, and be consistent in checking for cross-reference, citations of other books (are their titles correct?), the handling of figure and table captions, and so on.

A technical editor should read a draft three times:

- once for grammar and punctuation
- once for adherence to the style guide
- once for typographical errors

When suggesting rewording, editors must be very careful not to change the technical content of the information.

Timing of technical edits is important. On a new project, it is probably a waste of an editor's time to do detailed edits on a first draft, although it can be useful to examine the organization of a new document. A technical editor should examine a second draft of a manual, when three drafts are projected, and perhaps do a cursory edit of a final draft. Most projects won't be able to afford the luxury of full edits on every draft.

Tip ➤ *Try experiments.*

There are few good tools you can use today to examine your own text for wordiness or excessive use of the passive voice, but you may be able to experiment with some tools you already have to get some help in this area. For example, with an electronic editor of your choice, you may be able to search for passive constructions, perhaps by searching for "is" or "-ed." When you find these occurrences, read the surrounding text to see if you have a passive construction you can change.

For wordiness, read some of your text and identify your common wordy constructs. For example, you may use "in order to" or "was equipped with" a lot. With your sample of wordy constructs, search your files for the offending phrases and delete them. You will have to replace each phrase with the right word, of course, but this is sure to shorten your text and help make it more crisp. There are many sources of commonly overused phrases; any one of them can help. For a sampling, see Further Reading at the end of this chapter.

Experience shows that, depending upon project schedules and deliverables, a document usually receives the optimum review attention when you prepare three drafts. The first draft, patterned after the planned outline, is often rough and may not contain all needed information. But having a draft even in rough form lets you conduct a review and helps other members of the project team understand what you are trying to do. Your second draft should be as complete as possible, and your third draft is essentially a verification draft. If you are writing more than three drafts, both you and your reviewers may lose interest in accurate writing and review.

Tip ➤ *A first draft gets you valuable feedback.*

On many projects, particularly when software is not available, you can often get valuable feedback even with a draft that has many holes in it. The first draft gives reviewers an idea of what the document will contain, and how it is structured, even when they cannot comment on all details they will need to look at later. Early drafts can help get feedback started.

Bear in mind that your job is to write reviewable drafts; the iterative nature of the review process will help you improve each successive draft. When starting a review, establish what you expect of reviewers so they understand what you will accept or ignore. And don't just drop a review draft on someone's desk and expect to get the quality or quantity of feedback you need. You will almost always have to be proactive in getting the most from your reviewers.

Tip ➤ *Instruct your reviewers.*

Some writers conduct reviews entirely on paper; in such a review, you send out a draft with a due date for comments. You ask your reviewers to mark up the draft and return the marked-up copies to you. In other cases, you ask not only that reviewers mark up the draft but also that they attend a review meeting scheduled for the last day or the day following the last day of the review period.

Tip ➤   *A good time for a review meeting is when there are unanswered questions.*

A review meeting is particularly valuable when it is hard to clarify technical issues (that is, the reviewers disagree). The review meeting becomes the place where differences of opinion between members of the technical staff can be resolved immediately. This saves time both for you and for other members of the project team.

Tip ➤   *Write out your agenda for all to see.*

When you or your project leader start the meeting, it helps to let everyone know what will be done during the meeting, if you write up the agenda on a white board for everyone to see. This focuses attention on the goals of the meeting, and helps everyone know how the meeting is progressing.

Tip ➤   *Mark up a master.*

When you have received several reviews, it is often good practice to mark up a single master copy with review comments before beginning to edit your files. This way you observe conflicts between comments more easily and can resolve them without confusion.

Then you prepare your second draft, incorporating comments from the first review and any changes that are occurring in the product. At the right moment in the project cycle, you send this second draft to the review team for their next review.

Time this second draft to coincide with a real product in which all details have been established. If a product is still undergoing significant change, delay the second draft until major project or product issues are finalized. The alternative is to send your second draft to review too early. If you do, you must usually add another draft review to the cycle, which is costly both for you and for the project.

It is both a courtesy and good practice to return to your reviewers their earlier, marked-up draft review copies when you distribute your next draft for review.

Tip ➤   *Watch out for this horror story.*

I once saw a project where the writer went through twelve reviews in four weeks because the product's technical resource could not decide on certain product components and so essentially reviewed one page of the document each time a new draft was presented. Everyone got frustrated on this project! To avoid this situation, use the feature-freeze strategy.

Be firm in adhering to your freeze when you get to the assigned date. Your reviewers must understand that they will have another opportunity to see the document, and when they see it, they can add information about things that are currently true. If you don't get their cooperation, you will always be spinning your wheels and fighting fires, and you will be constantly interrupt-driven.

Your second draft, which should be complete with any illustrations and appendices, table of contents, and index, is perhaps the most difficult draft to time in a project. Timing of this draft is particularly tricky if several books must pass through review cycles almost simultaneously.

Tip ➤ ***Keep your technical resources on tap.***

As you get closer to the end of a project, technical resources you have worked with will very likely go off to other projects and no longer be available. For this reason, finalize your information as early as possible, and if possible, find ways to obtain input from resources when they are off on another project. When this is not possible, you may need to request other resources to answer your open questions.

Team Work

Most writers today work together with teams, not only their software development teams, but their full documentation team that includes the project leader, possibly a project manager, other writers, editors, graphics illustrators, possibly production people. Fostering cooperation and team spirit will help make everyone's work time more productive and more pleasant. Sharing of information between team members also makes the team more productive and flexible.

Testing

Several other processes can occur at this second draft stage in documentation development. One is documentation testing by people who are similar to those who will actually be using the document when the product arrives at the customer's desk. Many corporations use *field test* or *beta test* to achieve this goal and obtain feedback on the documentation directly from customers. Such testing must be planned for and executed within the project schedule.

Field test, or beta test (names for the same thing) is hardware or software product testing at selected customer sites. Alpha, or internal, field test precedes beta test and can only test the product in a more limited environment. Field test is an opportunity to see how the product performs in the environment where it is expected to be used. When your document goes to field test with your product, you can sometimes get valuable feedback from customers who follow your procedures and descriptions. Documentation testing can be done at any reasonable point in the project, but don't postpone such testing beyond the second draft stage or you will have no time to incorporate any changes you find needed in your information.

Online Testing   Many products today are prepared for delivery on a Windows or UNIX platform, both of which have online deliverables. On the Windows platform you may deliver WinHelp, and on the UNIX platform man (manual) pages. When writing for these platforms or for others, you will need to prepare your information using the appropriate online-delivery tool. For example, to deliver WinHelp files, you may use either Doc-To-Help or Robohelp. With any tool you use to create information that is to be read online, you should review online results to ensure that cross-references, pop-ups, titles, diagrams, tables, and word-wrapping all work as expected. If possible, review your online files at second draft stage and also have them reviewed by an editor. The accepted form of online material should be defined by your editor in the project style sheet.

Often your online form of the information is created directly from the same source you use for your hardcopy deliverables. The advantage of this is that you work with a single source for both paper and online. The disadvantage is that you cannot fully exploit the benefits of using an online form, such as color or animation, and you cannot rewrite all your material for online viewing. A compromise is to conditionalize your text so that some items are available in only the hardcopy form, and some only online. You won't, for example, typically include page numbers in your online form because page numbers don't have meaning online, and you won't include figure numbers for the same reason. A figure appears either where it should be in the text or is available in a popup window. Cross-references are handled by links that are visible in some way, such as colored and underlined words online.

In addition to customer or beta testing, sometimes you can conduct usability tests on books or parts of books, or tests on procedures you wrote. You must plan for usability testing so that time can be allocated for it.

Usability Testing   There are several ways you can perform usability testing. Each addresses different aspects of your document. These tests are like usability tests of other parts of the product, but address documentation specifically. They employ:

- Questionnaires
- Telephone interviews
- Read and locate tests
- Structured interviews
- Usability edits
- Summary tests
- Exploration of the user's environment
- Contextual inquiry

Before you begin a usability test, you must decide:

- What to test
- What to do with the results

Deciding what to test depends on your goals and the time and budget you have to conduct the tests. You won't be able to test everything in your document or in your documentation kit. The best way to decide what to test is to identify problems your reviewers have found with the documentation. For example, they may have seen no real difficulties in reading the text, but had lots of problems with the reading path or documentation map supplied with the documentation set.

Tip ➤   *Test what perplexes reviewers.*

This is a strong indication that you will get the greatest mileage out of testing the map to find out how it can be improved.

To prepare and use a *questionnaire,* decide on several things:

- Paper or electronic distribution
- Topics the questionnaire must address
- Sequence of topics
- Wording of questionnaire

Tip ➤   *Pretest a questionnaire.*

Always pretest your questionnaire before you use it in a real test. Keep it as short as possible and clarify ambiguous questions. You will need to tabulate questionnaire responses to draw any conclusions. Be sure you have time in your schedule to do this.

To conduct a *telephone interview,* start with a list of questions you prepare beforehand. There are three types of telephone interview:

- Interviewer has questionnaire.
- Both interviewer and respondent have questionnaire.
- Both interviewer and respondent have questionnaire and both are using the product.

The first type gives you the most limited feedback; the second is better; and the last is best of all, though the most difficult to arrange.

A *read and locate* test can be very helpful in establishing if your reader can find needed information. It is a little like an "open book quiz" where you ask users to read questions and locate information. This test can help you find buried information and identify information that is not in the documentation, so formulate your questions to get specific answers. Also, in developing your questions, focus on key tasks the users will perform, be sure you can get measurable results, have some easy and some hard questions, don't follow the organization of the book you are testing in the order of your questions, and test the questions before conducting the test. Listed below are questions you might ask in a read and locate test for a reference manual:

1. The logical name of the disk drive containing the system directory is:
2. [location of answer:]
3. You set the queue characteristics for a printer queue with command x:
4. [location of answer:]

A *structured interview* uses a questionnaire as well, but you visit the person of whom you ask questions. The most useful structured interviews are done with the respondent using or having used the product. Sometimes, on a questionnaire, a respondent will answer a question about how a book worked for her with "No problems with this." But when you sit with her and watch how she uses your book with the software, and how frustrated she gets trying to do something, you get quite another view. You may find out that the structure of your book, which looks wonderful to you, just does not work in the respondent's environment.

Use a *usability edit* when you want to evaluate a book containing procedures, for example, a tutorial, an installation guide, or a "getting started" document. In a usability edit, you observe an inexperienced user working with the product (hardware or software) using only the documentation. Have the user speak aloud while working. The user can also mark the documentation. Note problems the user encounters, paying particular attention to gaps in explanations or procedures, ambiguous information, problems doing a task, or problems finding information.

A *summary test* is a test for comprehension. You write down the main points you wish to get across, then test to see if those are the points your readers got. When you have the results, revise your document, if need be, and retest.

To *explore the user's environment,* you must visit users' offices and observe how they deal with documentation. Perhaps just a few books are within arm's reach, and others haven't even been opened. Perhaps they have lots of lists of system commands or tool menus placed strategically around the office. Asking what the users read to answer technical questions, whether they read manuals at all, whether the index or table of contents is helpful, and so on, can give you information that can cause you to change how you write and deliver documentation.

For *contextual inquiry,* your approach may be broader than documentation only; this technique is used to define system requirements, functional specifications, and designs. It can also be useful in determining what kind of documentation users require. You work closely with users in the context of their work to determine what they do and how they do it. From the information you gather, you develop ways to prepare the documentation.

Whatever tests you decide to use, you will find that testing always gives you ways to improve your documentation. Perhaps you will find that some tables are better set up one way than another, that some chapters need to be redesigned or reorganized, or that a document needs to be divided differently. Sometimes you misunderstand how readers will use the material, or you may approach the documentation problem from the wrong angle; you may have missed information or run into organizational problems. You will be able to correct such problems if you do your testing early enough. If you plan for one or more iterations, you can correspondingly improve your books.

As an example, Figures 4.4 and 4.5 show a documentation map and reading path before and after a usability test was run. The newer diagram was understood by everyone who saw it; the earlier diagram by none.

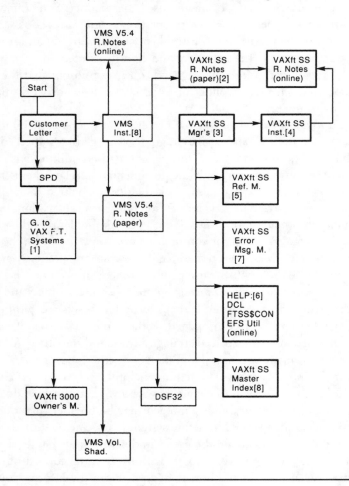

Figure 4.4
Map Before Usability Testing

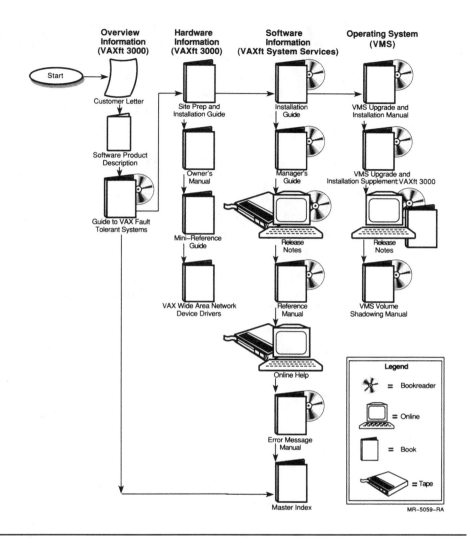

Figure 4.5
Map After Usability Testing and Modifications

Procedural Testing   There are three ways to test a procedure you have written:

- Try out, or have someone else try out, the procedure by following your text.
- Develop a flow chart of the procedure.
- Use a Nassi-Shneiderman diagram.

To *try out* your written procedure, give it to someone unfamiliar with the procedure and watch how well the person follows it. You will find out quickly if you have left out a step or if your instructions are confusing.

Sometimes, if your procedure requires a complex laboratory setup or equipment that is hard to obtain, you may be unable to use this method. If so, try one of the others.

To develop a flow chart, diagram each step of your written procedure using rectangles for action, diamonds for decisions, and arrows for direction. For example, the following procedure shows how to start your car:

1. Go to the car.
2. Open the door.
3. Get into the driver's seat.
4. Put the car in neutral.
5. Put the key in the ignition.
6. Turn the key in the ignition.
7. Press on the gas pedal.

Figure 4.6 shows this procedure in a flow chart.
Figure 4.7 shows this procedure as a Nassi-Shneiderman diagram.

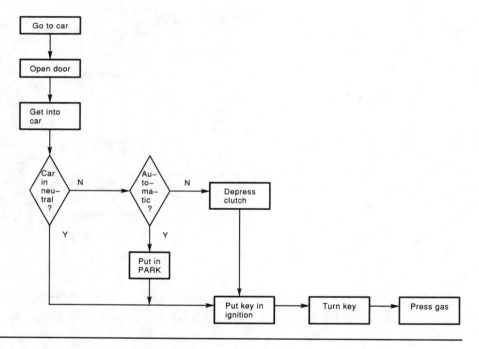

Figure 4.6
Flow Chart of Starting Your Car

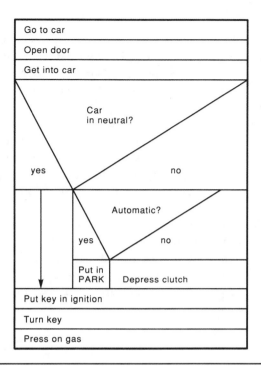

Figure 4.7
Nassi-Shneiderman Diagram of Starting Your Car

Notice that the procedure leaves out some decisions you might need, such as what to do if you get into the car on the wrong side, if you don't have the right key, or if the car is an antique that has a separate starter switch. So even this short example of a commonly understood practice contains many assumptions.

Editing

Another task is editorial review or proofreading of the document. An editorial review provides you with comments on the literary correctness of the document (grammar, spelling, and punctuation) and can include stylistic recommendations. Editorial/proofreading review requires three readings: one for sense, a second for phraseology and clarity, and a third for spelling and punctuation.

Your technical editor can provide a valuable service by commenting on organization and technical accuracy of a document or document set and, to have the greatest impact on the documentation, should be involved early in the review process. With limited staff, you may have to perform some of these tasks yourself.

Indexing

Indexing was virtually unknown in ancient times, became more common when printing evolved, and is now a necessity for all technical documents. Often your reader does not recall in which chapter or section an item was, but a good index can supply the answer. Computerized document access systems make indexes even more important.

A good index enhances the value of a technical document, regardless of whether the document is read as hardcopy or online. Even though you will prepare indexes for both these forms using similar tools, the importance of the index increases when a document is read online. Online documents are accessed rather than read through, and your index needs to serve the needs of both the experienced reader and the novice.

Your index must be appropriate for your book. Looking at other books you like for the same readers can help you decide what kind of index you need. You can create analytic or synthetic indexes or a combination of both.

You create an *analytic* index by identifying key topics in your book, reading and analyzing the text and graphics, and then arranging the topics in alphabetical order. Such topics you identify might be:

Daisy-wheel printer
Dot-matrix printer
Indexing
Passive voice
Planning
Rewriting

You can also add to your index by making *synthetic* connections between entries, by grouping entries about one type of subject. For example, you can group the entries about printers as follows:

Printers:
    daisy-wheel
    dot-matrix

Specialist scientific textbooks tend to have analytic indexes — the reader wants to look up a highly specific word. But most technical documentation benefits from a combined analytic and synthetic index. For example, you might select the words in small capitals in the following paragraphs for your index.

The DAISY-WHEEL PRINTER is a printer in which printing is done with a small wheel (that looks like a daisy); each character is placed at the outer end of each spoke in the wheel. The daisy wheel could be easily exchanged to use a different typeface for a document.

A DOT-MATRIX PRINTER is fast and flexible, but does not produce high-quality print. All dot-matrix printers form each character by a set of wires in a two-dimensional pattern set in a print head. The RESOLUTION of letters and clarity of printing depends on the number of wires in the print head. The more wires, the better the quality.

From this text, you then create several additional entries to help your reader find information by more than one route. Your final index could contain the following:

Daisy-wheel printer
Dot-matrix printer
Letter
    resolution of
Printer
   daisy-wheel
   dot-matrix
Resolution of letters

Sometimes you may need to create an *informative* index, to which you add information (names, dates, definitions, explanations). But such an index is rare in technical documentation. You might use such an index in a primer or tutorial.

A professional indexer can be valuable, but you should also be able to create a useful index yourself for a document you have created. As the writer, you typically know the subject so well that you are often the best person for the job. Some writers, however, prefer to have an independent indexer prepare the index for their work. It can be useful to ask technical reviewers or people who participate in your field test for terms they would like to see in your index.

There are three ways you can create an index:

- By manual methods
- With the assistance of your computer
- By automatic generation

When you create your own index manually, you mark a finished copy of your manuscript in a uniform manner for all items you think will be useful in your index. You then transcribe these entries onto 3-by-5 index cards, with their page numbers, and sort the cards in alphabetical order. You could also transcribe your entries on individual lines in a file and then use a sort utility to sort them alphabetically. When you transcribe your entries, you must make certain critical decisions:

- How to capitalize (always initial caps or only for certain items)
- How to sort (letter by letter or word by word)
- For individual entries, what major entries and subentries will be

Capitalization is often defined by the "house style" of your company or organization. Sorting method, whichever you select, must be followed religiously. When you sort letter by letter, you sort each entry starting with its leftmost letter, ignoring spaces and hyphens. A set of entries sorted letter by letter looks like this:

tenant
tenant farmer
ten-cent store
Ten Commandments
tend
10 Downing Street (sorted as "ten")
ten-speed
tens place

This same set of index entries looks different sorted word by word:

Ten Commandments
10 Downing Street (sorted as "ten")
tenant
tenant farmer
ten-cent store
tend
ten-speed
tens place

With some computer indexing systems, you can sort entries letter by letter, ignoring spaces and hyphens, and perhaps by numerical values. For example, you may see the following:

10 Downing Street (sorted with the D-words)
Ten Commandments (sorted with the T-words)
tenant
tenant farmer
ten-cent store
tend
ten-speed
tens place

An indexing system that uses the collating sequence and every character in each entry, including spaces and hyphens, may produce:

10 Downing Street
Ten Commandments
ten-cent store
ten-speed
tenant
tenant farmer
tend
tens place

If you create your entire index manually, you must eventually transcribe it in sorted order. But most writers preparing technical documentation use a computer to simplify this tedious chore. With a computer, there are several ways to create an index:

- by marking an entry with an indexing code
- by entering a word to be indexed with a menu pick
- by letting software create a full-text concordance of all words in your text
- by entering an index entry

How you actually create your index depends on the software you are using.

Some text processing software lets you indicate your index entries in your text with special indexing codes. For example, if you are using Microsoft Word, you indicate an index entry by marking a word or phrase using your mouse, and inserting it as an index entry using a menu selection. You can also add subentries or "See" references in a dialog box that appears when you begin to insert your index entry. Another text processing system might have you insert a control character such as "^" to indicate a single-word index entry. With a system like WordPerfect, you create a separate *concordance* file containing index entries, then apply that file to your written text. The concordance file and any words in your text marked as index entries then form your completed index with page numbers.

To obtain your sorted index, you may either invoke a separate utility, have your index processed when you output your finished or draft document, or create it on the fly as you need it. You may choose to process your index as you create intermediate drafts of your document or wait until the final draft. You must decide which choice works best for you. Some writers prefer to wait until their book is fairly close to its finished look before they do serious work on the index. If you are preparing an index manually, you must wait until you have final page numbers before you can complete the job. This is only one reason why doing indexes manually will soon be a thing of the past.

One area where computerized indexing needs improvement is the creation of permuted indexes, those that contain all the entries you supply plus the words of those entries rearranged as appropriate. With most software tools, you must supply your own permutations. For example, if you supply the entries "Deleting files" and "Deleting directories," an indexing utility that sorts and permutes these entries would create an index as follows:

D

Deleting directories
Deleting files
Directories,
    deleting

F

Files,
    deleting

Some computer software is available to scan your text and prepare an alphabetized list of selected words. These lists can help you identify words to add to your index, but so far no software can prepare an index that is as useful as one prepared by a person and edited. Some software tools such as Dynatext prepare an index of all words in a given text, on the fly. If you prepare information for use by such a tool, you won't have control over what goes into the index it presents to the reader. Research continues in this area, but few writers can take advantage of it yet.

Creating an Index   When you create your index entries, you need to bear in mind a few rules:

- Use nouns or noun phrases for your entries.
- Use appropriate terms, those your reader is likely to look for and terms you have used in your book. You can include terms not in your book if you think your reader will look for them as alternatives to the book terms.
- Keep each entry meaningful: base your selection on content, and consider what your readers will want to find.
- Provide multiple ways to reach important information, but don't have an entry with four or five subentries that all point to the same page.
- Do not overindex: don't include trivial entries in your index, and don't provide lots of references for an item that is only mentioned, not explained. An entry must lead the reader to text that contains useful information.
- For any index you prepare, whether it is a single document index or a subindex for use in a consolidated or master index, work with any other writers on your documentation team to index and spell words the same way. Don't, for example, use "Files, deleting" and "Files, deletion of." Use the same phrase for these two entries and be consistent in the way you write such entries throughout your index. A style sheet is helpful to ensure consistency.
- Keep your index accurate; delete old index entries when you delete text, and be sure your entries reflect the information you want to index.
- In general, don't index heads from your table of contents; this is redundant. Some heads represent tasks you may want to index, however, so use your judgment to decide what works for your book.
- Supply "See . . ." references to send your readers to the information they have looked up under another name. A "See . . ." reference should end with a period.
- Supply "See also . . ." references when you want your readers to seek additional information elsewhere. A "See also . . ." reference should end with a period.

You may encounter a new type of indexing if you work in a hypertext environment. *Hypertext,* made possible by the random access methods of computers, is nonhierarchical or nonsequential text. Traditional documentation, like books, is hierarchical and sequential.

In a hypertext system, readers follow no set order when reading text; they decide what they want to read next. Hypertext systems include web browsers such as Netscape, Microsoft Internet Explorer, the Apple Macintosh Guide, the

UNIX-based Intermedia, developed at Brown University, the Hyperties system developed at the University of Maryland (available as a commercial system on IBM PCs), and the Symbolics Document Examiner, among others.

As a writer for hypertext, you must keep in mind how your reader will access and read the information you provide. The usual method is to write information as short topics and use your authoring tool to provide the links that lead your reader to the topics. With hypertext, your topics must be short; thus you may need to decompose larger topics into smaller ones and supply feeder links to bring your readers through all the needed links. And your reader is more likely to use keyword searches than look things up in an index. We still have much to learn about creating effective documentation for this environment.

The user of a hypertext environment scans information differently from the reader of a book. Scanning from one chunk of information to another, traversing through many chunks, returning to previously read chunks or topics, is quite different from reading a book that is organized hierarchically. Readers learn differently when browsing cyberspace, and may need to construct the hierarchy on their own to understand the thread of what they are reading, or its basic structure. Online systems typically present top-level organization hierarchically to assist the reader in finding information, but this structure is soon forgotten when the reader delves down the information tree to find answers to questions. The reader of a book can flip back and forth in a book, perhaps keeping a finger at the table of contents while reading in the book, but the online reader must rely more on short-term memory to hold the hierarchical information needed to traverse the information tree. Short-term memory is our weakest mental resource. Unless fixed in long-term memory by being written down or otherwise fixed in our minds, information stored in short-term memory vanishes and is not retrievable.

In a largely electronic environment, the reader of technical material will no longer have a shelf of books from which to select but will be able to call up the pages of several books on a video screen at the same time and find references to associated information quickly and readily. You need to understand and anticipate the varied needs of a wide readership and encode these anticipated needs in the information you write and the index or keyword entries you supply.

When you prepare, review, edit, and complete your index, you must be consistent in your use of words and the terminology of the product you describe.

Your Final Draft

With testing complete and results incorporated into the last draft of your document, you can establish all the final details that need to go into the document and send it out for one last review. Normally, if you have completed all your testing, understood its results, and conducted all earlier reviews with full participation of the review team, at this point, you should have a very nearly perfect document.

Tip ➤ *Use your last review only to verify.*

This third and final review should be a verification review, not an opportunity for reviewers to ask for major changes. To achieve this goal, make it clear to your reviewers that the last draft is only for verification and last-minute changes, not for a fresh look at the book.

Once you have completed your final review and made those last small changes to your document, if your company has a group that prepares copy for printing, you may simply turn your files over to that group for processing as camera-ready copy. There is great variety in this part of the process. In some companies, or some departments of some companies, you won't be involved at this stage at all once you have handed over your files, and you often don't even see the printed document.

In other places, you may participate in the final process, verifying page breaks and title pages, checking final reprographic copy, and so on. Or you may be the one who creates the final sheets on your laser printer and takes them to the printer for copying in quantity. The amount of your involvement at this stage is extremely variable and depends on local procedures.

Receiving the Results

Once you have delivered your files or your pages, you are typically not directly involved until your final *result* becomes available. This can be a printed book, an online help file, a book intended to be viewed on a terminal screen, or any of a variety of other possible results. The moment when you receive your copy of the printed document, neatly covered and bound — the product of your unique labor — is one of considerable satisfaction and feeling of achievement.

Further Reading

There are many excellent books on technical writing; some address technical writing in general; others address business-oriented writing — memos, proposals, and the like. Some describe how to prepare reports, others describe the process, while still others address writing with computers. Some summarize work about technical writing or documentation. In the following lists, I have separated these books into categories. At the end, you will find a few books and papers on audience or reader analysis and indexing.

Business-oriented writing books:
Technical and Business Writing (Andrews, 1975), *Business Communication* (Andrews, Andrews, 1988), *Write for Results: How to Write Successful Memos, Letters, Summaries, Abstracts, Proposals, Reports, and Articles* (Andrews, Andrews, 1982), *Communication on the Job* (Comeau, Diehn, 1987), *Writing Effective Business Letters, Memos, Proposals and Reports* (Cypert, 1983), *The Guide to Better Communication in Government Service* (Falcione, 1984), *Writing: A Guide for Business Professionals* (Griffin, 1988), *Reporting Technical Information* (Houp, Pearsall, 1988), *The Business Writer's Handbook* (Oliu, Brusaw, 1987), *How to Write for the World of Work* (Pearsall, Cunningham, 1986), *Technical English: Writing, Reading, and Speaking* (Pickett, Laster, 1988), *Technical Writing for Industry* (Riney, 1989), *Writing on the Job* (Schell, Stratton, 1984), *Writing Handbook for Computer Professionals* (Skees, 1982), *Technical Writing: A Practical Approach* (Turner, 1984), *The Writing System for Engineers and Scientists* (Weiss, 1982), *The Random House Guide to Technical and Scientific Communication* (Zimmerman, Clark, 1987).

Books that address preparing reports:
The Technician as Writer: Preparing Technical Reports (Brunner, Mathes, Stevenson, 1980), *Guidelines for Preparing Computer Reports* (Girill, Perra, 1982), *Designing Technical Reports* (Mathes, Stevenson, 1976), *Technical Report Writing Today* (Pauley, 1979), *Technical Report Writing* (Souther, White, 1984), *Technical Report Writing* (Weisman, 1980).

Process books:
The Elements of Technical Writing (Alvarez, 1980), *Technical Writing: A Reader-Centered Approach* (Anderson, 1987), *Technically-Write!* (Blicq, 1981), *Technical Writing: Structures, Standards, and Style* (Bly, Blake, 1982), *Technical Writing: A Guide with Models* (Brinegar, Skates, 1983), *Handbook of Technical Writing* (Brusaw et al., 1987), *Technical Communication* (Carosso, 1987), *Technical Communication: A Practical Guide* (Dagher, 1987), *Effective Technical Communication* (Eisenberg, 1982), *Technical Communication* (Fear, 1981), *Writing for Science, Industry, and Technology* (Hirschhorn, 1980), *Don't State It ... Communicate It!* (Hochheiser, 1985), *Essentials for the Scientific and Technical Writer* (Hoover, 1981), *Effective Professional Writing* (Keene, 1987), *Technical Writing* (Lannon, 1988), *Strategies for Technical Writing: A Rhetoric with Readings* (Lay, 1982), *Technical Writing* (Levine, 1978), *Technical Writing: Forms and Formats* (MacKenzie, Evans, 1982), *Mastering Technical Writing* (Mancuso, 1990), *Technical Writing: Situations and Strategies* (Markel, 1988), *Technical Writing: Principles and Practice* (Miles, Bush, Kaplan, 1982), *Technical Writing*

(Mills, Walter, 1986), *Handbook of Technical Writing* (Oliu, Brusaw, 1982), *Technical Writing and Professional Communication* (Olsen, Huckin, 1991), *Principles of Communication for Science and Technology* (Olsen, Huckin, 1983), *Introduction to Technical Writing* (Rew, 1989), *Fundamentals of Technical Writing* (Robinson, 1985), *Strategies for Technical Communication* (Roundy, 1985), *The Technical Writing Process* (Samuels, 1989), *Scientific and Technical Writing* (Sandman et al., 1985), *A Guide to Technical Communication* (Sherlock, 1985), *Modern Technical Writing* (Sherman, Johnson, 1983), *Tools of the Mind* (Stibic, 1982), *Technical Writing: Process and Product* (Stratton, 1984), *The Technical Writer* (Stuart, 1988), *Basic Technical Writing* (Sullivan, ed., 1987), *Technical Communication* (Warren, 1978), *Technical Writing: Purpose, Process, and Form* (Warren, 1985), *Basic Technical Writing* (Weisman, 1985).

Books and papers on writing with computers:
Text, ConText, and HyperText (Barrett, ed., 1988), *The Society of Text* (Barrett, ed., 1989), *Mastering Documentation* (Bell, 1989), "The Shape of Hypertext Documents" (Bernstein, 1989), "Cognitive Tools and Computer-Aided Writing" (Carlson, 1990), *Document Databases* (James, 1985), *Word Processing for Technical Writers* (Krull, ed., 1988), *The Writer's Guide to Desktop Publishing* (Lang, 1987), "Standard Text Markup: What SGML Means for Technical Writers" (LaTorra, 1989), *Quick & Easy Guide to Desktop Publishing* (McNeill, 1987), "ZOG and the USS Carl Vinson" (Newell, McCracken, Robertson, Akscyn, 1980–81), *Hypertext and Hypermedia* (Nielsen, 1990), "The ZOG Approach to Man-machine Communication" (Robertson, McCracken, Newell, 1981), *Automatic Text Processing* (Salton, 1989), *Hypertext Hands-On!* (Shneiderman, Kearsley, 1989), "Anatomy of a Style Analyzer" (Stratton, 1989), *Desktop Publishing with WordPerfect 5.0* (Tevis, 1989), "The Role of Modularity in Document Authoring Systems" (Walker, 1988), "Authoring Tools for Complex Document Sets" (Walker, 1989a), "Hypertext and Technical Writers" (Walker, 1989b), "Intermedia: The Concept" (Yankelovich et al., 1988), *In the Age of the Smart Machine* (Zuboff, 1988).

Books on writing about computers:
Writing Better Computer User Documentation (Brockman, 1990), *Guide to Effective Software Technical Writing* (Browning, 1984), *Creating Technical Manuals: A Step-by-Step Approach to Writing User-Friendly Instructions* (Cunningham, Cohen, 1984), *How to Write Computer Manuals for Users* (Grimm, 1982), *Creating Effective Documentation for Computer Programs* (Hastings, King, 1986), *The Complete Guide to Writing Readable User Manuals* (Holtz, 1988), *Designing and Writing Online Documentation* (Horton, 1990), *Guide for Preparing Software User Documentation* (Miller, 1988), *Writing and Developing Operator Manuals* (Schoff, Robinson, 1984), *How to Write Papers*

and Reports about Computer Technology (Sides, 1984), *Developing Effective User Documentation* (Simpson, Casey, 1988), *Technical Manual Writing and Administration* (Walton, 1968), *How to Write a Usable User Manual* (Weiss, 1985), *Fundamentals of Procedure Writing* (Zimmerman, Campbell, 1987).

Books and articles on audience analysis:
Technical Writing (Andrews, Blickle, 1982), *Audience Analysis and Response* (Caernarven-Smith, 1983), "Commentary: The Myth of the Technical Audience" (Moxley, 1988).

Books on indexing:
Book Indexing (Anderson, 1971), *Indexing Concepts and Methods* (Borko, Bernier, 1978), *Introduction to Indexing and Abstraction* (Cleveland, Cleveland, 1990), *Basic Criteria for Indexes* (National Information Standards Series, 1984), *Abstracting and Indexing* (Rowley, 1982), *Indexing: The State of Our Knowledge and the State of Our Ignorance* (Weinberg, ed., 1989).

For the special considerations surrounding indexing in hypertext:
Indexing in a Hypertext Database (Clifton, Garcia-Molina, 1989).

For More Ideas

Research about technical writing, communication, and documentation:
"Minimalist Training" (Carroll, 1984), *Effective Documentation: What We Have Learned from Research* (Doheny-Farina, ed., 1988), "The Nature, Classification, and Generic Structure of Proposals" (Freed, Roberts, 1989), "What's Wrong with the Mathematical Theory of Communication" (Dobrin, 1982), "Writing in an Emergent Business Organization: An Ethnographic Study" (Doheny-Farina, 1985), "A Comparative Case Study of Technical Environmental Communication in Canada and the U.S." (Doheny-Farina, Karis, 1990), "A Conceptual Framework for the Augmentation of Man's Intellect" (Englebart, 1963), "Extracting Information from Printed and Electronically Presented Text" (Hulme, 1985), "Amplification in Technical Manuals" (Killingsworth, et al., 1989), "The Semiology of Documents" (Martin, 1989), "A Humanistic Rationale for Technical Writing" (Miller, 1979), "Invention in Technical and Scientific Discourse: A Prospective Survey" (Miller, 1985), "Wurd Processing" (Nelson, 1990), "Computer-Based Writing and Communication" (Olsen, 1989), "The Collaborative Process and Professional Ethics" (Raymond, Yee, 1990), "Application of Research on Document Design" (Rubens, Krull, 1985), "Document Design from 1980 to 1989" (Schriver, 1989), "Visual Markers for Navigating Instructional Texts" (Sullivan, 1990), "Can Research Assist Technical Communication?" (Wright,

1989), "Technical and Ethical Professional Preparation for Technical Communication Students" (Yee, 1988).

Finally, a few books you might like to look at on readability:
Readability (Gilliland, 1972), *The ABC of Style—A Guide to Plain English* (Flesch, 1980), *Tough, Sweet, and Stuffy: An Essay on Modern American Prose Style* (Gibson, 1966).

Exercises

1. What is usability testing?
2. What is readability?
3. What is a peer review?
4. When would you use a peer review?
5. When is a good time to obtain a technical edit?
6. What is a feature-freeze date?
7. When is it appropriate to use a metaphor?
8. Develop a documentation schedule for a single manual.
9. Develop a documentation plan for an information set of five manuals, three online help components, and a CDROM.
10. Describe how to prepare an effective questionnaire.
11. How does hypertext differ from a book for the reader?

Graphics in Technical Documentation　　　*5*

All colors at a distance are indistinguishable in shadow.
Leonardo da Vinci, *Notebooks* (ed. by Jean Paul Richter), c. 1519

This chapter addresses the basic goals and principles of technical illustration as used with technical documentation — how to specify, evaluate, and incorporate illustrations into your documents and files. The chapter also gives information on how you can produce passable illustrations without professional assistance. However, for many purposes, you enhance the quality of your technical information if you have a professional illustrator create your graphics.

I address graphics implications for print products in this chapter — how to make line drawings, when to use spot color — and what to consider when preparing material for online viewing. Moreover, I tell you how to do all this and still stay within schedule and budget. Impossible, you say? Well, computer tools help to make it possible, but you need to know what your tools are, how to use them, and when to be satisfied with what you have.

You use graphics in technical documentation for several reasons:

- To help explain something you can't describe in words (a picture is worth a thousand)
- To show physical equipment
- To attract the eye of your reader
- To enliven your text so your reader doesn't go to sleep or miss critical information

Illustrations, small or large, are one of the Great Attractors in technical documentation. (The others are described in Chapter 6.) Illustrations attract the eye of your reader because they introduce a change of pace and convey ideas or concepts that are hard to get across in words alone.

Both illustrations and white space attract attention; how you combine them affects the look of your document or online display, its readability and usability.

You can also use color to relieve boredom, but you won't use it frequently in technical documentation because it is expensive. The expense of color depends on how you prepare your copies in quantity. If you have a color printer and prepare only a single copy of your document, your major expense will be in the printer. But if you need to have your document copied in quantity, you will probably use offset printing where every color in addition to black and white requires a second film to be taken for each page with color.

If you add color to every page of your document, you will at least double your printing cost. And if you add more than one color to certain pages, the cost for those pages increases even further. However, some documents — product brochures, for example — need color to make them especially appealing. You won't always be able to avoid using color, but to reduce its expense, use it sparingly. When putting your information online, however, you may be able to use color extensively — it costs no more than black and white.

This chapter describes:

- How to design graphics
- How to use color
- How to prepare graphics
- How to use graphics
- How not to use graphics
- How to place graphics

How to Design Graphics

When designing graphics, either to draw yourself or to give to a graphics illustrator, consider the graphical information hierarchy described more fully in Chapter 3, Precepts of Technical Documentation. This hierarchy has the following order:

- Motion
- Size
- Brightness and saturation
- Position
- Color or hue
- Shape

For example, with a screen containing three items, a blinking date, the large word "Hello!" and a sentence "This is critical information", the eye looks first at the blinking date, then at the large word "Hello!, and finally at the small words "This is critical information" (see Figure 5.1). This hierarchy is based on the way human perception works and cannot be altered. Take it into account when you create information to deliver on screen. Except for motion, which you cannot use in a printed document, the hierarchy holds both for print and online media.

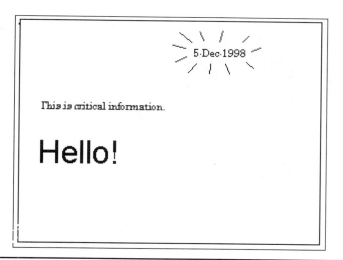

This is critical information.

Hello!

Figure 5.1
An Experiment in Screen Display Hierarchy

How to Use Color

Color terminology can be confusing, but generally you need to be concerned with only two attributes of color, its hue or intrinsic color, and its brightness.

A *color* is what you see either on screen or when you look at an object. The primary colors are red, yellow, and blue. They are combined to produce all other colors such as orange, or sky blue. Reds are often called warm and blues cool (for example, recall the heater/fan slide on your automobile dashboard, where blue indicates a cooler setting, and red, a warmer one).

A *hue* or tint is a particular shade of a color, such as light blue. For example, the hue of the summer sky is often light blue. The *brightness* of a color is its luminous aspect — how much it approaches the maximum luminosity of pure white or the lack of luminosity of pure black. To brighten a color, add white; to darken it, add black. For example, Figure 5.2 (in color on the back cover) shows three shades of blue: on the left, a standard blue, in the middle, a blue brightened by adding white, and on the right, a blue darkened by adding black. The values in the RGB (red, green, blue) and the HSL (hue, saturation, luminosity) systems are given. A fully *saturated* color is one that is made of the color itself, with no added white or black. Fully saturated colors are hard to read, so avoid their use for text. When in doubt, use achromatic colors such as gray, black, and white.

Minimize saturation difference between foreground and background — bright colors reach the brain before dimmer colors. Select background and foreground for

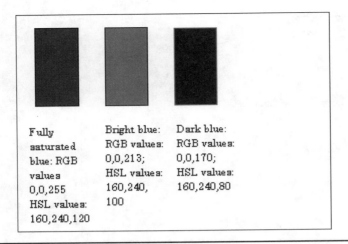

Fully saturated blue: RGB values 0,0,255 HSL values: 160,240,120

Bright blue: RGB values: 0,0,213; HSL values: 160,240, 100

Dark blue: RGB values: 0,0,170; HSL values: 160,240,80

Figure 5.2
Hue, Saturation, and Brightness

optimum contrast, noting that foreground colors are affected by backgrounds. Experiment with foreground/background combinations to see how they look before you make a final decision about color combinations. Keep the number of colors you use to a minimum. Colors don't have hierarchical meaning in expressing information, so use color occasionally to highlight items, but don't rely on color variation to be intuitively obvious to your readers.

How to Prepare Graphics

The traditional way to prepare a graphic was to draw a sketch of the diagram needed and hand it to an artist. The artist then drew the diagram on paper and perhaps inked it for final camera-ready copy. But complex paper drawings and the long hours spent creating them meant that few diagrams could be done within the schedules imposed by most projects. And any hand-drawn graphic had to be pasted onto the page when the time came to prepare camera-ready copy. Pasteup is a time-consuming manual operation prone to error. The wrong picture might be placed on a page, or the picture might be placed upside down. Your goal should be to create fully electronic documents, with all text, heads, and graphics in your files. Only with fully electronic documents can you eliminate pasteup.

When electronic editors came into use for technical documentation, writers experimented with them in creating artwork. Simple yet effective flow charts and box diagrams could be created using a few keyboard characters:

hyphen (-), vertical bar (|), plus sign (+), angle brackets (< >), square brackets ([ ]), slash (/), backslash (\), the letter V, and so on. Producing character or line art like this was tedious, but often such a simple diagram could convey an idea effectively. With most of today's text processing tools, you have several much easier ways to prepare simple diagrams. Once the diagram is in your files, you don't need to be concerned with last-minute pasteup, and your diagram will be there for all your draft reviews.

When a graphics package arrives at your company, you will find that at first everyone is delighted to have a tool that will make life so much easier. Everyone in your writing department will be able to get all the graphics they need in the books they write. Surprise! So many requests flood the illustrators, who have yet to become fully conversant with all the bells and whistles of the new tools, that books still don't have enough graphics. What is the answer? Let writers prepare their own!

This is not as strange as it may seem. You may enjoy doing your own graphics (this is not the same as doing someone else's), and because you control your book for a longer time, you can make changes closer to the end of your project. But don't become too enthusiastic about using graphics — you may use too many. And some diagrams are best left to an experienced graphics illustrator; you can benefit from their design skills and suggestions for simplifying and clarifying your diagrams.

There are many graphics tools available. The one you use depends on your system and perhaps on where you work. Adobe Illustrator, for example, runs on PCs and the Apple Macintosh; Paint, CorelDraw! and many others, run on Microsoft systems. Many text processing systems have fine graphics packages, and some graphics packages have excellent collections of clip art, prepared artwork you can place in your document without change. Some packages let you edit their clip art.

The more documents you create, and the more systems you use, the more likely you are to want to borrow graphics you create on one system and move them to another. Data exchange or data interchange software helps make this increasingly possible. If you create a graphic on an Apple Macintosh system and store it on a removable diskette, you can carry the graphic to another Apple Macintosh system and use it there, so long as the second system has the same graphics and text processing software as the first. Sometimes you may need special tools or use your network or the internet to move that Apple Macintosh graphic to your IBM PC. With a graphic on your own system, you can bring it into your document fairly easily.

Once you have a graphic on your system, you may be able to display it on your screen, or you may only be able to print it. To print a graphic that is not just character or line art, your printer must be either a dot matrix or laser printer. The ability of a laser printer to print the most complex graphics makes it the best for graphics, though, of course, it costs much more than a dot matrix printer. You cannot print professional quality graphics on a daisy-wheel printer.

PostScript

The preeminent language used with a laser printer to set up and print a graphic is PostScript, a page description language created by Adobe. Not all laser printers can interpret files written in PostScript, but many can. PostScript defines the letters and objects of your page and instructs the printer where on the page to print each letter and each object, how large to print a letter, whether to rotate it, or whether to shade it or fill it with black, and so on. The printer you use will be able to print rough work (perhaps 24 dots per inch), letter quality or better (300 dpi), or perhaps full publication quality (2400 dpi or higher).

You can include line drawings and perhaps image files. Image files are files that contain photographs or artwork, scanned into files with an electronic scanner, and use a high-resolution gray scale. Some captured-screen images are also bit-mapped image files. (For an example of such screen-captures, see Chapter 6.) If you want full gray-scale capabilities, you will need special editing software that lets you manipulate such images.

Some PostScript-capable printers can print in color, but color will add additional costs and complexity. Note that PostScript files, graphics, and color place heavy demands on disk storage.

How to Use Graphics

An effective illustration or graphic can assist your readers, focus their attention, highlight concepts, and help them grasp intricate relationships you describe in your text. An illustration can also aid recall, as people sometimes remember the "look" of a page where they read a piece of information when they cannot recall the page number or section reference. There are several guidelines for graphics usage:

- Place a graphic after the first paragraph where you mention it.
- Title all graphics.
- Number all graphics consecutively.
- Avoid busy graphics that are uncomfortable to look at or hard to understand.
- For a complex graphic, conduct a usability test to help ensure that your reader will understand it.

An effective graphic:

- Should cause the reader to think about substance, not graphic design
- Must be integrated with the text and any supporting data
- Must be clearly labeled, with legends and text written horizontally
- Can often be improved by making it smaller

A *data graphic* that conveys statistical or numerical information must:

- Show the data
- Use a consistent, defined scale
- Show the zero point of the scale
- Not distort the data
- Encourage comparison with other data sets
- Show how the data relate

Figure 5.3 conveys information about imports and exports. Following the rules for data graphics, the x and y axes are visible, labeled, and mark the consistent, defined scale that shows the zero point (0 to 500 million dollars on the left or y-axis); there is no distortion in the scale — it accurately represents the data for two years. The lines encourage you to compare the two sets of data, and the legend explains what the data show (a comparison of exports and imports for two years). The two different lines and the consistent scale effectively show how the data relate. Note also that this graphic illustrates the general graphics guidelines: it has a numbered title, it follows its citation in the text, and all its text is written horizontally.

Use pie charts rarely, only to show parts of a whole — never, for example, successive years of data. In a statistical graphic, a *gray scale* shows varying quantities better than a color scale because a gray scale has a natural visual hierarchy that is readily understood. For charts with both x and y axes, use the following conventions, taken from the JASA Style Sheet (Figure 5.3 is a graphic that adheres to all these rules):

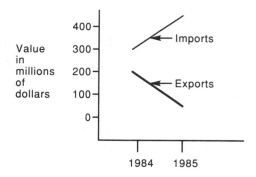

Figure 5.3
Sample Chart with X and Y Axes

- Label both horizontal and vertical axes.
- Where possible, place calibration lines or ticks inside and values outside axes — an acceptable alternative is to place both lines and values on the outside of the axes.
- Clearly differentiate between the meaning of line types, such as bold, fine, and broken lines, and dots and dashes, used for different data types.
- Identify lines either in the figure with an arrow and a label attached to each line, or in a legend showing a line segment and its description.

A title for a graphic can either precede or follow it. Titles tend to follow the graphic in technical material, but precede it in non-technical material. Keep your placement of graphics titles consistent throughout a document. Sometimes a title is incorrectly called a legend. A *legend* is an explanation of graphic symbols on a diagram or map.

How Not to Use Graphics

- Omit any graphic that conveys no information (a content-free graphic).
- Change or omit dizzying graphics that contain visually disturbing forms such as moiré patterns.
- Don't use an unexplained graphic.
- Don't waste pixels. When your graphic is for screen display, make every pixel count (screen real estate is premium territory).
- Avoid using a long series of sample terminal screens that convey little new information. A small number of samples should be sufficient. Help your reader to go to the real screen; don't try to reproduce an entire set of system screens in your printed book.

How to Place Graphics on Your Page or Screen

The best place to insert a single graphic on your page or screen is at the optical center. Because of an optical illusion, the real, or mathematical, center of your page or screen looks too low. So divide your page or screen with an optical center line about one-tenth of the distance from the true center to the top of the page or screen (see Figure 5.4).

For two pieces of art of equal sizes, place each an equal distance above and below the optical center line. For unequal pieces of art, place the larger, darker unit closer to the optical center than the smaller, lighter one. Depending on the

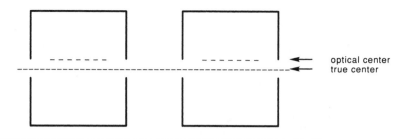

Figure 5.4
True and Optical Centers

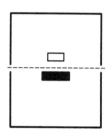

Figure 5.5
Placement of Two Graphics on a Page

nature of your material, you may violate some of the balance conventions in your layout. Figure 5.5 shows the placement of two diagrams around the optical center of a page.

If you have more than one graphic, particularly for less formal materials such as brochures and newsletters, use the TOYSUC ("toys you see") forms. Place several graphics on the page in the shape of a large T, O, Y, S, U, or C. Use whichever one works best for the type and number of diagrams you have. Always consider how the eye of your reader travels when reading the page — in multi-column work, place graphics at the top or bottom of columns.

For example, to use the T form, place your graphics as shown in Figure 5.6. You can follow the other letter forms for placement of several graphics on a single page.

Traditional rules for placement of graphics follow conventions adopted over many decades in the print industry. Today so much material is being placed online for viewing on the internet, and online display opens up several options that were prohibitively expensive in the print world, that a great deal of experimentation is still underway. There are few hard and fast rules that work effectively in every situation. The first question to ask yourself when creating material to be viewing on screen is: can readers find what you want them to find? But see additional discussion of this

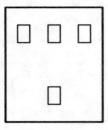

Figure 5.6
Placement of Graphics in T-Shape

burgeoning topic in Chapter 6. Testing the effectiveness of an online display can help you determine if it does what you need it to do.

Visualization

When you decide to create a graphic, you must visualize what you want to present. Often a graphic represents a physical object — a disk drive, a terminal, and so on. Sometimes, for example, when you want to show demographic data, a map is a good way to convey information. If you like bar graphs, use them for fine detail; if you like pie charts, use them only for rough comparisons — they don't convey fine detail very well.

Most software concepts are more abstract than hardware concepts, but you can still produce reasonable software graphics. For example, the graphics in Figures 5.7, 5.8, and 5.9 illustrate a stack, a linked list, and a hypertext environment, respectively; all are abstract computer concepts that exist only as virtual realities. Their graphical representations are quite different from each other.

Documentation maps that show the relationships between books in a set, or reading paths that show the order you recommend your reader to follow when reading a set of documents, are very instructive. For any document that is part

Figure 5.7
Stack

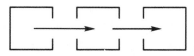

Figure 5.8
Linked List

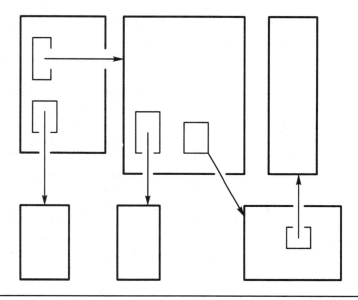

Figure 5.9
Hypertext System

of a set, a map or reading path is essential. If you create a complex map, however, be sure to conduct a usability test to see if others will understand it. For an example of a documentation map, see Figure 4.5.

Further Reading

The premier books that provide advice and examples of how to represent data in graphics are *The Visual Display of Quantitative Information* (Tufte, 1983) and *Envisioning Information* (Tufte, 1990). The latter gives many fine examples of the excellent use of color in graphics. Tufte's latest book *Visual Explanations* (Tufte, 1997) provides many examples of constructing charts to maximize information content. *Interaction of Color* (Albers, 1975) is excellent for many examples that show how colors work together. Albers spent many years experimenting with squares of contrasting colors and documented his considerable experience in this book. *Color for the Electronic Age* (White, 1990) provides many illustrations of the use of color with appendices on all standard color systems. "Color as Communication" (Gribbons, 1997) provides an excellent set of tips on the use of color, and includes a selective bibliography. The "JASA Style Sheet" (JASA, 1976) advises how to use graphics to show statistical data honestly, as does *Statistical Graphics Design Principles and Practices* (Schmid, 1983). *A Practical Guide to Technical Illustration* (Batho, 1968) gives basic advice; others with similar content include *Introduction to Scientific Illustration* (Beakley, Autore, 1983), and *Technical Illustration* (Bethune, 1983), and *Technical Illustration* (Earle, 1978). *Scientific Illustration* (Jastrzebski, 1985) is outstanding. *Technical Illustration & Graphics* (Mracek, 1983), *Illustrations* (Richardson, 1985), and *Technical Illustration* (Thomas, 1978) all show how to develop technical illustrations manually.

Books and papers about design, layout, and formatting:
"Guidelines for the Identification and Formatting of Technical Periodicals" (Haag, 1989), *Designer's Guide to Creating Charts and Diagrams* (Holmes, 1984), *Layout* (Hulbury, 1989), *The Technology of Text* (Jonassen, 1982), *Bookmaking: The Illustrated Guide* (Lee, ed., 1980), *Publication Design* (Nelson, 1987), "The 25 Worst Desktop Publishing Mistakes" (Parker, 1989), *Graphic Layout and Design* (Silver, 1981), and *Methods of Book Design* (Williamson, 1983).

For More Ideas

A book that can help you think about how you use graphics is *Exercises in Visual Thinking* (Wileman, 1980). For an example of using a decision graphic in technical documents, see "Visualizing a Procedure with Nassi-Shneiderman Charts" (Weiss, 1990). For a comparison of U.S. and Japanese newspaper graphics, see "Japanese and U.S. Media" (Beniger, Westney, 1981). *The Computer Graphics Glossary* (Hubbard, 1983) tries to standardize terms on this topic. A well-known book that presents graphics effectively is *Anatomy, Descriptive and Surgical: Classic Collector's Edition* (Gray, 1977).

Documents attempting to show that graphics are their own language, a suggestion still subject to scholarly dispute:
Graphics and Graphic Information-processing (Bertin, 1981), *Semiology of Graphics* (Bertin, 1983), "Extending the Expressive Power of Language" (Gross, 1990), "Communicative Functions of Icons as Computer Commands" (Krull, 1985), and *Graphics in Computer Documentation* (Krull, Rubens, 1982). For ideas on how humans process information, see "The Semiology of Documents" (Martin, 1989) and "The Visual Development of Documents" (Martin, 1988).

Information about computer typography:

T$_E$X and METAFONT (Knuth, 1979), *Digital Typography* (Rubinstein, 1988), "Typography for the Desktop" (Tinkel, Will-Harris, 1989), "T$_E$X: Typesetting for Almost Everybody" (Whidden, 1984), and *How to Spec Type* (White, 1987).

Documents about the effective use of color:

Color and the Computer (Durrett, ed., 1987), *Using Computer Color Effectively* (Thorell, 1990), and "Investigating the Effects of Color" (Hoadley, 1990). *Techniques for Computer Graphics* (Rogers et al., eds., 1987) is a collection of papers that describe work in human factors, user interface design, and online documentation. "Add Color Impact to PC Publishing" (Venit, 1990) advises how to use color in printing with a PC.

A periodical for the display of scientific concepts and visualization:

Pixel.

Exercises

1. Why use a graphic in a technical document?

2. What is the graphical information hierarchy?

3. Name and describe a system used to define colors.

4. What is PostScript? Why might you use it?

5. Discuss the use of moiré patterns in graphics.

6. Give an example of how to place diagrams on a page.

7. When might animation be useful?

Information Presentation 6

This chapter on information presentation covers page layout (including orthography and punctuation), book design (including typography), printing (including papers), and screen layout. The chapter also briefly discusses alternative media because you are likely to encounter them in your work.

When you prepare information for your readers, consider what your result will look like when it reaches them. If you work with systems that present information in print, you will be concerned with page layout and book design; if you work with systems that present information on screen, you will be concerned with screen layout. You may also need to consider new forms for presenting information such as voice (audio), interactive video, video film, or animation.

You need to modify information you present in book form that your readers will access on screen. Where a book usually contains, for example, a table of contents, a screen display (containing fewer lines and larger characters than a page of typeset text) may be more usable with a menu. While reading a book, your readers can flip quickly back and forth through the pages, using the fingers of one hand as bookmarks. Reading a book through the remote medium of video screen, keyboard, and perhaps mouse is quite different.

Information presentation standards can help your readers, and you may need to follow such standards in your writing. For example, the United States Department of Defense Military Specification Standard (MIL-STD) defines topics and document organizations for specifications and manuals of several kinds. The methods of Information Mapping also provide standard ways to present your topics. Standards exist for the major formatting languages HTML (Hypertext Markup Language) and SGML (Standard Generalized Markup Language). These standards are further described in the appendices.

The Military Standard defines information by content and output style. It specifies distinct forms for design information, test information, development information, and so on. When you create material to conform with the standard, you need to be aware of what information you must convey and the form you must use. But how you lay out information on a page or screen for greatest effectiveness remains more an art than a science.

The Great Attractors of Technical Documentation

You can use several representational devices to attract the eye of your reader to locations on your page or screen. These devices include:

- Pictures, graphics, photographs, drawings, icons
- Questions
- Color
- Lists
- Tables
- Typographical change (italics, boldface, change in font size)
- Animation, video
- Audio

Each of these has a different impact on your readers, but all can help them find information on a page readily. Most of your readers will only quickly skim material to solve a problem. Thus effective use of these Great Attractors can help make your document easy to use.

Page Layout

How you arrange material on your page affects how easily your reader can find a piece of information. To help you decide what to place where, consider what your readers can remember. For example, a newspaper editor uses several rules that work for readers of English:

- Put important stories on the front page.
- Put the most important story in the top right column.
- Use headlines or large titles to catch reader interest.

How you lay out a page for a newspaper, however, with its headlines and multicolumn text, is quite different from how you lay out a page for a magazine or book. Books have varying page layout criteria based on their projected readership, and often are classed by their readers' level of educational achievement. Page layout is also dictated by writing direction. For example, English reads from left to right, whereas Hebrew and Arabic read from right to left.

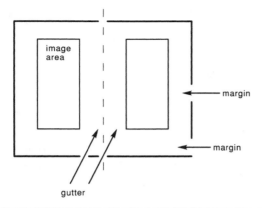

image area

margin

margin

gutter

Figure 6.1
Image Area, Gutter, Margin

The area on a page that can receive print is called the *image area.* The white space on the inside of the image area, near the binding, is the *gutter* (this term is also used for the white space between columns in a table). The white space on the outside of the image area, opposite the binding edge, is the *margin* (see Figure 6.1).

Space between lines of text is called *leading* (rhymes with "heading"); between letters on a line, *kerning.* Chapter titles and headings, set in a larger font size than the main body of text, are sometimes said to be in *display type.* Headers and footers are often set in a different typeface than text. These visual elements contribute significantly to continuity of thought and provide access markers for your readers.

Text on a page can be *justified* (aligned so that the image area presents a block-like look with left and right edges filled, that is, flush left and flush right) or *ragged* (having an uneven appearance on one margin). In work such as English that reads from left to right, a ragged right margin is common. The text in this book is justified, but the long quotations from other sources, such as those on p. 137, are ragged right. In scripts that read from right to left, the left margin tends to be ragged.

You can place work that is too wide for a page on a *turnpage,* sometimes called *landscape,* but this is not easy for your readers. The normal presentation of a page, longer than it is wide, is called *portrait.* (See Figure 6.2 for illustrations of both these page orientations.)

You can sometimes place very wide material on a *foldout.* For example, in a hardware document you may want to present a single diagram of all the machine components at a high level — not all the nuts and bolts but all the major parts. To do so requires an 11-by-17-inch sheet to contain all the pieces

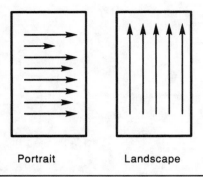

Figure 6.2
Portrait and Landscape Orientations

without making them too small to be legible. Because this is only one diagram in a small document, perhaps 8 1/2 by 11, you can use a foldout. However, a foldout must be hand-collated into your final document and thus adds significantly to the expense of production. In general, avoid foldouts if possible. You can often separate the information into smaller segments that can each fit on a single 8 1/2-by-11 sheet.

Tip ➤   *Foldouts are cumbersome.*

Page Details

An illustration or intentional mark that continues outside the image area and may be trimmed during binding is said to *bleed*. For example, a *bleed tab* is a mark representing a tab placed at the edge of the image area (see Figure 6.3). Sometimes you can place words in white in a bleed tab. Bleed tabs are an inexpensive alternative to physical tabs on heavy paper stock.

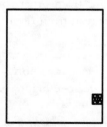

Figure 6.3
Bleed Tab

With the right software, you can create your own bleed tabs on each page, or you can have bleed tabs added by hand to the sheets of your book when you prepare your copy for the printer. A *page* is one side of a *leaf;* leaves (sometimes sheets) are the pieces of paper that make up a book. Text processing systems automatically set up illustrations, heads, and tables as *page elements* in the image area of a page; *page breaks* in your source files determine where pages begin and end. In older typesetting systems, page *makeup* is the arrangement of page elements by hand to create a page. The permanent positioning of page elements to form reprographic copy is called *pasteup.*

Right-justified text prepared with *monospaced* typeforms such as a type-writer-style font is harder to read than ragged-right text. The next two examples below show this. Both passages contain the same sentences represented in a proportional and a monospaced font, respectively. The text is the first few sentences from Charles Darwin's *The Voyage of the Beagle,* 1859 edition.

What follows is the proportionally spaced sample.

After having been twice driven back by heavy South-western gales, Her Majesty's ship *Beagle,* a ten-gun brig, under the command of Captain Fitz Roy, R.N., sailed from Devonport on the 27th of December 1831. The object of the expedition was to complete the survey of Patagonia and Tierra del Fuego, commenced under Captain King in 1826 to 1830 — to survey the shores of Chile, Peru, and of some islands in the Pacific — and to carry a chain of chronometrical measurements round the World.

Here is the monospaced sample.

```
After having been twice driven back by heavy South-western gales,
Her Majesty's ship Beagle, a ten-gun brig, under the command of
Captain Fitz Roy, R.N., sailed from Devonport on the 27th of
December 1831. The object of the expedition was to complete the
survey of Patagonia and Tierra del Fuego, commenced under Captain
King in 1826 to 1830 — to survey the shores of Chile, Peru, and of
some islands in the Pacific — and to carry a chain of chronometrical
measurements round the World.
```

It is easier to read proportional text because of the way our eyes work. Our eyes move forward along a line of print in small, rapid jerks called *saccades,* with short fixations, and backward movements called *regressions.* With difficult material, more regressions occur. The experienced reader grasps whole words or phrases at a glance during the fixation time.

Once you have read one line of print, your eyes make a long return regression to fixate the beginning of the next line (Hulme, 1985). When reading text that is both monospaced and justified, your eye must move farther and therefore takes longer to view the words.

In monospaced type, each character has the same width; in proportional or variable-spaced type, width depends on the individual character. For example, *i* and *m* take up different amounts of room in a proportional font but the same amount of room in a monospaced font:

```
jimmy
```
jimmy

Note how much space remains in the monospaced example between the *j* and the *i*.

Online Layout

When creating material for online display, you need to consider both the medium and the goals of the presentation. The medium is a rather poor-resolution device, generally, but it has the great advantage of being able to use both color and animation. Material online can often be changed more frequently than printed material.

Just as with the page layout of printed books, to some extent what is pleasing and effective online is a matter of opinion. But today it is easier than ever before to look at many examples of screen layout simply by surfing the web, looking at internet web sites for ideas and examples.

Some web sites are informative but dull; others are messy yet informative. On such a site, the reader may need to work hard to find the information needed. For an example of a beautifully designed and informative web site, visit the Virtual Garden Marketplace; it has lovely and appropriate graphics, even including a reed-thin line that unifies items in categories, and appropriate colors and graphics that lead the eye easily and comfortably to find, say, garden tools (a pair of yellow garden clippers heralds this section), or chairs (this section opens with a wooden garden chair). The site menu bar under the banner (complete with a graphic of a wheelbarrow) has tasteful green buttons. There is lots of white space and sections are clearly defined. There is no animation and no crackle. The site projects a peaceful, pleasant, lovely atmosphere, just perfect for its intended audience. You can visit this site at http://www.vg.com — click on Marketplace to see this part of the site. For a short section of the site, see Figure 6.4, A Superb Web Site.

Other extremely effective sites appropriate to their audiences are certain automobile sites, for example www.porsche.com and www.rollsroyce-bentley.com. Both clearly project their respective corporate images and do it with elegance and reserve. As is appropriate for the sporty Porsche, its site contains some flashy animated graphics used to help the reader navigate the site.

Some sites are dedicated to strictly technical information and contain virtually no graphics: everything is presented as running text. Some sites very clearly categorize text so that it is easy to find, but with others you have to work hard to find answers to questions. A good site presents a clear categorization of

Figure 6.4
A Superb Web Site

information with both a table of contents and a search capability. Support sites that customers access to get answers to software support problems can usefully contain FAQs (frequently asked questions) that may take care of many support calls. FAQs are straightforward to code in HTML. Don't rely only on a search tool to help your readers find information at your site; provide a reasonable and visible organizational structure.

When creating material for a web site, understand the goals of your client for putting information in this form. A corporate client may first and foremost want to project the corporate image. The Porsche and Rolls Royce sites do this effectively and appropriately. Their goal is to get people sufficiently interested to contact a sales person, although few people will buy an expensive automobile directly off a web site.

The goals for a site like Virtual Garden Marketplace are both to project the image of its line of merchandise, and also to provide contact or purchasing information when a reader has decided what to buy. Another alternative is the direct sell: www.amazon.com exemplifies this approach. A huge bookstore, Amazon.com lets you order books over the internet and employs enticing features such as discounts, the ability to add and remove items from your shopping cart, surely a great enticement for the perennial book buyer.

Thus the guidelines for screen layout for web sites are:

- understand client goals to create an appropriate web site
- use color carefully and as appropriate to the audience
- use animation only where it can be meaningful and helpful to your reader
- avoid gratuitous use of color, animation, decoration — it will detract from the effectiveness of your site
- provide clear and consistent navigation cues (menu bars, buttons, lists, and so on)

If you are creating online material for display on a specific computer system, for example UNIX or Windows 95, your online material should follow the conventions of that system. You'll need to use the tools required by that system, and you won't have a great deal of flexibility in changing the overall design of your online material. But organization of the material, and providing clear navigational cues will still be of critical importance.

Animation

Animation is frequently used in promotional materials distributed on the internet, included with software, and in demonstration packages. It can be very useful to help the user visualize the flow of data, illustrate a process (for example, copying a file, opening a folder), understand abstract and complex topics. Animation and multimedia tools continue to interest many technical documentors, and we still need to develop a consistent rhetoric to identify how best to use them.

Reader-Level Formats

Regardless of whether you use proportional or monospaced type, lay out a book or screen for a young reader with most of each page containing a picture and three or four short lines of simple text in moderately large type, and repeat new words frequently in several contexts. Too much glitz impedes learning, so be cautious in using colors or motion.

As the educational level of your readers increases, include fewer illustrations, increase the vocabulary, and decrease the type size you use.

To see a page layout for a readership with a fairly high level of education, look at some scientific journals. *Science,* for example, presents research written by original experimenters in a two-column format, with diagrams and photographs to illustrate concepts, and footnotes and bibliographies in fine print. College-level and state-of-the-art textbooks are often produced with similar layouts.

Research shows that we read word by word or phrase by phrase, not letter by letter. The amount your eye grasps depends on your level of reading proficiency. When a child starts to read, she begins by learning to recognize the individual letters, but rapidly progresses to recognize words by their shape. Subsequently, reading proficiency increases with the ability to recognize phrases by their shape

(Tinker, 1955, 1965). But the capacity of the eye to capture several words at a glance has limits; this is why a line of text is not extremely long.

To use an extreme, who could read at a glance a line of text that was 20 inches long? Or even 10 inches? Experience shows, and research supports, that the most readable lines are no more than 5 1/2 inches long. Depending on typeface and word length, a line of 5 1/2 inches contains ten to twelve words.

Lines in literary material are typically shorter than 5 1/2 inches, and lines in scientific or technical material may be a little longer. Type of material also dictates the width of columns when information is presented in a two-, three-, or multicolumn format. Note that you must use special care in the placement of illustrations in multicolumn work. Place them so that there is no confusion where the reader's eye is to travel after looking at the illustration. In general, this means at the top or bottom of a column. For examples of intelligent placement of illustrations, see *Scientific Illustration* (Jastrzebski, 1985).

Large pages filled with solid-looking panels of print repel all but the most hardened scholar. Some books printed in such a fashion are virtually unreadable, though they may contain much useful information.

The format of this book is one example of page layout. I chose it because it had nicely proportioned pages with wide margins where I could place notes or small figures to attract your eye. I also liked the variations of typeface for different levels of headings. Running feet are a feature I believed you would find useful for getting quickly to the chapter of interest.

Dictionaries and encyclopedias show material in different page layouts; they are designed for easy access to segregated topics of information. Large encyclopedias use extensive indexes to help readers find a particular piece of information. An encyclopedia index usually provides access to a topic not only by the topic name itself but by alternative terms — sometimes terms that are not in the topical article. This, too, increases reader access to the information.

When you create a document, consider how your readers will access the information. For sequentially accessed documents, provide a clear hierarchical organization and smooth transitions. For nonsequential documents, such as hypertext and chunks of information read on line, provide extensive indexes, conceptual maps of information content, and multiple access paths. Particularly when you provide lots of information, you need to provide readers with multiple access paths: tables of contents, indexes, and perhaps permuted tables of contents are all helpful.

Readability

Readability, not to be confused with legibility, is an attribute of good technical documentation. A character that is *legible* is one whose shape or form you can make out. Sometimes you cannot tell if a letter you are reading is *o* or *a*. Then you say the letter is not legible. So legibility is an attribute of individual letters, and perhaps of entire words, if you are looking at a page of very poorly printed material.

Readability is an attribute of content and the ability of the reader to understand that content; if you read a sentence and understand it fully, the sentence is readable; you have comprehended its content. Tests have been developed to evaluate the readability of a document, although such tests don't yet look at all aspects of comprehension, and there is no universal agreement on their efficacy. Readability formulas use factors such as:

- The average number of words in a sentence or paragraph
- The number of syllables per 100 words
- The percentage of words with three or more syllables

Two frequently used readability formulas are the *Fog Index* and the *Clear River test.* Another formula, developed by Rudolph Flesch, which he calls the *readability index,* uses the average number of words per sentence and the average number of syllables per word.

The Fog Index, developed by Robert Gunning in the 1940s, uses the average number of words in a sentence (AWS) and the ratio of difficult words (three or more syllables) to total words (#DW), calculated for a sample of 100 to 200 words with the formula:

$$\text{Fog Index} = (\text{AWS} + \text{\#DW}) \times 0.4$$

The higher the index, the less readable the material for a given audience. For example, a Fog Index of 20 means that the material is suitable for junior college to college graduates, while a Fog Index of 5 means that the material is suitable for perhaps fifth graders.

As examples, consider the following paragraphs, Case I and Case 2. Case I has a readability score of 51 and a Fog Index of 22:

CASE 1

With today's page formatting software tools that accept large files of text and format an entire page at a time, there is opportunity for software to be developed that considers all the orthographical and typographical conventions of a given language, and format each page of text in the optimum fashion. The syllabic structure of every language is different, and the typographical conventions used by writers in each language are different. For example, a moderately sophisticated software tool for performing page formatting must hyphenate words correctly according to the conventions of the language of text.

There are three sentences in this paragraph; the first contains 60 words, the second 24, and the last 20, giving an average of 34 words per sentence. In the three sentences, there are 22 words of three syllables or more. The average words per sentence (34) plus the number of difficult words (22) is 56. Multiply 56 by 0.4 for a Fog Index of 22.4, or 22, leaving off the fraction.

To lower the Fog Index or increase the readability score on this information, you need to rewrite. Case 2 shows how you might rewrite the Case 1 text.

CASE 2

Today's page formatting software formats a whole page at a time. Such software takes into account both the spelling and typography used with each language. Every language has a different syllabic structure and different typographical conventions. So a software tool that does page formatting must hyphenate words using the conventions of the language.

There are now four sentences in this paragraph; the first has 11 words, the second, 14, the third, 11, and the last 17. Thus the average number of words in a sentence is 14. The number of words of three syllables or more is 10, for a Fog Index of 9.6 or 10, or a readability score of 78 if we round up to the nearest whole number. This score suggests that the paragraph as revised is much more readable than the earlier paragraph. You must decide if it conveys the same information.

The Clear River test, developed by John Morris in the 1970s, uses more factors (words in a sentence, words in a paragraph, syllables per 100 words, words per punctuated pause), and compares the results to acceptable average scores (25 words per sentence, 75 words per paragraph, 150 syllables per 100 words, 12 words per punctuated pause), yielding several scores rather than a composite. The writer can use the separate scores to identify areas that may need improvement.

Using the Case 1 and Case 2 examples, you can see how each fares against the Clear River averages (see Table 6.1) and how their scores differ when using the Fog Index or the readability test.

Table 6.1
Readability Tests

Factor or Test	Clear River Averages	Case 1	Case 2
Words per sentence	25	34	14
Words per paragraph	75	104	53
Syllables per 100 words	150	168	93
Words per punctuated pause	12	12	11
Fog Index		22	10
Readability		51	78

Another approach, suggested by Walker Gibson, which he calls "Tough, Sweet, and Stuffy," contains sixteen criteria for prose discourse. These criteria comprise other aspects of text readability such as how you use pronouns, verbs, adjectives, and punctuation.

Each readability index has its proponents, although some people believe none have any real value (Stratton, 1989). Some suggest that readability tests may be less useful to the author than tools for correcting spelling and grammar, but that they undoubtedly have value in helping serious writers consider how their work is perceived by others.

Others see the readability tests as examining only the surface features of writing, not its deeper linguistic structures, and suggest that more tools are needed to examine writings' rhetorical structures and the design that goes into good writing. Tools that help the writer grasp and comprehend large amounts of information would also be useful.

If you like readability tests, use them; if you hate them, ignore them.

Orthography of Foreign Words

With today's page formatting software tools that accept large files of text and format an entire page at a time, there is the opportunity for software to be developed that considers all the orthographical and typographical conventions of a given language and formats each page of text in the optimum fashion. The syllabic structure of every language is different, as are the typographical conventions used by writers in each language. For example, a moderately sophisticated software tool for performing page formatting must hyphenate words correctly according to the conventions of the language of text.

English text has certain rules for text formatters, which don't apply to, say, Spanish text (Mañas, July 1987). The hyphenation algorithm is not applicable to both languages. The basic orthographic and syllabic conventions that govern hyphenation are one level of language the formatting tool must understand. The traditional conventions of word partitioning are another. A third level is the aesthetic parameter that lets the user balance the percentage of hyphenations against the volume of spaces for a page of text. Some tools allow flexibility in modifying the rules to please the individual who decides on the correctness of the formatting.

Foreign Terms

Avoid using foreign terms in technical documentation. They don't clarify. See Table 6.2, Foreign Terms, for terms to avoid and their English alternatives.

Spelling

Good spelling must be part of your linguistic repertoire. The next few paragraphs list a few commonly misspelled words I have often seen in technical documents, and briefly summarize the rules for forming plurals and compounds.

Table 6.2
Foreign Terms

For	Latin	Use
cf.	confer	compare
e.g.	exempli gratia	for example
et al.	et alii	and others
etc.	et cetera	and so on
i.e.	id est	that is
q.v.	quod vide	see
via	via	through, with, by — whichever applies
vice versa	vice versa	conversely
vis-à-vis		opposite to, face to
viz.	videlicet	namely
vs.	versus	instead of, rather than, against

Words I have often seen misspelled in technical documents are shown in Table 6.3.

Table 6.3
Misspelled Words

Wrong	Right
kernal	kernel
seperate	separate
hexidecimal	hexadecimal

Form plurals of words and acronyms with *s* or *es* as shown in Table 6.4, which shows some of the trickier plural formations.

In compound nouns, make only the principal word plural, as shown in Table 6.5.

If all the words are equally important, make them all plural: woman engineer, women engineers. But note these exceptions: notary public, notaries public; attorney general, attorneys general.

Do not change compound adjectives when forming plurals, as illustrated in Table 6.6.

Form plurals of Latin-derived words with Latin plurals, but use the anglicized plural if that is your local house style. Table 6.7 gives both Latin and English forms. I prefer Latin plurals for more technical material. Whichever style you choose, use it consistently.

Table 6.4
Troublesome Plurals

If The Word Ends In	Add	Examples
a vowel	s	Ada, Adas; CPU, CPUs
e	s	queue, queues; tape, tapes; file, files; drive, drives
two vowels	s	studio, studios; radio, radios; rodeo, rodeos; zoo, zoos
a vowel + a consonant	s	computer, computers; processor, processors; server, servers; VIP, VIPs; FORTRAN, FORTRANs
two consonants	s	butt, butts; PC, PCs; disk, disks
a consonant + a vowel	es	potato, potatoes; hero, heroes; torpedo, torpedoes (exceptions: zeros, mementos)
certain "s-oriented" consonants: s, x, ch, sh, z	es	boss, bosses; bus, buses; box, boxes; UNIX, UNIXes; beach, beaches; crash, crashes; rush, rushes; fez, fezes
y preceded by a consonant	change y to i, add es	activity, activities; authority, authorities; category, categories; company, companies; policy, policies
y preceded by a vowel	s	attorney, attorneys; key, keys; play, plays; quay, quays

Table 6.5
Plurals of Compound Nouns

Singular	Plural
add-on	add-ons
B-tree	B-trees
built-in	built-ins
by-product	by-products
client-server	client-servers
daughter-in-law	daughters-in-law
dial-up	dial-ups
pop-up	pop-ups
state-of-the-art	states-of-the-art
three-year-old	three-year-olds
vice-president	vice-presidents

Table 6.6
Plurals with Compound Adjectives

Singular	Plural
client-server architecture	client-server architectures
object-oriented database	object-oriented databases
point-and-click input	point-and-click inputs
stand-alone compiler	stand-alone compilers
three-schema architecture	three-schema architectures

Table 6.7

Latin and Anglicized Plurals

Singular	Latin Plural	Anglicized Plural
agenda		agendas
antenna	antennae	antennas
appendix	appendices	appendixes
axis	axes	
crisis	crises	
criterion	criteria	
datum	data	
focus	foci	focuses
formula	formulae	formulas
index	indices	indexes
matrix	matrices	matrixes
medium	media	mediums
memorandum	memoranda	memorandums
nucleus	nuclei	
phenomenon	phenomena	
stimulus	stimuli	
stratum	strata	

Suffixes and Prefixes

When you add a suffix that begins with a vowel, such as *ing* or *ed,* to a stem that ends with a single vowel plus a consonant, *double* the final consonant. Table 6.8 shows examples of this construction.

If a word ends in a double consonant, keep both letters before a suffix, as shown in Table 6.9.

If a word ends in *l,* keep the letter when adding *ly,* as shown in Table 6.10.

If a word ends in *n,* keep the letter when adding *ness,* as shown in Table 6.11.

If a prefix ends with the same letter that starts the stem, keep both letters, as shown in Table 6.12.

Words that end in silent *e* usually drop the *e* before a suffix that begins with a vowel, but note the common exceptions to this rule, as shown in Table 6.13.

For words that end in *-sede, -ceed, -cede:* only one word ends in *-sede*— "supersede"; three words end in *-ceed*— "exceed," "proceed," "succeed"; and all others end in *-cede*— "precede," "secede," and so on.

Table 6.8
Doubling a Final Consonant

Stem	Suffix	Compound
run	ing	running
regret	able	regrettable
commit	ed	committed
swim	ing	swimming
grin	ed	grinned
	ing	grinning
remit	ed	remitted
rip	ed	ripped
put	ing	putting
excel	ence	excellence
occur	ence	occurrence
refer	ed	referred; but: reference
transfer	ed	transferred; but: transference
prefer	ed	preferred; but: preference
model	ing	*Exception:* modeling
	ed	*Exception:* modeled
focus	ed	*Exception:* focused
	ing	*Exception:* focusing

Table 6.9
Words that End with a Double Consonant

Stem	Compound
butt	butting
install	installing
spell	spelling

Table 6.10
Adding *ly*

accidental	accidentally
perpetual	perpetually

Table 6.11
Adding *ness*

thin	thinness
stern	sternness

Table 6.12
Adding a Prefix

Stem	Prefix + Stem
serve	disserve
shape	misshape
similar	dissimilar
sonant	dissonant
spell	misspell
spend	misspend
state	misstate
step	misstep

Table 6.13
Words that End with Silent e

Follow Rule	Exceptions
durable	manageable
usable	noticeable
irresistible	knowledgeable
likable	

Accents and Diacritical Marks

The accents and diacritical marks required in many languages are part of correct spelling, and you must use them if your text includes foreign words. For example, you may need to refer to the CCITT (Comité Consultatif Internationale Télégraphique et Téléphonique). While no universal system of diacritical marks is available and mutually agreed upon, the International Character Set available in many software packages contains the marks needed for many modern European languages. This is an area where more software tools are still needed — for example, tools that can handle multiple scripts together including those that are written right to left as well as left to right.

Treatment of Numbers

You need to treat numbers uniformly in technical documentation. For example, you can follow the *ten rule* in text, spelling out the name of any number that is ten or less. If you used the ten rule, your text reads as follows:

The console panel contains five switches and 11 lamps.

You can also adopt the *five rule,* in which case the above text reads:

The console panel contains 5 switches and 11 lamps.

However, don't begin a sentence with a numeral. For example, don't leave a sentence as:

8 switches on the console are toggle switches to key in bits.

Rewrite such a sentence so that it begins with "Eight," or rephrase it, perhaps as follows:

You use the 8 console toggle switches to key in bits.

The ten and five rules don't apply to tables. Always use numerals in tables. Everyone in your group should follow the same convention for presentation of numbers, as your readers will expect consistency in these details. At minimum, be consistent within each document you write.

Use of Voice Systems

If you write for or use a voice system, you may need to become familiar with the International Phonetic Alphabet (IPA). This alphabet, containing about 180 characters, can record the *sounds* of any language and represents vocal sounds more accurately than other alphabets.

International Character Standards

To help standardize how computers deal with characters and character sets, the International Standards Organization (ISO) has developed several standards defining how machines represent characters. The most important of these standards include Latin-1, Multi-Octet Character Set (MOCS), and Unicode. Appendix B lists some of today's standards.

Capitalization

In titles, capitalize the first and last word, and any nouns, adjectives, and verbs, and make articles and short prepositions lower-case. If you aren't sure of the rules for capitalization, see your grammar book or style guide. For examples of capitalization for titles, see the title of this book and the chapter, section, and subsection titles.

Punctuation in Technical Documentation

You are already familiar with the usual English punctuation marks (otherwise you probably wouldn't be reading this book). The next few paragraphs address the special importance of punctuation marks in technical documentation. The recommendations here apply to both printed and online presentation. If you need to refresh your knowledge of how to use the period and exclamation point in writing English, see a grammar book.

I describe the punctuation marks in alphabetical order by name to ease your future access: apostrophe, backslash, brackets and braces, colon, comma, dash, ellipsis, exclamation point, hyphen, parentheses, period, question mark, quotation marks, semicolon, space, and underline. You will find information on other marks and symbols in the next main section, Special Notation.

Apostrophe

Use an apostrophe (') to show possessive case, but not to form plurals or with "it." (The contraction "it's" means "it is," not "of it." This is a common error, one you should avoid.)

To show possessive case, write "The operator's task is to put paper in the printer." But don't anthropomorphize inanimate objects — don't write a sentence that makes an inanimate object appear active. For example,

Incorrect: Check the system's console lights.

Better: Check the system console lights.

Best: Check the lights on the system console.

Use an apostrophe to form contractions, but follow your house style if it does not allow this construction. When forming a contraction, include enough letters to avoid ambiguity.

Incorrect: I'd like to see that.

Better: I'ld like to see that.

Be careful when forming the possessive of a plural that ends in "s":

Incorrect: Schedule the writer's meeting for tomorrow.

Correct: Schedule the writers' meeting for tomorrow.

Backslash

You won't use a backslash (\) in normal text, but you may need one in describing computer language syntax or in examples. For example, the following fragment of computer language syntax shows a backslash:

```
.
.
.
while (lastc != '\n') {rdc();
}
.
.
.
```

The backslash is common today in Microsoft syntax, such as file specifications. For example, the following file specification references a file on a Microsoft Windows 95 system:

```
D:\The Book\Revision 1997\Chapter1.doc
```
Note that spaces are valid characters in this file specification.

Brackets and Braces

Brackets and braces are common punctuation marks in technical documentation; they come in several forms: angle brackets (< >), square brackets ([ ]), and curly brackets or braces ({ }). Parentheses sometimes do similar work in syntax descriptions. Brackets, braces, and parentheses usually occur as *closed forms,* with both left and right members present and required, but sometimes you find them as *open forms,* with only one member present.

Using angle brackets as a closed form:

```
Use the <TABLE> tag to start a table.
```

Using right angle brackets as an open form:

```
When you see the console prompt >>>, press B RETURN to boot the system.
```

For more information on using brackets and braces, see the Special Notation section, p. 158.

Colon

Use a colon (:) to introduce a list, whether the items in the list are in paragraph form, separated by commas, or in a numbered or bulleted column. You will often use a colon as part of command or statement syntax; in syntax, take care to check all uses of this mark. For example, on several operating systems, the file specification contains colons.

Using a colon in an example:

```
NODENS::swdsk: [directory.subdirectory] filename.extension
```

In the above example, the word before the double colon is a node or processor (CPU) name, while the word before the single colon is a disk drive name.

Using a colon at the start of a list:

```
The system contains several devices: a processor, a disk drive, a
    printer, and a terminal.
```

Do not break a sentence with a set-off procedure or list introduced by a colon:

> *Incorrect:* The system contains the following devices:
>> Processor
>> Disk drive
>> Printer
>> Terminal
> which you can connect together.

Correct: The system contains several devices:

    Processor
    Disk drive
    Printer
    Terminal

Note that this second list does not end with a period.

Comma

In technical documentation, use the comma (,) sparingly — to separate main clauses or to separate an introductory, long phrase from a main clause. You can also use commas to separate more than two items in a list and adjectives in a long string. However, beware of long strings of adjectives; you may clarify your meaning if you rewrite the sentence to eliminate some of them. You can use commas instead of parentheses with less formal documentation. You will often use a comma in technical documentation in computer language syntax descriptions.

Using commas to separate more than two items in a list:

> The book describes knowledge representation, models, learning rules, and neural networks.

But:

> The book describes learning rules and neural networks.

Using commas to separate a string of adjectives:

Incorrect: The course introduces multiple state-of-the-art object-oriented database products.

Better: The course introduces multiple, state-of-the-art, object-oriented database products.

Dash

The capabilities of your text processing tools may limit your ability to discriminate between en and em dashes.

Use an en dash (–) to join letters and numbers, but never as a substitute for "to" or "and." For example, write "1 to 4," not "1–4." Do this even in tables.

Use an em dash (—) to mark a break in thought, set off a summary, or set off an abrupt parenthetical element or an element containing commas. The em dash does not cause as abrupt a transition as a colon, which might often be a reasonable substitute. For example, the following shows use of an em dash to mark a break in thought or a sentence element containing commas:

> The system disk contains many applications — the system executive, system utilities, device drivers, and so on.

But try this with a colon instead:

The system disk contains many applications: the system executive, system utilities, device drivers, and so on.

You can also use an em dash to avoid awkward punctuation:

Awkward: "Use this when you prepare text for a two-column doctype.", a longer presentation of the same information.

Better: "Use this when you prepare text for a two-column doctype." — a longer presentation of the same information.

Ellipsis

Use horizontal ellipsis (. . .) to show where text is missing. Also use it in syntax descriptions to avoid repeating the same information many times. Use vertical ellipses to indicate missing lines. The following example shows use of horizontal ellipsis:

```
adv -m resource -d description | [clients ...]
```

The ellipsis after "clients" indicates that several client names can follow.

Use vertical ellipsis to show missing lines:, as shown in the following example:

```
PORT RESPONSE
   00040032
   0001000A
   .
   .
   .
   002D2F29
```

When you omit lines from a working example, you emphasize the information you present; but be sure you keep any data that is critical to your readers' understanding. For example, the above "Port Response" example shows the first few lines the computer port presents, so when your readers use the system and see the actual response, they can match up what the computer presents and what is in your book. The vertical ellipsis leads readers to look further down the column for the relevant piece of information.

Exclamation Point

You will find exclamation points used in some computer languages to set off comments. When you illustrate such languages, you can use the comments to help explain your examples.

Using an exclamation point to set off comments:

```
<!DOCTYPE book SAMPLE "filespec .dtd" A comment in SGML.
[
<!ENTITY bookinfo SAMPLE "/directory/path/bookinfo.sgm">
<!ENTITY chapter1 SAMPLE "/directory/path/chapter1.sgm">
]>
<BOOK>
&bookinfo;
&chapter1;
</BOOK>
```

Hyphen

Use a hyphen (-) to join two words into one, particularly when coining a new word or forming an adjective with a numeric value. Also use it in a series of words having a common, unrepeated base. You will often use a hyphen to join an adjective and a noun. For example, the word "dial-up" shows such use. You can use a hyphen and a minus sign interchangeably.

Using a hyphen to join an adjective and a noun:

Shared-memory parallel processors provide entry to the world of vector processing.

Using a hyphen to coin a new word:

There was noise on the dial-up line.

Using a hyphen to show keystroke combinations:

Press Control-C to kill the program.

Using a hyphen as a minus sign in math equations:

q = log y *-log y

Note that you use a hyphen in a compound verb that acts as an adjective,

I have a follow-up question.

but not in a compound verb that acts as a verb:

I will follow up with a question.

Using a hyphen to form an adjective with a numeric value:

The telemetry processor collects incoming data in a 1000-word buffer.

Using a hyphen in a series where you do not repeat the series base:

The system has fault-, error-, and surge-detection algorithms.

However, don't use a hyphen just to avoid repeating a morpheme, an inseparable word fragment.

Incorrect: You can enter both upper- and lowercase characters.

Correct: You can enter both uppercase and lowercase characters.

Tip ➤ ***Consider possible ambiguities when you use a hyphen.***

Parentheses

Use parentheses (()) to set off supplementary or explanatory information you could omit without destroying the meaning of the sentence or clause. Sometimes it is easier to keep such information within a sentence than to devote another sentence to it.

Use parentheses to set off explanatory information. For example:

Begin a new column of print (2-column doctype).

You could expand this to "Begin a new column of print. Use this when you prepare text for a two-column doctype" — a longer presentation of the same information. The original text, though a bit "telegraphic," was appropriate for the document it came from, a summary handbook. You will also use parentheses in syntax definitions for computer languages.

Period

Use a period at the end of a sentence and after a few common abbreviations (Mr., Mrs., Ms., ed. (editor), Co. (Company), Inc. (Incorporated)). Don't use periods after postal abbreviations of states (MA, NY, and so on) or in acronyms (ACM, IBM, and so on). Use periods as appropriate and required in language syntax (see the example for colon). Also see foreign terms to avoid (such as viz., etc., and so on) in Table 6.2.

Question Mark

Use a question mark at the end of a sentence that asks a question and where appropriate in examples, as dictated by messages or syntax that use this character.

Using a question mark in an example:

The system displays the following error message:

```
?Command unknown
```

Quotation Marks

You won't have much opportunity to use quotation marks (",") — also called quotes — in most technical documentation, though you might use them to enhance clarity.

Using double quotes to enhance clarity:

<le> (meaning "list element")

You might use a single quote (') to represent the keyboard character in an example. For example, you could describe the use of the single quote character as follows:

To translate a symbol, precede the symbol by a ' character.

To the computer, the double quotation mark is an ASCII 34 and the single quote is an ASCII 39. If what you produce is sorted by computer, double quotes will come first. You may also use a single quote for clarity: for example, "Press the 'Cancel' button." But you may find better ways to do this, such as "Press the CANCEL button." The flexibility you have to present such detail depends on the text processing system you use.

Semicolon

Use a semicolon (;) as a period (almost). In most English texts, the semicolon acts like a period, but often joins two closely related sentences. You can either use a semicolon the same way in technical documentation or avoid it altogether and use a period instead.

Using a semicolon to join two closely related sentences:

Basic operating system utilities should not crash; they might exit with sparse error messages, but should not core dump.

Use semicolons as appropriate in computer language syntax.

Slash

The slash (/) is also common on many computer systems. For example, the following cites a specific web site:

```
http://www.digital.com
```

Spaces

In addition to normal use of spaces in all your natural language writing, you use a space as appropriate and required in computer language syntax. That use is illustrated in the program and syntax examples throughout this book. When you create such examples, think of the space as a special, invisible character. To the computer, a space coded as ASCII 32 is as "visible" as any other character.

Underlines

Sometimes you use an underline (_) in examples, particularly if you write documentation for an application or system that uses the underline in syntax. Check your underlines carefully to be sure you haven't used hyphens.

Using an underline in a command example:

```
$ show cluster/continuous RETURN
Command> add rem_proc RETURN
```

Incorrectly using a hyphen means your example won't work:

```
$ show cluster/continuous RETURN
Command> add rem-proc RETURN
```

Punctuation for text differs from punctuation for bibliographies, indexes, notes, and other specialized forms. If you need to use these forms, consult a local copy editor or, if you have no local editor, decide on your own conventions and stick to them. A punctuation mark (except for colons, parentheses, and brackets) is generally printed in the same font or style as the character it follows (that is, lightface, italic, or bold). Punctuation marks for all scripts are language-specific.

Special Notation

Technical documentation often requires special notation to clarify information and present text concisely. Usually you adopt this special notation when describing language or command syntax; sometimes you use it for mathematical formulae.

Notation for Syntax

Although part of punctuation, certain characters have special uses in computer documentation.

Use square brackets ([ ]) and curly brackets or braces ({}) in *syntax* descriptions. Syntax descriptions are typographical constructs you use to show how command or language elements combine to form software commands or statements in computer languages.

The usual convention is to use square brackets for optional items and braces for a list of items from which your user must select one. This, however, depends on the conventions of the system or application for which you are writing. If no conventions have been established, decide on some and stick to them.

Figure 6.5 shows the syntax for the FIND command in a database system using both square brackets and braces.

As an alternative to using parentheses, brackets, and braces in syntax definitions, and if the syntax permits, you can use the *Backus-Naur Form* (BNF) of syntax definition (De Morgan et al., 1976). The BNF notation uses the characters <, >, ::= (is defined to be), := (assignment statement), and | (or).

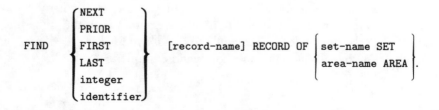

Figure 6.5
Use of Braces in Syntax

Figure 6.6
Railroad Diagram

For example, you could write the previous database FIND statement in BNF as follows:

```
FIND {NEXT | PRIOR | FIRST | LAST | integer | identifier}
[record-name] RECORD OF {set-name SET | area-name AREA}.
```

Railroad Diagram

Another way to show syntax is with a *railroad diagram.* As shown in Figure 6.6, the FIND statement looks quite different when presented this way.

Using square brackets to indicate that an "ELSE statement" is optional:

```
IF condition THEN
    statement-list
    [ELSE
    statement-list];
```

Mathematical Notation

Special mathematical characters and symbols also are part of your typographical repertoire. You use mathematical expressions to represent equations and phrases that are part of your text — for example, to describe the theory behind certain analytical software packages. However, don't use mathematical expressions in material for novices; they will find them intimidating.

Rely on your technical resources to provide you with any mathematical expressions you need. For standard forms, see a math textbook. Perhaps you will need to represent mathematical equations with summation or integrals in your text. With the appropriate software, this is easy to do, as the following fragment shows:

$$\int_{n=1}^{\infty}$$

Tables

Technical documentation commonly contains tables, a condensed and succinct way to present information. Often a table presents information in a more user-accessible form than text, but it can be quite a challenge to reduce a large mass of information to tabular form. Put information in a table when you want your readers to look at the numbers or compare items directly.

Guidelines for the use of tables:

- Title each table.
- Place your table title before the table.
- Number tables consecutively.
- Place a table after the first paragraph in which it is mentioned.
- Label each column in a table (these labels are called column heads).

Depending on your table, you may also need to label every row.

Construct a table so your readers will read it down the page, in the same direction as when following the text. A very wide table can be placed on a turnpage, but avoid this if possible.

Tip ➤ *Split tables that are too wide for a page.*

A better solution for your readers is to separate the large table into two or three smaller ones that you can present without a turnpage. For a very long table, try to group the information in logical sections.

Book Design

Book design goes beyond the layout of material on a single page. It addresses features such as how heads fall on the page, how running heads or feet appear (headers and footers) throughout the book, and how tables, the table of contents, indexes, and appendices are laid out. The book designer also considers and plans for those pieces of a document that constitute its *front matter* and its *back,* or *end, matter.*

Front matter includes:

Title page

Copyright and trademark description

Reading path or documentation map

Table of contents

Preface

Back matter typically contains:

Appendices

Glossary

End notes

Bibliographical information

Index or indexes

The order of elements in front matter is usually as shown in the preceding list, but the order of back matter can vary, although the index should always be last. Sometimes you will find an index placed before the table of contents. If you decide to do this, do it uniformly for all books in your set. American audiences tend to expect a table of contents in the front matter and an index in the back matter, but in some countries the order is not the same — for example, a table of contents may be in the back matter. Just be consistent in how you place these elements.

Do not overlook the possibility of placing reference information, such as lists of commands or frequently consulted items, inside the back cover of a document.

Design your book so that your readers find information quickly. For example, use horizontal lines to help your readers find something quickly on a page, because horizontal lines on heads or subheads guide the reader's eye. Also use lots of tables and figures, particularly in reference material. With material that is to be read through, and less used for reference, provide plenty of white space and clear headings.

Tabs, either on especially heavy paper or cover stock or as bleed tabs, also enhance accessibility. Consider what information they should hold. For example, if you place tabs between chapters, don't just put abbreviated chapter titles on them — include chapter numbers as well. When your reader finds an entry in your index with a chapter and page number, the tab chapter numbers will make it easy to find the right page.

Tip ➤ *Put chapter numbers on tabs.*

Consider page layout and book design together. Strive to have text, heads, notes, references, bibliographies, appendices, title pages, table of contents, lists of illustrations, and so on, all suitable for the material. You may need to decide, for example, whether each chapter and appendix is to begin on a *recto* (right-hand) or *verso* (left-hand) page. This aspect of book design is as much an art as a science. Your objective is to design a document that is a unified whole, with all pieces in harmony with each other.

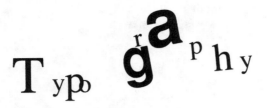

Figure 6.7
Odd Sample Head

Typography

Typography is the art and technique of composing printed material from type-forms. With computers, typographers have found a new flexibility in creating new typeforms. Writers who need special effects or a new design for a particular purpose can sometimes obtain exactly what they need with computer typography.

When you have a choice of several typeforms in your text processing system and printer, understanding the features of each and how it will look on a page or serve your purpose can help you decide which is best. However, over-enthusiasm can lead to using too many typeforms in a single document, which can give a ransom note appearance to your page layout and introduce clutter and confusion in your readers' minds. Note how odd the head in Figure 6.7 looks. Use typeforms conservatively for most technical work.

Published information needs to be user-accessible, and increased conformance to design standards is a reality for many writers of technical documentation (Haag, 1989).

Typography began, in the fifteenth century, when Gutenberg and his contemporaries found ways to create metal type in molds and use assembled letters for printing text. There is some evidence that the idea of movable type originated in Korea and found its way to Europe through trading connections (Burke, 1985, McKerrow 1965). Early European designs intentionally mimicked the fine calligraphic styles practiced at the time, complete with heavy and light lines, minimal punctuation, and abbreviations of common terms. But handmade or even machine-made metal fonts remained cumbersome to prepare, and setting up type for printing remained labor-intensive. Today computer typography is a reality.

Some of the earliest experiments in computer typography were done by Donald Knuth, who defined a standard typographic language he called T_EX. He based T_EX on his earlier work in mathematical typography, which had been inspired when he realized that "Mathematics books and journals do not look as beautiful as they used to" (Knuth, 1979).

Knuth extended his work in typography, the mathematical representations of individual characters, into alphabet design, described in "METAFONT," the last section of his book. For his original mathematical designs, he adapted fifteenth-century designs developed for the first European printers. He found ways to define aesthetically pleasing letter forms mathematically, at a computer terminal. He called one font he developed *Computer Modern.*

With the computer programs Knuth developed using the language he devised, the typographer can define the font for the alphabet, format pages, and build documents. For font design, the typographer can control about twenty parameters, such as the size and proportions of various letter parts. These include *x-height* (the height of your lowercase x), height of *ascenders* and *descenders* (letter fragments that ascend above or descend below the x-height), and length of *serifs* (fine lines at the ends of letter shapes to improve legibility). By changing these parameters, the typographer can obtain an infinite number of *typeforms* for a specific font, all related and blending harmoniously with each other.

Computer font design eliminates many time-consuming processes that a type designer working with drawings and metal molds has to follow, and it enables designs to be developed and tested with great rapidity.

One pleasing result is the ease with which a designer can prepare a complete font consistent throughout its full range of characters. In the past, a type designer often had to be content with incomplete fonts, borrowing from other similar fonts for special characters, such as those needed for mathematical symbols, subscripts, or superscripts. Computer typography helps to eliminate such borrowings and inconsistency. Today's computerized fonts can be more self-consistent and aesthetically pleasing, and more readily and inexpensively created, than old-style metal fonts.

Knuth's work also included the development of entire new alphabets with specialized characteristics, and he was able to imitate virtually every style of typography that had been used for printing books, weaving letters in tapestries, or painting.

With today's *bitmap graphics* (graphics or characters formed by groups of bits mapped into the right shape), typographers can develop almost any form of *typeface* (all the characters in one typeform) and alphabet, and ways are being found to use bitmap graphics for languages beyond those written with the Roman alphabet. Specialized software is becoming available for virtually every type of *script,* such as Cyrillic, Arabic, Hindi, Hebrew, Japanese, Chinese, Korean, and even for ancient scripts such as Egyptian hieroglyphics.

Each script has unique requirements for how letters are formed, how *ligatures* (joined letters) are represented, and what attributes are most important for the aesthetic appearance of the script. If you have access to typographic software, you can experiment with creating specialized and beautiful scripts and forming entire alphabets from them.

However, if you create a new typeform, your nearby laser printer must be able to print it. Some printers can print only the fonts that are permanently stored in them. For example, a daisy-wheel printer can only print the characters you see on its daisy wheel. A laser printer either has resident fonts stored permanently or in interchangeble ROMs, or can accept fonts loaded from another system (downloaded or downline loaded fonts). A printer that accepts downloaded fonts is more flexible.

The PostScript language used with a PostScript-capable printer can let you download your fonts at print time. For example, you may prepare your document on an Apple Macintosh and select an exotic typeface for your heads, say Lubalin Graph. This looks wonderful on your screen, but when you print your document on your attached printer, surprise! All your heads are in Helvetica! What happened? Your printer ROM did not have the typeforms for Lubalin Graph and used the *default* typeform.

However, if you use software that creates an output file in PostScript, and print on a PostScript-capable printer, you may be able to print your Lubalin Graph heads. You will usually work with software that sets up your typeforms for you, but you need to understand how your output is handled by your printing device.

Printing

Mass production of books became possible when metal font types were used with a press much like a linen press and paper became commonly available. Printing would not have developed had leather, parchment, or vellum been the only available media; while these surfaces were fine for handwritten manuscripts, they did not hold the thinner inks needed for the printing press.

Over time printing devices became more automatic, ways were found to create an entire line of type from a keyboard (Monotype and Linotype machines), photo-offset printing developed, and paper was produced not in individual sheets but as huge rolls that could be fed into the large presses used for printing newspapers, magazines, and large print-run books. Efforts such as computer-file-to-film and CALS continue to eliminate manual processes and use electrons, not paper, for both intermediate steps and final results.

Today relatively inexpensive equipment for text processing and printing has moved at least simple printing capabilities from the realm of the master printer to the desktop. However, personal printing devices are not suitable for large print runs but are generally used to create a single copy of a document for use as a reprographic master for quantity printing. If you are interested in the history of printing, a topic beyond the scope of this book, see the readings suggested at the end of this chapter.

Types of Paper

The type and finish of paper used for printing your final product is also part of book design. Paper is available in many types for use in publishing: *book papers* for books or journals; *text papers* for leaflets and advertising; *cover papers* for covers of pamphlets, journals, and paperback books; *newsprint* for newspapers, catalogs, mass-market paperbacks, and similar short-lifetime materials; and *bond* largely for office work. A variety of finishes and qualities is available in all categories.

Paper is measured by physical stock size, weight, and thickness. The thickness of a piece of paper is measured in *mils* (thousandths of an inch) at the paper mill and is converted to *ppi* (pages per inch or *bulk*) when sold. The range is from 200 to 1000 ppi, with commonly used paper around 500 ppi. Paper is sold by *basis weight*, which in the United States is the weight of 500 sheets of paper of a given *basis size*. The basis size of paper stock (for example, 50-pound book paper) is 25 by 38 inches. For cover stock, basis size is 20 by 26 inches, while for bond, basis size is 17 by 22 inches (four 8 1/2-by-11-inch sheets). Thus 50-pound book paper is about the same weight as 27-pound cover paper and 20-pound bond.

Standard paper sizes differ in the United States and abroad. European stock paper sizes are based on the metric system, while U.S. sizes retain the older English system with measurements in inches and weights in pounds. Descriptions of sizes and some conversions are given in Appendix B. If you work in a large organization, you may not need to consider paper type when you develop your books, but if you are a single writer in a small company, you may have to.

Bindings

When you package your documents, you can select from four binding methods:

- Three-ring binder
- Perfect binding
- Wire-o binding
- Saddle staple

If you update your documents frequently, and your readers don't mind inserting sheets of paper into a notebook, you can use a three-ring binder. Perfect binding is inexpensive, but does not stand up to heavy use. Wire-o is a good binding for ease of use but more expensive than perfect binding. You can use saddle-staple only for documents with a small number of pages.

Screen Layout

Creating material intended for screen display is different from creating material for paper. Screens have fewer lines than the pages of most books, and fewer characters per line, because of their larger screen character sizes. A screen also has significantly lower resolution than the printed page (75 dpi compared with 1200 dpi or higher). How your readers interact with the screen depends largely on the software that drives the screen display, whether it contains *context-sensitive* capabilities, and whether it is *menu, window,* or *command* driven or a combination of the three.

A *context-sensitive* system responds to a user inquiry considering user context. For example, in a context-sensitive system when you receive a brief error message, you can press the Help key to see a recovery procedure. A *menu-driven* system shows you a selection of choices (like a menu), from which you select one with a keystroke. A *windowing* system lets you view several parts of your system or application in several windows. Each window can contain a menu or a command interface. Windowing systems and the Apple Macintosh, for example, present you with many pull-down window menus from which you select your tools or actions.

A *command line interface* lets you enter commands by typing them and executing them by pressing the Return or Enter key. For example, MS-DOS, or its equivalent on Microsoft Windows 95, is a command line interface. A command line interface requires the reader to enter commands at a keyboard. A character-cell interface may use a command line interface for some of its functions and lets you use a mouse for others. Figure 6.8 shows a character-cell interface.

A *menu-driven* system displays choices as *nested* or hierarchical lists. A windowing system provides several levels of choice in *pop-up* windows (*tiled* or *overlapping*) or menus, perhaps *pull-down* menus, selected with a *mouse.*

A mouse is a device attached to your system, supported on a rolling ball, with clickable switches. You move the system cursor by moving the mouse on your table or mouse pad, and click the mouse switch to select a menu, window, or action.

Pull-down menus or other pieces of information are activated by *hot spots,* or links, in the text. A hot spot is a place where you can access more information than you see on your screen. Because of their different characteristics, online media

```
Func: ▮------------------   *** DECintact System Menu ***   12-MAY-1989 14:44:53
Key:                                                                DECintact V1.1


SOFF      Sign off DECintact System    VIEW       View a Report File
EXFM      Examine a Screen Form        PSWD       Change DECintact Password
SECA      DECintact Security Add       SECD       DECintact Security Delete
SECI      DECintact Security Inquiry   SECU       DECintact Security Update
SECS      DECintact Security Summary   SET_HOST   DECintact Remote Access
TEST      Test DECintact Application   DCL        DECintact DCL Interface
CALSET    Calendar Set Function        HELP       Online DECintact Help
SAMPLE    Sample Application
```

Figure 6.8
Character-Cell Interface

require a different approach to creating text and graphics than that required by the printed page. A screen can display changing colors and changing figures (animation), or flash (blink) words or symbols to attract readers' attention. Searching online information is also different from searching printed material.

Combined Media

Combined uses of various media are being developed in both the publishing and broadcasting industries. Capabilities already exist to combine text and voice, and hypertext shows the potential for a multimedia approach to information gathering and storage.

One fascinating application of the use of CD-ROM technology is the recording of images of illuminated manuscripts initially captured on high-resolution photographic film, so that readers who cannot handle the precious documents directly can read them through the medium of the CD and a video screen (Fox, 1989). Such new ways to access rare materials will certainly be more frequently used in the future, and more information will be available to more scholars than ever before (Frenkel, 1989).

Some computer corporations provide CD-ROMs containing technical manuals, marketing manuals, and training materials accessible with a graphics display terminal. Particularly where information changes rapidly and there are many pages and many readers, a CD-ROM distribution device is extremely useful and cost-effective.

Information Retrieval

Information retrieval is the obtaining of texts, books, illustrations, or any prepared intellectual materials from storage locations. If you go to a library and select a book from a shelf, you retrieve the book. When you open the book and read its contents, you retrieve the information it contains that was placed there by the book's author.

In a large library with thousands of books, it takes you a long time to find anything, unless the books are organized in some easily understood fashion. Methods that use computers have helped to make information retrieval more flexible, rapid, and effective than the manual, paper-based methods that libraries have long had to rely on.

Information retrieval is of critical importance in business settings, and technical documentation often makes up a large part of the information base of a business. Part of your work in creating technical documentation might be keeping track of document versions and maintaining and updating the document information base.

To understand how others will retrieve information you and other writers squirrel away, you should know something about how others may use your documents.

Modern retrieval systems depend heavily on computerization and require that those who put information into the system understand how the data are to be used. Many systems, both public and private, are becoming accessible from home terminals; this makes the collections they serve increasingly available.

The retrieval systems you will use in your technical documentation work fall into three major classes:

- Hardcopy
- Softcopy
- A combination of the above

Fully hardcopy retrieval systems have a card catalog for finding printed documents. A partially computerized system has a search system like the card catalog.

Online access to the catalog makes it easier for the searcher to browse by keyword, author, or title, and it permits a variety of search capabilities that are limited or nonexistent with a card catalog. For example, a computerized catalog might let you search not only by keywords (subjects) but by call number. You are not likely to find a hard copy card catalog that lets you do this.

Once the searcher finds an item of interest, the system explains how to obtain a document — perhaps by alerting a librarian who retrieves the document from the stacks and either brings it to the circulation desk or puts it in the mail to the requestor.

A fully softcopy retrieval system provides online access to both the card catalog and the texts themselves, and perhaps to bibliographical references. In the world of technical documentation, you will find that you often help to build libraries of technical documents and work with the documents of others in online forms.

With the internet, many online search techniques and tools have become increasingly available. Learning how to use the character-cell forms such as Lynx can get you started, but most users today will use a PC or a Mac and connect with a web browser such as Netscape or Internet Explorer. These tools do a fine job of reaching the desired web site and providing you with the information you see. Both also include email capabilities. Once you have access to a web service, you can search the internet for many pieces of information. Most people will use a search tool such as Altavista (www.altavista.digital.com) or Yahoo (www.yahoo.com). These sites change frequently and from time to time introduce new ways to search the internet, that vast data repository.

Hypertext Systems

The web *is* hypertext. Hypertext and hypermedia systems can present more complex information than traditional databases and provide new ways for users to access data (Clifton, Garcia-Molina, 1989). Hypertext systems use the concepts of *browsing* and *active objects,* in which the user can choose new data while looking at existing data items. A hypertext system provides information in chunks, and if you write for a hypertext system, you provide the chunks of information and the links between them. An active object is linked to another part of the database so that the user can move directly from one chunk to another.

Browsing in a hypertext environment lets you skim through presented information, and you can work with active objects while other, inactive objects remain in view or in process. The *scope* of a hypertext inquiry is determined by how you as a writer set up the links in your hypertext system.

Hypertext systems can require you to use *multiple attribute* indexing, which is unlike the simple keyword attributes used in traditional indexing. With multiple attribute indexing, you need to provide multiple paths to the information you provide. The tool you use to create your hypertext information also provides capabilities for you to create such paths.

Special algorithms are needed for this type of indexing search, and more remains to be done to improve the relevant algorithms and enhance accessibility. A hypertext system is intended only to be used in an active, online environment, never as a printed book (but see the interesting hypertext-like document *Hypertext Hands-On!* [Shneiderman, Kearsley, 1989]), and readers need to feel comfortable using the mouse and keyboard to search for information in the system.

Early hyptertext systems included Intermedia, the Symbolics *Concordia* and Document Examiner system, and *Hyperties,* which has been well described in several publications.

The information on screen can contain *hot spots,* where the user can place the mouse cursor and click to see the next level of information. A hot spot might contain a reference to a table — clicking on it brings up the table for viewing. Another hot spot might contain a graphic.

A HyperCard system, a programmer's environment, can provide multimedia capabilities, including live-action video; still images stored on laser discs; audio track for output from a CD player; high-resolution color images; music, speech, and color scanners; music synthesizers; and touch screens. While these media are not widely used in technical documentation, they are becoming increasingly useful in demonstrations, promotional material, and tutorials.

Human-Computer Interfaces

The design of any computerized information system must consider the effectiveness of the human-machine interface in terms of human physiology and cognition (Rubinstein, Hersh, 1984). Since systems must be designed to interact effectively with human beings, a designer must take into account human needs and capabilities. For example, some designers believe that command interfaces are easier to use than menus; others prefer menus. The reality is that some people prefer one, and some the other. And sometimes the same person prefers one interface while learning a system and another interface after having mastered it.

Tip ➤ *Ease of use and ease of learning are not the same.*

Experience shows that ease of use and ease of learning are not synonymous. So an interface designer needs to prepare different interfaces for different user needs. When you write technical documentation, you may have many opportunities to influence the design of the interface on the system about which you write.

How We Remember

What a person can remember easily can be important in interface design. For example, for quick recall, people can typically remember *seven plus or minus two* items (Miller, 1956). Thus an effective system should be designed so that the user need recall no more than that. It can be very difficult to so segment the information on a complex system to achieve the seven-item limit. With training, however, users can remember more than seven items.

When presenting a system that contains a very large number of items, develop ways to collect the items in natural or logical groups. Recognition is quicker than recall, so one way to present a large amount of information, for example, the hundred or so UNIX commands, is to present it alphabetically. With a list in this well-understood order, the user can read through to find the item needed.

Tip ➤ *Use mnemonics.*

You can use *mnemonics,* memory aids, to improve the ability of your readers to find items. We all learn the alphabet and the multiplication tables by a conscious effort when we are young, and with enough experience, these become almost automatic. Anyone who knows the alphabet, for example, can easily use a dictionary or an encyclopedia, or find a computer system command in an alphabetical list.

Rhymes help us remember odd bits of information. This typical rhyming mnemonic helps us recall the number of days in each month:

Thirty days hath September,
April, June, and November,
All the rest have thirty-one
Except February alone . . .

Once you know this rhyme, you need only remember that February usually has 28 days, except for leap years when it has 29. The rhyme helps you remember because if you get it wrong, you know it right away — the lines do not scan or sound right. The rhythm aids recall as well.

Another common example is a mnemonic to help you spell:

I before E
except after C
or when sounded like AY
as in *neighbor* and *weigh.*

Other memory aids include developing mental pictures to help you remember long strings of numbers or objects. For example, to remember a long number, you might associate an object with each digit and then place each object around an imaginary room. With practice you can remember amazingly long numbers.

Of course, with practice most of us can recall several seven-digit phone numbers, our nine-digit Social Security number, and so on. So we can take these average usages into account when we determine how much we can expect our readers and the users of the computer interfaces we describe to recall.

How We See

The research into human cognitive capabilities shows us that humans have capacity limits. For example, vision is the most acute human sense, surpassing hearing in the fine divisions it can distinguish. So the physiology of vision (Tinker, 1955) is important when you use different presentation forms.

The human eye focuses on *red better than blue* (Glass et al., 1979). This is because of the physiology of the eye and on how humans discriminate between colors. So when you decide on colors for printing fine detail in a document or for displaying information on a terminal screen, choose red if you can; blue will be less effective. Good use of color can reduce the amount of time your readers take to find information in tables, pie charts, and bar graphs, and it can improve readers' accuracy in finding information.

The human eye is also attracted to *things that move.* (The great popularity of television demonstrates this daily.) Consider this when deciding how to display something on a terminal screen. For example, don't just place a piece of information on a screen and leave it there; if it is important, have it flash, blink, or change color. Then even if the user is not watching the screen when an event occurs, the movement on the screen will attract attention.

A display that uses color effectively can be helpful, but beware of too many, or meaningless, colors.

Tip ➤ ***There is no obvious color hierarchy.***

There is no universally accepted color sequence to represent importance or hierarchy other than a gray scale (Tufte, 1990). If you wish to use color to show importance, perhaps use size as well. For example, if you have three important events to show to the user, use red for the most important, orange for the second-most important, and yellow for the least important. Then make the red items large and blinking, the orange items all uppercase and normal size, and the yellow items a normal size mix of uppercase and lowercase. This will clearly distinguish between the items in a hierarchical fashion. For more information on the use of color, see Chapter 5.

Alternative Media

Many writers today must not only consider the content and structure of the information they write for presentation in a printed form; they must also show how the information is to appear or to be used with other media—for example, as part of an online system. This will continue to be an increasingly important medium for future writers, some of whom may create material entirely for online distribution.

With the trend toward online materials, media other than printed books and papers are becoming increasingly common. While there is very likely no good, direct substitute for a nicely printed book, handsomely bound and easily held in the hand, not all information is needed, useful, or even desirable in this form. When a person wants something to sit at home and read, a book is best, but for reference material and material that changes frequently, printing is costly, not as effective, and can often be avoided by using other methods.

Many catalogs and parts lists, for example, are now more often available in microform than on paper. The method is inexpensive and portable (though a microform reader must be available), and it makes possible frequent updating of large stores of data, as well as the exchange of information that in the past could only be consulted in a single location.

Computer access to text files can make it quicker for the readers to obtain a given piece of information, and it provides additional ways to access the information. For example, the current paper version of the UNIX operating system documentation set fills a large bookcase with about fifty large three-ring binders. But the online set fits on a single Compact Disk Read-Only-Memory (CD-ROM) and is accessed like any other disk drive by the operating system. A reader accesses the CD-ROM with a command and can view any document, or any page in a document, by searching with a mouse through index entries, hot spots, or table of contents entries.

The new technology of the CD-ROM has also increased the capabilities of certain computer systems that can access data on these devices. Today's CD-ROMs can hold up to 600 million characters (megabytes) of data and essentially obviate the use of magnetic tapes or diskettes for some data with permanent storage requirements.

WORM (write-once read-many) technology and optical disks also make the archiving of large data sets possible, with improved long-term reliability over magnetic tapes and traditional disk drives. We have some evidence that magnetic tapes and disks have lifetimes of a decade or more, but data stored on them can be damaged by *degaussing* or loss of magnetism, accidental or intentional. Optical disks are said to have much longer lifetimes than magnetic media.

A major advantage of online methods is that they provide additional flexibility for searching materials that are extremely difficult if not impossible to use for other media. It would be impossible to find anything in a large encyclopedia, for example, if the material were not organized in a readily understandable fashion. No one could read and remember all the information in such a large set of volumes. Considerations for storing information for effective use are discussed in the next section on information retrieval.

Further Reading

The most fundamental works on vision as it relates to how we read and distinguish items are *Vision* (Marr, 1982) and the works of Tinker: "Prolonged Reading Tasks in Visual Search" (1955), *Legibility of Print* (1963), and *Bases for Effective Reading* (1965). *Visual Perception* (Cornsweet, 1970) is also an excellent source for real data on the subject.

"The Magical Number Seven, Plus or Minus Two" (Miller, 1956) is a classic paper providing insights that are valuable for the computer field and user interfaces in general. In particular, Miller points out that there are significant differences between the capacity of each human sense. Some of Miller's conclusions have been superseded by later work. *Eye Movements in Reading* (Rayner, 1983), *Visual Perception of Form* (Zusne, 1970), *The Psychology of Reading* (Crowder, 1982), "The Effects of Extended Practice on the Evaluation of Visual Display Codes" (Christ, 1983) all contain additional data on how we read and perceive.

For More Ideas

Books and papers on speech and cognition:
"Speech Communication" (Bailey, 1985), *Cognition* (Glass, et al., 1979), *Self-Organization and Associative Memory* (Kohonen, 1988), *Fundamentals of Human-Computer Interaction* (Monk, ed., 1985), *Language as a Cognitive Process* (Winograd, 1983).

Books and papers on how people retrieve information:
"An Evaluation of Retrieval Effectiveness for a Full-Text Document Retrieval System" (Blair, Maron, 1985), "Probability and Fuzzy-Set Applications to Information Retrieval" (Bookstein, 1983), "Systems Design and the Psychology of Complex Systems" (Brehmar, 1986), "The Coming Revolution in Interactive Digital Video" (Fox, 1989), "The Next Generation of Interactive Technologies" (Frenkel, 1989), "Author/Publisher/Reader of the Future" (Haramundanis, 1989), "On-line vs. Manual" (Haramundanis, 1981), "The Visual Development of Documents" (Martin, 1988).

Books about how libraries and online systems work:
Libraries, Technology, and the Information Marketplace (De Gennaro, 1987), *The Electronic Library* (Dowlin, 1984), *Introduction to Cataloging and Classification* (Downing, 1981), *Multiple Thesauri in Online Library Bibliographic Systems* (Mandel, 1987), *Online Text Management* (McGrew, McDaniel, 1984).

Books that address human factors:
The Human Factor (Rubinstein, Hersch, 1984), *Designing the User Interface* (Shneiderman, 1987), "Future Directions for Human-Computer Interaction" (Shneiderman, 1989), *Screen Design Strategies for Computer-Assisted Instruction* (Heines, 1984).

Books that address machine translation of natural languages:
Machine Translation Systems (Slocum, 1988).

A paper and book that provide information on BNF:
"A Supplement to the ALGOL 60 Revised Report" (De Morgan et al., 1976). *Forth-83 Standard* (1983).

Books you can obtain to satisfy your curiosity about the history of writing and the development of printing:
The English Common Reader (Altick, 1957), *The Day the Universe Changed* (Burke, 1985), *The Book before Printing* (Diringer, 1982), *Semitic Writing from Pictograph to Alphabet* (Driver, 1976), *A Study of Writing* (Gelb, 1963), *The Sumerians* (Kramer, 1963), *An Introduction to Bibliography for Literary Students* (McKerrow, 1965), *Orality and Literacy* (Ong, 1982), *Amusing Ourselves to Death* (Postman, 1988), and *Reform of the Chinese Language* (1958).

Books and journals on information retrieval:
You can find more material on information retrieval in publications such as *Communications of the ACM, Journal of Communication, Information Design Journal,* the *International Journal of Man-Machine Studies,* the *International Journal of Online Information Systems,* and the *Annual Review of Man-Machine Studies.* Hypertext or Memex delivery systems will more significantly change what writers do than even word processing or electronic text processing systems have. Publications such as the *Journal for Information Science, Visible Speech,* and *Technical Writing and Communication* are also excellent sources for current work in the field.

Exercises

1. What is the difference between readability and legibility?
2. What are three of the great attractors of technical documentation?
3. What is the image area on a page?
4. Is monospaced or proportional spacing preferable?
5. What is the resolution of a printed page? Of a video monitor?
6. What is the Fog index?
7. Why be concerned about accents and other marks on foreign words?
8. Name three punctuation marks that have special importance in technical documents, and describe their use.
9. What is BNF and when might you use it?
10. What is a character cell interface? Give an example.
11. What is a command line interface? Give an example.
12. What is a windowing interface? Give an example.
13. What is HTML? When might you use it?

Tools 7

Every tool carries with it the spirit by which it has been created.
Werner Karl Heisenberg, *Physics and Philosophy*, 1958

This chapter touches on the software tools you may use to create technical documentation and the issues around their selection. You won't find information here about older technologies such as the typewriter (even the electronic typewriter).

As a technical writer, editor, or course developer, you will encounter many software tools. Such tools are continually being improved and enhanced, and new ones become important for new environments and uses.

Tools include word processing software, text editors, graphics editors, page layout tools, language (translation), and file management tools. You select your tools based on your requirements or those of your project or of the company where you work. Requirements can include author's requirements such as ability to specify a standard template, create a table of contents and index, automatic spell and grammar checking, and so on. Requirements often include delivery requirements such as the ability to create files that can be viewed with a specific browser on a specific operating system. For example, your project may have a requirement to create material to be viewed with Microsoft Internet Explorer or Netscape Navigator on Windows NT systems.

These requirements, which must be determined before tool selection, thus drive tool selection, and the tool you select will drive the process you use throughout your research, writing, review, test, and production process. Be sure you know the full writing-to-production process so you know what you will need to do at each stage in the process.

If no product or project requirements can be established, select a tool you know that has the capabilities you require as an author, such as automatic page numbering, creation of table of contents, automatic cross-referencing, WYSIWYG capabilities, and so on. If you come onto a project where tools are already selected, and those tools are not in your repertoire, get training immediately. Training can be formal, one or two day training, self-paced training, or even spending the time you need to become familiar with the tool using its documentation. If at all possible, obtain a copy of the documentation to use for reference. For many tools, particularly if you have previously learned another tool that helps with the same tasks, even a day or a half day of training is enough to get you started using the tool. With additional day-to-day experience you will increase both your proficiency and expertise in use of the tool. Become an expert on one tool at a time. Have someone in your group standardize templates and processes to streamline things for the entire team. If possible, have a system manager or system management team support your systems to help with system problems when they arise.

Never change tools or add new tools in the middle of a project. This will cause many problems, most of which will be unforeseen, and may even seriously impact your project schedule.

Consider the graphics tools, the tools to be used by graphics illustrators who prepare art for your project. Such tools must meet the compatibility requirements of the project, or at least of the document on which you are working. A graphics tool must be able to produce art in files that can be accepted by the tool you and your team are using. There may also be requirements from the delivery system to which your final product is dispatched.

All the tools mentioned here are implemented on a computer, and when you use them you work more with electrons than with paper. You may still think of what you do as producing paper, however; it is a hard habit to break, even when you know that most of what you do will not be printed but rather recorded in computer files or on a CD-ROM.

The software tools you use in your daily work provide options and capabilities that have not always existed. Sometimes you may have so many options that it can be hard to choose between them. For many writers, the ideal solution would be to have available and immediately accessible all tools needed to do the job; each tool would be easy to learn and easy to use, and you could select any one at will. On the other hand; some writers prefer to have a single tool, or at least the illusion of a single tool, to meet all their needs. But most are like skilled carpenters — they need a wide variety of specialized tools to do their job.

Why is it so much easier to write with electrons than with a typewriter? Mainly because it is so much easier for you to make changes to your material and because you gain so much control over your final result. Consider these parts of your technical documentation:

- Text
- Graphics
- Information structures (table of contents, index, headings)
- Text formatting
- Page layout

When you create a technical document, you consider all these aspects of your work and modify what you produce as you go along.

Think about how hard it is to make changes to any of these when you use a typewriter — even if you don't do the typing yourself. Making changes on a typewriter is so time-consuming and laborious that you usually won't make any that aren't absolutely essential. But with electrons — why, that is another matter. You can revise, rework, discard, bring back, move, polish, and buff any part of your document. You can see a need for a new graphic and add it; you can find ways to improve reader access by adding new index entries or better headings.

The wonderful thing about this technology is that it truly frees you from the non-creative chores associated with writing that take time and energy. You can try out different ways to present information or describe something and then select the best one. If you are not sure which is best, you can perform usability tests on certain sections and then revise accordingly. You have the time and energy to examine your document and make improvements.

And if you use page layout or text processing systems, you'll be able to see what your book will really look like before it is printed in quantity. It is amazing how often, as your reviewers see successive drafts, they keep "finding" errors that were there all along. When you provide a review draft that looks like the finished product, they find those things early.

So the boon of using electrons, even when you ultimately produce a document on paper, is the time you save, the improvements you can make, and the control you can exert over your finished document. Once you have found these gems, you won't want to give them up.

You will also discover some system tools that are invaluable in your work — for example, directories that assist file management, programs that let you sort or compare files, and windowing systems.

Windowing systems are the outgrowth of much work in educational institutions such as Massachusetts Institute of Technology, Carnegie-Mellon University, and Brown University. With a windowing system (X-windows, MS-windows, and others) and suitable hardware, you can edit a file in one window, call up a second file in a second, verify an example in a third, look at a web site in a fourth, and read a new mail message in a fifth — all at the same time. This can be really convenient when you must verify examples or read mail without exiting from your text processing system. Windowing systems can significantly enhance your productivity because they let you use and control more than one process tool at a time.

In addition to the usual electronic editors, text processing systems, and page layout systems, this chapter touches on other tools you may encounter such as spelling and grammar checkers. Other tools enable you to work with and organize information in ways appropriate to electronic, online media, as well as authoring tools and software or database management systems that help you share files with other writers and prepare materials such as a master index for a large documentation set.

I separate tools into arbitrary groups: support for information structures, text editors, graphics editors, text formatting software, page layout systems, where I discuss printers, language tools, and file or document management systems. Of course, some tools can fit into more than one group.

A tool that supports *information structures* helps you prepare, say, your table of contents automatically — you don't have to type it in and enter page numbers for entries. A *text editor* lets you create and edit text only — it does no formatting. A *graphics editor* lets you create graphics and a variety of illustrations. A *text formatting system* formats your text on a page, while a *page layout system* formats all your document elements — text, graphics, headers, footers, and so on for presentation on your final delivery medium, a printed page or an online screen. How printers handle printing the pages of your hardcopy document fall into this category. Language tools assist you in preparing material that is internationalized and ready for localization or translation into a foreign language. Document or file management systems assist you, your team, and your project in dealing with the many files generated by your project.

But first, what are the considerations for selecting a tool? These must be based on your requirements.

Tool Selection Based on Requirements

Before you select a tool or a suite of tools to create technical documents you must understand the requirements the tool must satisfy. The requirements come both from yourself as the author or member of a publications team and from the client for whom you are creating the technical documentation. Requirements typically include:

- client requests
- client requirements
- delivery requirements (operating systems, delivery channels)
- use of legacy data
- expected future use of information
- file-sharing within project (other writers on the same team)
- file-sharing with other projects

For example, Table 7.1 lists several requirements and tools that can meet those requirements.

Table 7.1
Requirements and Tools that Meet Them

Requirement	Tools that Meet the Requirement
PostScript output for printed document	Word with PostScript print driver, DECdocument, FrameMaker
SGML output viewer	ArborText Publisher, Frame5+SGML
SGML source	SoftQuad Author/Editor
HTML source viewable with web browser (Netscape, Internet Explorer)	EDT, vi, HotDog, MS Internet Assistant
PC screen capture	Paint, Robohelp
WinHelp	Word + Doc-To-Help, Robohelp, Bristol Technologies
Online help on Windows NT	Word + Doc-To-Help
Online help on Windows NT, using legacy ASCII files	Conversion to Word + Doc-To-Help

Support for Information Structures

To deal with the information structures of your document, you need much more than an electronic editor. You need both a text processing and a page layout system, or a combination of both.

The information structures you provide in your document are critical to its ease of use. With the right tools, you will have information structures for both yourself and for your readers.

For example, information structures for your use as an author include cross-referencing, ways to permute index entries automatically, and ways to conditionalize your files. Information structures for your readers include index entries, table of contents, headings and subheadings, and the captions or titles for figures, tables, and examples. You use all of these to help your reader find information.

When you prepare complex technical documentation, you need facilities that support your information structures: cross-references to all headings, tables, figures, examples, and steps within procedures, page numbers, footnotes, bibliographical references, endnotes, and glossary terms. The software you use should provide this support, but the available tools vary widely in their ability to do so. Table 7.2 lists typical information structures you are likely to need and may require of your tools.

Table 7.2
Information Structures

Table of contents	*Conditionalizing files for:*
Index	printed output
Permuted index	online delivery
Headers	ASCII output
Footers	
Footnotes	*Symbolic referencing for:*
Endnotes	Chapters
Cross references	Headings
	Tables
Tool should support automatic numbering of:	Figures
Pages	Examples
Headings	Footnotes
Tables	Bibliographical references
Figures	Glossary terms
Examples	Page numbers
Lists	
Steps in procedures	
Footnotes	
Endnotes	
Callouts	

Text Editors

The earliest electronic or text editors were used primarily for writing computer programs and gradually were adopted for creating text and writing manuals. Primitive text editors let you capture your words in a file and do no more, and some very early ones could only handle uppercase letters. Happily, such limitations are gone forever. The early text editors were also called line editors because you could only see one line of text at a time and worked on that one line. Today you are not likely to use a line editor, but you might use an editor with a video screen or computer terminal only to place words in a file, and not process or format that file in any way. Examples of such text editors include EDT, EMACS, and vi.

You can generally choose your electronic editor from those on your system. And if you are familiar with a particular word processing system, you can often customize the system editor to use those same keystrokes you know and love. However, often your editor of choice changes even as you become used to it, and relearning it, or learning an entirely new editor, can be a part of your work.

Many text editors are command editors, which means you explicitly enter commands to add, delete, search for text, and so on. You execute commands by entering a keystroke such as ESC or CTRL/Z. You are likely to use a text editor if you are creating material that need only be an ASCII file, without any invisible control characters. This can be a requirement of files you need to send in email correspondence on some legacy systems, or of a processing system that accepts an ASCII file as input.

You only need to use a text editor for a short time to see that the processes you use to create text and include graphics are quite different from the purely mechanical processes of writing by hand or copying text on a typewriter. You keep several things in mind as you create text with an electronic editor: the words and phrases you want to write, the commands to the editor, perhaps the markup tags you need, and the final look of the page. Thus your thinking must encompass several activities that operate in parallel.

Graphics Editors

Graphics editors typically require some sort of windowing system software, although some do not. Examples of graphics editors include SuperPaint, and Adobe Illustrator.

Most editors you use to create graphics are WYSIWYG systems. Some let you prepare both text and graphics and assemble these elements together in a compound document. If you know PostScript, you may be able to edit your PostScript files to create or edit a graphic, but this is a tedious way to prepare illustrations.

A WYSIWYG editor displays both text and graphics and lets you view your file in close-to-finished form directly on the screen, as you make your edits. The page you create is adjusted by the WYSIWYG system as you make changes. Some writers find that a WYSIWYG editor is perfect for what they do; others feel that "what you see is *all* you get" — that is, what you cannot place in your file and view on the screen, for example, non-keyboard characters, you cannot use in your document. But improvements in WYSIWYG systems have removed most of these restrictions

Precise differences between screen and print can be significant in a WYSIWYG system, although this is becoming less important as technologies improve. For example, if you view your text on a high-resolution screen, you may see your letters as bit-mapped graphics, with stair-step edges. These are "jaggies," jagged edges. *Antialiasing* is a technique that removes these jaggies. It uses a smoothing algorithm that sharpens and smooths out letter edges before printing by making bits adjacent to the black bits of a bit-mapped character gray.

Graphics File Formats

There are three basic graphic file formats: *vector, metafile,* and *raster.* Vector graphics are described in mathematical formulas, have device-independent resolution, and are smaller in terms of file size than other formats. Metafiles contain information about each object in a figure, have device-independent resolution, and are larger than vector files, smaller than raster files. Raster graphics are created with the number of pixels per inch required by resolution of the output device. Graphic data is stored for each pixel, which makes these the largest of the file formats (Barrett, 1995).

The three types and some tools that produce them are listed in Table 7.3, Graphics File Formats.

Table 7.3
Graphics File Formats

File Format	Attributes	Tool Examples
Vector	• written in mathematical formulas • device-independent resolution • smallest file size	Adobe Illustrator Freehand Autodesk AutoCAD
Metafiles	• information about each object • device-independent resolution • smaller than raster files	CorelDraw! MS Powerpoint SuperPaint
Raster	• data stored for each pixel • device-dependent • largest file size	MS Paint Adobe Photoshop Corel PhotoPaint

Including a preview image when saving a vector drawing increases file size three to five times, but may be needed to let another person view the image before editing it. When working with raster graphics, color depth has a significant effect on file size; more colors means larger file size. Most authoring tools cannot use more than 256 colors, and for most purposes 16 colors or monochrome (black and white) is all you can use.

Many conversion tools are available to move graphics files from one tool to another, for example TechPool Transverter Pro is a PostScript translator, Inset HiJaak Pro is a raster or metafile translator, and Lview Pro (shareware) is a web graphics translator.

Graphics Requirements

Before selecting a graphics tool, consider the following:

- Identify all output requirements for graphics on your project.
- Create graphics to conform to the highest level requirements (a graphic can always reworked to a lower requirement, but often cannot be reused for a higher level requirement).
- Understand color requirements of your processing, production, and delivery systems.

• Consider the impact of using TrueType fonts, even unintentionally. Some processing and delivery systems rely on receiving pure PostScript fonts; some page layout applications use default TrueType fonts for spaces and blank areas in a document, even when the font is not used for text. To avoid this problem, select a common PostScript font before starting a document.

Table 7.4 lists examples of tools applicable to different levels of graphics requirements, from highest to lowest. Most tools are available for both the PC and the Mac.

Table 7.4
Tool Examples for Graphics Requirements

Graphic Requirement	Possible Delivery	Tool
3D rotatable wire frame	printed documentation, several views	Autodesk AutoCAD
3D rotatable solid	3D full animation multiple views of solid models	Autodesk AutoCAD Micrografx Designer
3D full animation	CBT (Computer Based Training) kiosk demonstration disk	Autodesk 3D Studio Adobe Premier
3D line art	printed documentation online help	Adobe Illustrator
16.8 million colors	CBT kiosk printed documentation	Adobe PhotoShop Adobe Illustrator
256 colors	CBT kiosk 2D animation web	Adobe Photoshop Adobe Illustrator CorelDraw! Corel Photopaint
16 colors	CBT kiosk demonstration disk EPSS online help web GUI icons	Paintbrush Microsoft Paint
2D animation	CBT kiosk demonstration disk animated presentation	Autodesk Animator Pro Macromedia Director Peripherals Plus Astound
screen captures	printed documentation CBT	HiJaak Pro Robohelp Microsoft Paint
presentation graphics	overheads or slides printed documentation	Microsoft Powerpoint

Text Formatting Software

Software for the simplest *text formatting* takes the file you prepare with your electronic editor and makes certain formatting decisions based on text and a few commands or control characters. For example, text can be indented or margins changed; or a heading may be printed with the same typeface but in bold. You may define how long each page is to be, say sixty lines, and the text formatting software can then insert a page-eject command after every sixtieth line. But that is the extent of what this kind of software can do. If you are preparing material for web viewing, you can add HTML markup to your text using a simple text editor. Formatting is done by the web browsers when the file is viewed.

An example of text formatting software that lets you do some page layout is troff, a version of RUNOFF that runs on UNIX systems.

With a *markup system,* you place explicit markup information in your source file and format your text by processing your file. If you are using a dedicated text editor, simply saving your file prepares it for printing appropriately formatted. Markup systems are well suited for long, formal, and standardized publications. As a general rule, a *markup* system can be preferable for large, complex documents that require several layers of internal and external cross-referencing and for writers sharing a common database such as master title indexes or common document segments. You can use a markup system with a character-cell terminal.

A *WYSIWYG system* is preferable where you must control page layout and need great flexibility in the size and number of fonts and in the placement of photographs and diagrams. A WYSIWYG system is the better choice for preparing brochures or newsletters, for example, though not all WYSIWYG systems can handle photographs. WYSIWYG systems are also easier to learn to use than markup systems.

Using a batch system lets you do other work while your text is processing; it lets you process multiple chapters of a book simultaneously (a *bookbuild*) and perhaps create your table of contents and index at the same time; and it makes it possible to standardize page layout across an entire book or document set. Markup systems can let a writing team create a master index for their document set, and they typically have graphics inclusion capabilities. A disadvantage of markup systems is that you must process and print your file to verify page formatting. You can sometimes view the content of your document on your character-cell terminal, without the actual fonts that will be used in printing.

Tip ➤   *Software with more features takes longer to learn.*

As with any software, the more features present in a text processing tool, the more time it takes to learn.

One feature of early text processing systems was the ability to justify lines of text so that the formatted page had flush left and right margins. Justifying was a primitive attempt to make the output of a text processor look like a page in a printed and typeset book. However, the added spaces in a line made a document harder to read, and, particularly in a text with an unusual number of long words, they created rivers of white where the spaces on succeeding lines appeared to join together in vertical or slanted lines.

Printers

The printer you use dictates what your final printed document will look like. There are certain things you cannot do with a limited device such as a dot matrix or daisy-wheel printer. But with the greater capabilities of a laser printer, for example, you can create pleasing documents with a page layout and typography suitable to your purposes.

Choice of printer is often, but not always, dictated by initial purchase cost. Quality is also an important consideration. What is fine for when you just want to look at your own work can be quite inadequate for correspondence-quality work or the development of technical manuscripts. And if your needs extend to printed brochures requiring several colors, you will need even more expensive and complicated equipment. The next few paragraphs guide you through the forest of printing devices.

Since the 1940s, when computers began to print information on paper, several types of inexpensive printing devices have evolved, including character, line, page, daisy-wheel, dot-matrix, ink jet, laser, and loadable-font printers. All but the last three of these are called *impact* printers, because they print a character by striking the paper.

The *character* printer prints a single character at a time. A typewriter is a character printer; when you press a key on the keyboard, a single character is imprinted on paper. Early typewriters had a basket of uppercase characters, with each letter on a separate wand. Such a system was also used by early Teletype machines. When the shift key was invented, the basket of characters grew to incorporate uppercase and lowercase letters, and typewriters were modified to work with the larger character set. A few commonly used special characters, such as #, $, and % were added to typewriter keyboards for convenience. The carriage of the typewriter carried the paper past the place where each letter struck the paper.

The requirements of fast typists, along with the larger character sets, imposed severe demands on this mechanical system, and many innovative designs were developed to meet these demands. The *typeball,* a golf-ball-sized interchangeable element that moved along the carriage track and held the letters, was one such device; the *daisy-wheel* device (so named because it looks like a daisy) was another.

The daisy-wheel printer is a character printer. Its printing mechanism is a small spoked wheel, with each spoke holding a character at its outer end. Each daisy wheel, like each typeball, held a different typeface, and daisy wheels could easily be exchanged depending on the typeface chosen for a document.

These mechanical devices helped typists type faster. Eventually, however, the act of printing a character on paper was separated from the typing process itself.

Electronic typewriters that help the typist by lifting off an error with sticky tape and overprinting with white ink, and checking spelling became common. But the storage capacity of an electronic typewriter couldn't compare with the capacity of even a small computer or word processing system.

Around the same time that daisy-wheel printers became popular, the *dot-matrix* printer also became available. The dot-matrix printer is fast and flexible, but cannot produce high-quality print.

All dot-matrix printers work on the same principle: each character is formed by a set of wires or their equivalent in a two-dimensional matrix, and the *resolution* of letters and clarity of printing depends on the number of wires in the print head. Print heads typically have 7 by 9 or 9 by 12 wires (dots). The figure below shows a typical 5-by-7 dot-matrix representation of the lowercase letter *h*. A dot-matrix printer can be instructed to make characters double-width (double size), which gives them flexibility not found in character printers.

Dot-matrix printers print with ribbons, either single-use mylar or multi-use cloth, or perhaps on special thermal paper. An *ink jet* printer uses a dot-matrix design for forming characters, but jets of ink, not wires, form the characters. Rather a dinosaur of the 1960s, a *line printer* that could print an entire line of up to 132 characters at a time evolved from the character-printing device. Such printers were designed more for printing reports, particularly reports containing lots of numerical data, than for printing text, and they had no graphics capabilities. Some high-speed printers were called line printers, but this was incorrect because in reality they only printed one character at a time.

With the introduction of *laser* printers, using the technology of *xerography* and memory chips that could hold information about how each character was formed, printing technology moved into an entirely new realm. Laser printers made possible an extremely high quality of printing. Characters in such printers are specified either by a ROM in the printer, in a bit-map graphics form, or with a page description language. A bit-mapped form takes a lot of storage space, but can handle moderately complex graphics well. The figure below shows a letter in a simulated bit-mapped form.

Printer capabilities extend to both text and graphics and make possible a wide variety of publications with pages automatically formatted by page layout software. Specific fonts chosen for particular audiences can be loaded into the target printing device, and the final printed piece can have a quality high enough to be sent to a printing vendor as a master for mass copying or printing.

Laser printers are characterized in dots per square inch (dpi). For creating reprographic or camera-ready copy, a laser printer should have a resolution of at least 300 dpi. Printers with resolutions of up to 2400 dpi are available, but the higher resolution is typically more expensive.

Some printing devices are unable to print all possible unusual characters, so verify your printer's capabilities before you decide which unusual characters to use. For example, if you are creating material that includes examples in a programming language such as Ada or Algol that requires special characters, you'll need to find a printer that can print such material. You may easily find a loadable font to use with your software to write the material and view it on screen, but printing it on paper may be more difficult. Sometimes the easiest way to check what your printer can do is to run a test.

Tip ➤ *Test your printer for unusual characters.*

Along with the capabilities of font creation and storage in the target printing device, programming languages also evolved in which fonts and page layouts could be specified. One such page description language (PDL), as these printer languages are called, is PostScript. This is a high-level language, based on Forth, which can produce complex graphics. Forth, developed in the late 1970s, is a real-time control language similar to artificial-intelligence languages like LISP (List Processing System). The functional definitions of Forth are documented in the Forth-83 Standard (1983).

PostScript has become an integrated component of desktop publishing systems and is used by several popular software packages. With PostScript capabilities, your printer can create a wide variety of documents that earlier could only be created by typesetting machines and laborious manual paste-up of master pages (masters) for printing.

Page Layout Systems

Page layout software processes your source file and presents the information laid out on a page for printing. Fully capable page layout software adjusts for font sizes in headings, examples, and tables, and can place graphics in just the right place on each page. Examples of page layout software include PageMaker and FrameMaker; Word provides page layout capabilities adequate for much technical documentation.

Interactive Page Layout Systems

A WYSIWYG system normally uses a screen that shows a page or two at a time and has graphics capabilities. With a batch-based markup system, you use a character-cell terminal where you see only the markup source file. With a markup system, you must process and print, or perhaps display, the output to see the resulting formatted material. With a WYSIWYG system, you view changes to a file interactively. WYSIWYG gives you more detailed control of the look of your output than does a batch-based system. For example, you can change page size or fonts for headings on the fly and see the results on your screen. For many purposes, such a system is ideal, although where standardization of output form is important, a WYSIWYG system may not be the best choice.

A WYSIWYG system gives you immediate feedback on page layout, lets you see fairly closely what your document will look like when printed, and lets you change format easily and see the results quickly. With increasingly powerful PC systems, many of the processing limitations of interactive systems have disappeared, and they play an increasingly important role in the preparation of technical documents.

Language Tools

You will find many software tools to assist you in improving your spelling, style, or grammar. These include electronic dictionaries, spelling checkers, translation aids, and language analyzers. Many of these tools, briefly described in this section, are still very primitive, but they hold the promise of new capabilities to come.

Electronic Dictionaries

Electronic dictionaries are part of several tools you may use. For example, most desktop publishing systems contain a dictionary and can alert you to spelling errors as you type. You can use electronic dictionaries to verify spelling and to guide hyphenation. Some tools let you use more than one dictionary at a time, which can be useful if you are working on a multilingual document or a document such as a medical textbook that uses specialized terms. Thesauri can be useful and are integrated with some WYSIWYG systems.

Spelling Checkers

Spelling checkers, which read a text file and display words that appear to be misspelled, are useful aids, particularly if you don't spell well. However, they cannot discriminate between the correctness of "their" and "there" or "boy" and "buy," for example, and thus are not a substitute for proofreading a document for sense — a task only a human being can do.

A spelling checker works with the dictionary that comes with it, and many spelling checkers let you add to the dictionary. This is a useful feature because once you add your own special, unique terms such as file names ("Release_notes.txt") or software utility names ("SYSGEN"), you can use the spelling checker to make sure they are spelled correctly throughout your text.

Some spelling checkers present you with alternatives when they flag a word that may be misspelled. This feature lets you select the correct word rather than go elsewhere for verification. A spelling checker does not provide you with word definitions, only spelling verification and flagging, so it is still up to you to be sure you have used the right word.

For example, the following passage taken from *Alice's Adventures in Wonderland* by Lewis Carroll, shows how a spelling checker might highlight your spelling errors, shown in caps. Some systems highlight errors with color, a better method than capitalization.

> The Hatter was HTE first to break HTE silence. "What day of the month is it?" he said, turning to look at Alice: he had taken his watch out of his pocket, and was looking at it uneasily, shaking it every now and then, and holding it to his ear.

Grammar Checkers

A grammar checker can help you verify the grammatical correctness of your text. It is typically interactive, letting you display a document, select a region of text to be checked, read the displayed grammatical comments, and make corrections with some editing functions.

A grammar checker processes for grammatical form, not for meaning, analyzing sentences to determine if the relationships between words are correct. For example, it can find split infinitives ("to boldly go"), subject-verb disagreement ("ideas flows smoothly"), too many noun adjuncts (adjectives or adjectival phrases: "high-performance mainstream computer environment"), and clustered prepositional phrases ("reference text appears on the bottom of each page in the update to the system service").

A grammar checker might flag a sentence as shown here:

```
Once a complete copy of the entire
document HAS BEEN
=> PASSIVE VOICE
printed on the output device, the sheets
can BE USED to create
=> PASSIVE VOICE
multiple copies.
```

The grammar checker lets you know you have a couple of phrases that are very likely in passive voice. You can then examine the phrases and decide if you want to change them. Some grammar checkers will not work with a source file that contains markup tags.

A grammar checker cannot check for meaning and would not flag a nonsense sentence such as "colorless green ideas sleep furiously," nor can it identify errors of logic, poor flow of ideas, or ambiguities. A sentence like "Repair and wash the carburetor and filter mechanisms," for example, would not be flagged by a grammar checker.

Grammar checkers for personal computers include Grammatik IV from Reference Software, Inc., RightWriter, available from RightSoft, Inc., and Perfect Grammar from Lifetree Software, based on CorrecText. A grammar checker included with some versions of UNIX is part of the AT&T Writer's Workbench.

Translation Aids

Translation tools include editors that enable the translator to view more than one file at a time and preprocessors that help prepare a source file for translation. For example, when you create your source file, you can then send it to the person who is the translator along with your text in the original language.

If your translator can use the same text processor for preparing the translated book, the translator won't need to change any markup tags, but can concentrate solely on translating the text. A preprocessor that highlights the tags so they are easily recognized and ignored by the translator can make the work of translation easier. So too can electronic dictionaries that help ensure consistent spelling.

Tools for translators are in the experimental stage, and much work remains to be done to simplify the technical translator's task.

Most translation tools are either direct machine-translation systems or machine-assisted systems. A machine-translation system accepts text in one language and prepares a partial translation in a target language largely by direct word substitution. A machine-assisted translation system lets the translator view the text as it is translated. The translator can then accept or revise the translation directly on the terminal. Some translation tools translate the source language into an intermediate language first (Esperanto or InterLingua, for example), then translate from the intermediate language to the target language (Slocum, 1988).

Language Analysis Tools

Several tools help you evaluate your writing. There is no agreement among language analysts as to whether these tools are truly effective, but some writers feel they can help them improve the clarity of their prose. The tools range from those that examine a text for educational grade level to those that compute an index of readability. All tools currently available separate the text to be analyzed into character strings and use rules or algorithms based on string searches and matches (Stratton, 1989).

The information you can obtain from a style analyzer includes the number of words in your text, the average number of words per sentence, the number of unique words in the text, and the number of times each unique word appears. Some provide the number of words in each sentence and paragraph, and the number of sentences in each paragraph.

Style analyzers have their drawbacks. For example, many fail to recognize that "Dr." is a word and not the end of a sentence, and deal incorrectly with such text elements as headings, titles, and captions. Some deal incorrectly with misspelled words as well.

Readability scores based on formulas such as those developed by Rudolph Flesch and Robert Gunning are a feature of some style analyzers. However, the results of such scores vary between analyzers and may not always be helpful. For more discussion of readability scores, see Chapter 6.

Some style analyzers provide recommendations for you to consider. The analyzer may display a phrase it considers wordy or that appears to contain jargon and suggest a substitute phrase or deletion of the original. Writers often find that a style analyzer helps to improve their writing by coaching them to follow standard rules, but after they have used the analyzer a few times, they no longer learn from it and set it aside.

If you can benefit from a style analyzer, it can be a boon. If you can't, no amount of experience with the tool can make you like it. There is little evidence that style analyzers improve writing style, but if judiciously used, they may help to make you aware of things that you can do to improve, or at least reexamine, your writing.

File Management

When you work with any software system manipulating files, you need flexibility in copying, naming, renaming, and appending those files. If you work with several writers on a team and need to share files, you may also need access to code or text management systems. All systems provide basic copying functions, but some provide greater capabilities and are easier to use than others.

Sometimes you need to be able to move files from one system to another, or perhaps create a graphic on one system and then move it to a second system to make it part of a document. The greater the capabilities of the computer system you use, the more flexible your work environment, and thus the easier it is for you to accomplish your tasks.

System Features

When you use a single-user system such as a home computer, you may need to store a large document as segments on multiple diskettes. However, if you work on a multiuser computer system with large storage capacity, you typically do not have to manipulate and keep track of multiple diskettes or tapes, nor do you have to be concerned with preparing backup or archival copies of your work. In a multiuser environment with operations support, this task is done by someone else.

A production publishing environment is one that produces multiple copies of multiple documents on a fixed schedule. Such environments can be exceptionally demanding, and they place a high premium on tools and devices that help ensure high quality in the shortest possible time. Tools for illustrators (for example, Adobe Illustrator) and high resolution, high quality printing devices are often required in such production environments, but they aren't treated in any detail in this book.

Nevertheless, if you prepare files for a production system, you need to understand both the tools and the requirements of that environment. The more you do to ensure that last-minute changes are avoided or kept to a minimum, the smoother and more error-free will be the final process for preparing camera-ready copy.

File Management Strategy

Your own work process to some extent will dictate how you manage your files. In a typical work environment, you will deal with multiple files and multiple versions of those files. And the philosophy of file management of the computer system on which you work will have an impact on how you do your work.

For example, on some systems multiple versions of files are retained automatically, with a version number. On others, only the current copy of a file is kept; the previous version vanishes. Depending on the software you use, data from a previous version may be retained in the current file as hidden data, viewable with revision tools. Check on how your system handles new generations of files before deciding on your file management strategy.

In working in the Windows 95 and in other windows environments, using the file management tool Windows Explorer makes it easy to view the structure of files on your system, and to add new folders (or sub-directories) as required. I like to start a new folder for a new project, giving it a distinctive name, not a generic one. For example, when starting a new project dealing with IEEE standards, I would create a new folder at a top level on a large disk drive called IEEE, not Project1. If I anticipate several drafts of the document, I create subfolders starting with Draft1. I also like to include draft dates on the title page of any document. A date on the front of your draft is a quick check to verify which version of a document you or a reviewer is referring to when providing a comment or responding to one.

Tip ➤   ***Date your drafts to avoid confusion.***

When I begin the second draft of the document I make an explicit copy of the current draft and place it in a folder named Draft2, and so on. This way I can always revert back to a previous version of the document if necessary. If system backup is available, I can rely on that backup for old versions of documents; alternatively, I keep my own backup of files on diskette.

I also prefer to create chapters each in a separate file, which makes processing and updating easier. But again, this depends on your own work process and style, and perhaps on the practices of your team. On a team where writers share files, an agreement on basic file management practices is essential.

File and project management practices can also have an influence on business processes such as ISO 9000-series certification. If this is important in your environment, you and your team will need to put appropriate procedures and practices in place.

File Transfer

When you need to transfer files from one system to another, you will typically have several alternatives: copying files to a diskette, tape, or removable disk, CDROM, or transferring files over the network.

If the files you need to transfer are small, and the systems on both ends of the transfer have diskette drives, you can copy your files to diskettes and send the diskettes in the mail or by courier. When files are too large to be placed on diskette, in many cases you can use a compression tool such as WinZip to place them on and read them from diskette. When files are too large for such compression to work, you can consider using removable disk cartridges that have multi-megabyte capacities, or perhaps tape cartridges. And for large files that you need to transfer in a short period of time, consider doing file transfer over the network. For this to be useful, you should have at least a 50 kilobaud line or modem. A 14.4 kilobaud modem is probably too slow, although it may work in some environments. (For baud rate definition, see the Glossary.) If your network connection is too slow, you may lose your connection before the file transfer is complete due to network time-outs, and have to initiate the same transfer all over again. For example, it can take over an hour to transfer a 6 megabyte file over a 14.4 kilobaud line.

The basic rule for file transfer is: both ends of the transfer must have the same equipment.

For example, both ends must have floppy disk drives, or both must have removable disk drives, and so on. If you are doing a network file transfer, both ends should be able to send and receive at the same speed, for example both should have 14.4 kilobaud (Kbps or kilobits per second) modem capabilities. If you transmit at 14.4 kilobaud and the receiving modem can only receive at a lower rate, you are likely to have file transfer problems. When transferring files between corporations, or between a corporation and a vendor, agreements must be reached and procedures established beforehand about how to transfer files across corporate firewalls.

Code Management Systems

A code management system is a software tool that helps control and monitor activities in files it manages. Such a system typically provides an edit history for any document under its control and determines who edits a specific element in the system.

Where writers work together to create documentation and share common files, a code management system can be useful or even essential. Elements that are candidates for file sharing include:

- Lists of titles
- Lists of symbolic names for titles
- Glossary terms
- Common overview text
- Common critical tables
- Common illustrations
- Chapters or sections of a book being prepared by more than one writer

Code management systems are often based on those used by software developers who work collaboratively. Software, like documentation, contains many source code modules, and developers require control of the editing functions. The need for a code management system arises when several writers or developers must collaborate to prepare material in parallel. Without a code management system, the edits of one writer may be lost if two writers begin to edit the same file to which both have access.

Say there is a file called TEXT.TEXT on the computer system two writers use, and both writers need to make changes to it. At 9:00 A.M. Writer A calls the file with her editor and obtains the version TEXT.TEXT;1, with a generation number of 1. She does her editing and then saves the file back in the common area at 10:00. This becomes generation 2 of the file or TEXT.TEXT;2. Before Writer A is done, Writer B takes a copy of the file, also TEXT.TEXT;1, generation 1. He begins editing at 9:30 and finishes at 10:30, when he returns his new version of the file to the common area. The file is now at generation 3, and the generation 2 edits have been lost because Writer B did not begin with TEXT.TEXT;2 but with TEXT.TEXT;1. Such a problem can cause total chaos, but it can be avoided by a code management system, which acts as an effective "traffic cop."

Typically, a code management system has at least two features: the ability to automatically generate an audit trail, or edit history, of work on any file in the system, and the ability to require that no file can be edited by more than one person at a time. One way the system ensures this is to lock a file once it has been checked out by one writer, thereby preventing another writer from making edits to it.

Such a system imposes requirements on how individuals do their work, but it can improve the quality of a collaboration and simplify the processes of team work. You know that files cannot be corrupted unexpectedly by simultaneous edits, and you recognize that cooperation in making edits is enforced by a neutral traffic cop, the code management system.

Further Reading

You can find much comparative information about computerized tools in the *Datapro* reports available in many technical and large public libraries. Occasionally Consumers Union will prepare comparative reports on home computers or tools. Other reporting organizations include *Auerbach* and *Faulker Technical Reports.* Manufacturer's literature can also provide detailed information on specific tools. You can find comparative reports on software for IBM personal computers, clones, and other personal computers in *Software Digest Ratings Reports.*

To learn about new tools, become familiar with the periodicals in the field, including *PC World, PC Magazine, Computer Shopper, MacWorld,* the *Proceedings* of the International Technical Communications Conference (ITCC), the *Communications of the ACM,* other software magazines.

Even advertisements from local software sources can provide information on software tools.

For More Ideas

For information about controlling your PostScript printed output:
First read *PostScript Language Tutorial and Cookbook,* and then, when you become proficient, *PostScript Language Reference Manual* (both from Adobe Systems, 1985).

For more information about word processing software:
Microsoft Word User's Guide (Microsoft Corporation, 1993-1994), *Guide to Microsoft Word* for the Apple Macintosh (Jacobs, 1989), *Using Microsoft Word 4*, Macintosh (Pfaffenberger, 1989), *The WordPerfect Question and Answer Book* (Stone, Doner, 1989), *WordPerfect 5.0 On-Screen Help Book* (1990), or *WordPerfect 5.1 "On-line Advisor."*

Exercises

1. What is a WYSIWYG system?
2. What is a template?
3. How should you select a word or text processing tool?
4. What are information structures?
5. Name two graphic file formats and describe their attributes.
6. What is antialiasing?
7. How do you decide if a printer can produce camera-ready copy?
8. What is PostScript?
9. When might you use network file transfer?

Societies, Conferences, Journals, and Internet Resources   A

This appendix lists societies, conferences, and periodicals that might interest you as you continue your career in technical documentation. It also contains starting points for you to use the internet for finding resources related to technical writing. These resources may be web sites, list servers, or chat rooms. Many of the societies focus on topics of interest to people who work with computers, so if your area of expertise is elsewhere, you can ignore them. However, societies and organizations that are dedicated to the technical writing field should be valuable to you.

The key conferences for technical communicators are ACM SIGDOC, ITCC (hosted by STC), IPCC (hosted by IEEE PCS), ACM CHI, INTERACT, local STC chapter meetings, and other ACM and IEEE related conferences including SIGGRAPH.

Students with an interest in the pedagogic aspects of technical writing may also be interested in ATTW.

Most societies publish at least a newsletter, and some produce books, journals, and a wide variety of publications. Most have at least an annual conference or symposium. Take opportunities in your local area to find out about meetings, seminars, and other ways to communicate with others in the field. You are bound to benefit.

Societies

- American Association for Artificial Intelligence
  445 Burgess Ave., Menlo Park, CA 94025
     Publishes *AI Magazine.*

- American Medical Writers Association (AMWA)
  9650 Rockville Pike
  Bethesda, MD 20814
     Publishes the *American Medical Writers Association Journal.*

- American Society for Information Science (ASIS)
  1424 16th St., NW, Suite 404, Washington, D.C. 20036
    Publishes *Annual Review of Information Science and Technology, Bulletin, Database Directory, Handbook* and *Directory;* also *Jobline, Journal, Proceedings,* and various monographs. Holds two meetings annually.

- American Voice Input/Output Society (AVIOS)
  P.O. Box 60940, Palo Alto, CA 94306
    Publishes proceedings, *AVIOS Journal, AVIOS News.* Holds annual meeting.

- Association for Business Communication (ABC)
  100 English Building, 608 South Wright St., Urbana, IL 61801
    Publishes the *Journal of Business Communication.*

- Association of Computer and CD-ROM Users
  P.O. Box 3336, Yuba City, CA 95992
    Publishes *CD-ROM Report* and *Computer Consultant Newsletter.* Holds annual conference.

- Association for Computing (ACM)
  1515 Broadway, New York, NY 10036
    Supports numerous Special Interest Groups (SIGs) that are valuable for the technical documentor. Publishes *Communications of the ACM,* many computer journals, and conference proceedings. A SIG typically publishes a newsletter, organizes technical symposia and sponsors technical sessions at computer conferences. The relevant SIGs include:

    SIGART: Artificial Intelligence

    SIGCHI: Computer and Human Interaction (Sponsors annual conference.)

    SIGDOC: Computer Documentation
    Publishes a refereed journal, *Asterisk (*), the Journal for Computer Documentation,* sponsors an annual conference, a web site (www.acm.org/sigdoc), and other member services.

    SIGGRAPH: Computer Graphics (Sponsors annual conference.)

    SIGIR: Information Retrieval (Sponsors annual conference.)

- Association for Information Management (ASLIB)
  Information House, 20–24 Old St., London EC1V 9AP, England
    Publishes *ASLIB Book List, ASLIB Monthly, ASLIB Proceedings, Computing,* and *Journal of Documentation,* as well as handbooks, directories, monographs, reports, and bibliographies. Holds periodic conferences and conducts seminars and training sessions.

- Association of Professional Writing Consultants
  3924 S. Troost, Tulsa, OK 74105
    Publishes *Professional Writing Consultant* newsletter and membership directory. Holds annual conference.

- Association of Teachers of Technical Writing (ATTW)
  c/o Dr. Carolyn D. Rude, Dept. of English, Box 4530, Texas Tech University, Lubbock, TX 79409
    Publishes *Technical Communication Quarterly*. Holds annual meeting.

- Council for Programs in Technical and Scientific Communication (CPTSC)
  Prof. Marilyn M. Cooper, Michigan Technological University, 1400 Townsend, Houghton, MI 49931
    Promotes programs and research in technical and scientific communication.

- Graphic Communications Association (GCA)
  100 Daingerfield Rd.
  Alexandria, VA 22314-2888
    Affiliated with Printing Industries of America. Sponsors conferences and expositions with a publications focus, including SGML conferences.

- Human Factors and Ergonomics Society
  Box 1369, Santa Monica, CA 90406-1369

- Institute of Electrical and Electronics Engineers (IEEE)
  345 East 47th St., New York, NY 10017
    Publishes *IEEE Transactions on Professional Communication, IEEE Spectrum, IEEE Computer Graphics and Applications,* and many other journals. IEEE's Professional Communication Society (PCS) hosts the annual International Professional Communication Conference (IPCC), often linked with ACM SIGDOC. Supports web site at www.ieee.org/pcs.

- Linguistic Society of America
  1325 18th St., Suite 211, Washington, D.C. 20036
    Publishes *Language* and the *Meeting Handbook of the Linguistic Society of America,* the program and record of its annual meeting.

- National Council of Teachers of English (NCTE)
  111 W. Kenyon Road, Urbana, IL 61801-1096
    Holds annual Conference on College Composition and Communication (CCCC); provides a forum for critical work on the study of college level reading and writing. Publishes journal *College English*.

- Publishing Systems Group (Computer Users) (PSG)
  c/o Henry Simons, Trentypo, Inc., 304 Stokes Ave., Trenton, NJ 08638
    Publishes *Publishing Systems Group — Newsletter* and a directory. Holds two conferences annually.

- Society for Documentation Professionals (SDP)
  P.O. Box 2298, Woburn, MA 01888
    Offers local programs.

- Society of Indexers (SI)
  16 Green Road, Birchington, Kent CT7 9JZ, England
    Publishes *The Indexer, Microindexer, Training in Indexing,* and various books, papers, and reading lists. Holds biennial meeting. Affiliated with American, Australian, and Canadian societies.

- Society for Technical Communication (STC)
  815 15th St., NW, Suite 506, Washington, D.C. 20005
    Publishes *Technical Communication, Journal, ITCC Proceedings,* and *Intercom Newsletter.* Sponsors annual International Technical Communications Conference (ITCC). The preeminent society for the technical communicator.

Conferences

As a technical writer, you have a great many conferences to choose from. This selection emphasizes those conferences of interest to you if you work in technical documentation with a focus on the computer industry. You won't be able to go to every conference, but this list may get you started thinking about attending the most worthwhile.

- ACM Conference on Computer Graphics and Interactive Techniques (SIGGRAPH).
- ACM SIGACT, SIGMOD, SIGART, and Symposium on Principles of Database Systems (PODS). Sponsors: ACM SIGACT, SIGMOD, and SIGART.
- ACM SIGCHI Conference on Human Factors in Computing Systems (CHI). Sponsors: ACM SIGCHI, SIGGRAPH, Human Factors Society, and IEEE-CS.
- ACM SIGDOC Conference on Computer Documentation.
- Computer Graphics International (CGI). Sponsors: Computer Graphic Society and British Computer Society.
- Conference on Office Information Systems (COIS). Sponsors: IEEE-CS and ACM SIGOIS.

- Electronic Publishing 90. Sponsor: National Institute of Standards and Technology.
- Human-Computer International (HCI). Sponsors: various. HCI International '97 was held jointly with the Symposium on Human Interface (Japan) in cooperation with the Chinese Academy of Sciences, EEC-European Strategic Programme for Research and Development in Information Technology, ESPRIT, the Human Factors and Ergonomics Society, IEEE Systems, Man and Cybernetics Society, the International Ergonomics Association, the Japan Ergonomics Research Society, the Japan Management Association, and the Software Psychology Society.
- Human Factors in Computer Systems (CHI). Sponsor: ACM SIGCHI.
- Hypertext 89. Sponsors: ACM SIGIR, SIGOIS, and SIGCHI.
- IEEE Professional Communications Conference. Sponsor: IEEE.
- INTERACT — Human-Computer Interaction Conference. Sponsor: IFIP. Held every three years. Hosted in 1996 by the British Computer Society and the BCS HCI Specialist Group.
- Interactive Multimedia. A conference and exhibit on training, education, and job performance improvement. Sponsored by the Society for Applied Learning Technology.
- Interactive '97 conference and exposition. Sponsored by Softbank Forums.
- International Conference on Research and Development in Information Retrieval. Sponsor: ACM SIGIR in cooperation with AICA-GLIR (Italy), BCS-IRSG (UK), GI (Germany), and INRIA (France).
- International Technical Communications Conference (ITCC). Sponsor: STC.
- National Federation of Abstracting and Indexing Conference.
- Seybold Expo: Seybold.
- SGML Conference. Sponsor: Graphics Communications Association (GCA).
- TechDoc. Sponsor: Graphics Communications Association (GCA).
- Conference on Computer-Supported Cooperative Work (CSCW). ACM sponsored.

Journals and Magazines

Apart from the ACM, IEEE, and ITCC proceedings, you won't find many journals that relate directly to the work you do. However there are a few, and I list them below. For addresses of STC, ACM, and IEEE, see the section on societies. If you are lucky enough to work in a company that maintains a good technical library, you may have ready access to these journals. If not, you may find them at a large public library near you.

- ACM *Asterisk (*), Journal of Computer Documentation.*
- *AI Expert,* Miller Freeman Publications, 500 Howard St., San Francisco, CA 94105.
- *Byte,* McGraw-Hill Information Services Co., Byte Publications, One Phoenix Hill Lane, Peterborough, NH 03458.
- *Cognitive Science,* Ablex Publishing Corp., 355 Chestnut Street, Norwood, NJ 07648
- *College English,* National Council of Teachers of English, 1111 Kenyon Rd., Urbana, IL 61801.
- *Electronic Publishing,* Dept AC, John Wiley & Sons, Inc., 605 Third Ave., New York, NY 10158.
- *HyperLink,* P.O. Box 7723, Eugene, OR 97401.
- *Hypermedia,* Taylor Graham, 12021 Wilshire Blvd., Suite 187, Los Angeles, CA 90025.
- IEEE journals, especially *IEEE Transactions on Professional Communication* — see the previous section on societies.
- *InfoWorld,* C.W. Communications, Inc. (Menlo Park), 1060 Marsh Rd., Ste. C-200, Menlo Park, CA 94025.
- *Journal of Business and Technical Communication,* Sage Publications, 2455 Teller Road, Thousand Oaks, CA 91320
- *Journal of Technical Writing and Communication,* Baywood Publishing Co., 26 Austin Ave., P.O. Box 337, Amityville, NY 11701.
- *Language,* published by the Linguistic Society of America, 1325 18th St., Suite 211, Washington D.C. 20036
- *MacUser,* Ziff-Davis Publishing Co., (Belmont), 11 Davis Drive, Belmont, CA 94002-3001.
- *MacWeek,* Ziff-Davis Publishing Co. Computer Publications Division, One Park Ave., New York, NY 10017.
- *Macworld,* Macworld Communications, Inc., 501 Second St., San Francisco, CA 94107.
- *PC Magazine,* One Park Avenue, New York, NY 10016.
- *PC World,* PC World Communications, Inc., 501 Second St., #600, San Francisco, CA 94107.
- *Personal Computing,* Business Publications, Inc., Ten Holland Dr., Hasbrouck Heights, NJ 07604.
- *Personal Publishing,* Hitchcock Publishing Co., 191 S. Gary Ave., Carol Stream, IL 60188.
- Seybold Reports (*Desktop Publishing, Office Systems, Publishing Systems*), Seybold Publications, P.O. Box 644, Media, PA 19063.
- *Technical Communication,* Journal of the STC — see the previous section on societies.

- *The Technical Writing Teacher,* c/o Dr. Carolyn D. Rude, Dept. of English, Box 4530, Texas Tech University, Lubbock, TX 79409.
- *Verbum,* VERBUM Subscriptions, P.O. Box 15439, San Diego, CA 92115. Covers design and PCs for personal computer enthusiasts.
- *Visible Language,* Sharon Poggenpohl, Rhode Island School of Design, 2 College Street, Providence, RI 02903
- *Written Communication,* Sage Publications, 2455 Teller Road, Thousand Oaks, CA 91320

Internet Resources

There are web sites and list servers (correspondence tools) you can use to contact and keep in touch with your colleagues in the technical communications field. A web site lets you read information and possibly send email to an individual or subscribe to a list server where you expect to find discussions of interest. A list server lets you exchange messages with others who subscribe to the list. Usually these services are free to the user. A good book to learn about doing research on the internet is the *Official Netscape Guide to Internet Research* (Calishain, 1997), and using any good internet search engine such as www.altavista.digital.com can bring much information directly to your online viewer.

Web Sites
- ACM SIGDOC web site: www.acm.org/sigdoc
- IEEE PCS web site: www.ieee.org/pcs
- Writing department at Oklahoma State University: http://bubba.ucc.okstate.edu/artsci/techwr
- Technical writing at Rennselaer Polytechnic Institute, with a list of list servers to which you can subscribe: www.rpi.edu/~perezc2

List Servers
- TECHWR-L: at Oklahoma State University, subscribe by sending email to list-serv@vm1.ucc.okstate.edu
- SHARP-L: at Indiana University, Bloomington, subscribe by sending email to LISTSERV@IUBVM.UCS.INDIANA.EDU, maintained by the History Department for the Society for the History of Authorship, Reading, and Publishing

Standards

The major standards groups in the United States are the American National Standards Institute (ANSI), the National Bureau of Standards (NBS), and the National Institute of Standards and Technology (NIST). The primary international standards associations are the International Organization for Standards (ISO) and the Comité Consultatif Internationale Télégraphique et Téléphonique (CCITT). (ISO is not an acronym, it stands for "iso" meaning equal or standard, as in isometric, or isobar.) These organizations work together to help ensure that standards are developed, adopted, and revised periodically.

You will find many of the standards relevant to the field of technical documentation listed in this appendix, organized by topic.

Visit www.iso.ch/VL/standards.html for the ISO catalog of all standards. For information on SGML, visit the SGMLOpen web site at www.sgmlopen.org/sgml/docs.

Standard Printer's Measures (U.S.)

- 6 picas equal 1 inch
- 12 points equal 1 pica
- 72 points equal approximately 1 inch
- 6 points equal 1 nonpareil (half pica)
- 1 point equals about 1/72 inch

Character Set Standards

- ISO 8859-1: 1987, Part 1: Latin Alphabet No. 1
- ISO 8859-2: 1987, Part 2: Latin Alphabet No. 2
- ISO 8859-3: 1988, Part 3: Latin Alphabet No. 3
- ISO 8859-4: 1988, Part 4: Latin Alphabet No. 4
- ISO 8859-5: 1988, Part 5: Latin/Cyrillic Alphabet
- ISO 8859-6: 1987, Part 6: Latin/Arabic Alphabet
- ISO 8859-7: 1987, Part 7: Latin/Greek Alphabet
- ISO 8859-8: 1988, Part 8: Latin/Hebrew Alphabet
- ISO 8859-9: 1989, Part 9: Latin Alphabet No. 5
- ISO 8859-10: 1992 Part 10: Latin Alphabet No. 6
- ISO 8859-13, Part 13: Latin Alphabet No. 7
- ISO/IEC 10586: Georgian Alphabet
- ISO/IEC 10646-1: 1993 Universal Multiple-Octet Character Set (UCS)
- Unicode Standard, Version 2.0, 1996

Romanization Standards
- System for the Romanization of Japanese: ISO 3602: 1989 (Kana script)
- System for the Romanization of Arabic: ISO 9036: 1987 (7-bit encoded)
- System for the Romanization of Slavic Cyrillic Characters: ANSI Z39.24-1976
- System for the Romanization of Hebrew: ISO 8957: 1996
- System for the Romanization of Lao, Khmer, and Pali: ANSI Z39.35-1979
- System for the Romanization of Armenian: ANSI Z39.37-1979
- System for the Romanization of African: ISO 6438: 1983

Color Standards
- Inter-Society Color Council and the National Bureau of Standards (ISCC-NBS) method of color definitions
- Munsell color notation (visual intervals on Color-Aid paper) defined by hue (spectral wavelength, based on composition), value (white, 9, to black, 1) and chroma (saturation) or purity of color from neutral to a maximum; based on five colors: red, yellow, green, blue, purple. Shown in a Munsell Globe or Munsell Tree.
- Pantone Matching System (PMS), a set of 500 to several thousand numbered and named colors. Useful because they are standardized, widely available, and extensively used by printers, designers, and computerized technology.
- Natural Color system, the Swedish standard color notation. Based on yellow, red, blue, green, white and black.
- CIE (Commission International de l'Eclairage) standard based on accurate measurement of light. Colors are defined on an x-y grid

Information Science Standards
- Basic Criteria for Indexes: ANSI Z39.4-1984
- Writing Abstracts: ANSI Z39.14-1979
- Title Leaves of a Book: ANSI Z39.15-1980
- Preparation of Scientific Papers for Written or Oral Presentation: ANSI Z39.16-1979
- Guidelines for Thesaurus Structure, Construction, and Use: ANSI Z39.19-1980
- Identification Code for the Book Industry: ANSI A39.43-1980
- International Standard Serial Numbering: ANSI A39.9-1979
- MIL-STD-490A: Military Specification Standard
- ISO 8879-86: Information Processing — Text and Office Systems — Standard Generalized Markup Language (SGML), Amendment A1: 1988
- DOD-STD-2167: Department of Defense standard including Data Item Description (DID) specification standards.

Paper Stock Standards
The metric A-series is based on a rectangular sheet of paper. The A0 size is one square meter in area; half this sheet is the A1 size, half the A1 is the A2, and so

on. All sheets are the same shape (the ratio of short side to long side is always the same). There is also a B-series, with sheet sizes intermediate between the A-series sizes. Standard paper sizes are shown in Tables B.1, B.2, and B.3.

Table B.1
U.S. Book Paper Standards

Sheet Size (inches)	Before Trimming Folds To	Trim Size
35 × 45	5 $^5/_8$ × 8 $^3/_4$	5 $^1/_2$ × 8 $^1/_2$
38 × 50	6 $^1/_4$ × 9 $^1/_2$	6 $^1/_8$ × 9 $^1/_4$
45 × 68	5 $^5/_8$ × 8 $^1/_2$	5 $^1/_2$ × 8 $^1/_4$

Table B.2
U.S. Bond Paper Standard

Size (inches)	Folded Size
17 × 22	8 $^1/_2$ × 11

Table B.3
A-Series (European) Paper Sizes

Name	Millimeters	Inches (approx.)
A0	841 × 1189	33 $^1/_8$ × 46 $^3/_4$
A4	210 × 297	8 $^1/_4$ × 11 $^3/_4$
A5	148 × 210	5 $^7/_8$ × 8 $^1/_4$

Phonetic Standards

- International Phonetic Alphabet (IPA). (See *Language,* 66, no. 3 (September 1990): 550–552.)

HyperText Markup Language (HTML)   C

The HyperText Markup Language (HTML) tags are what you use to tag text for displaying information on the internet. Tags continue to be added and modified, and some browsers won't display every tag. Most of the tags in this list work with both Netscape Navigator and Internet Explorer. For complete lists of information from these tables, documents to support them, and the latest information, see the web sites http://www.w3.org/pub/www/MarkUp/html-spec_toc.html, the web site of the World Wide Web Consortium which maintains the HTML definition, or http://www.tac.nyc.ny.us/manuals/html/html-spec_toc.html.

This appendix contains five tables; the first table groups commonly used tags by category or function, for example tags you use to specify the structural components of your document such as <HEAD> and <BODY>, tags you use to specify color of a document component such as TEXT=*color*, tags you use to format characters such as <B> and <I>, and so on. The second table lists valid hypertext references you can use to link to locations on the Internet. The third table lists tags in alphabetical order and provides syntax of each tag. Not all these tags work with all browsers. The fourth table lists selected colors you can use, with color names and their hexadecimal values. The fifth table provides codes for inserting special characters not present on many keyboards.

Table C.1
Tag Categories

Category	Tags and Attributes
Structural	<HTML>, <BODY>, <HEAD>, <H1>, <H2>, <H3>, <H4>, <H5>, <H6>, , <P>
Document Attributes	ALINK, BACKGROUND, BGCOLOR, BGPROPERTIES, LEFTMARGIN, LINK, TEXT, TOPMARGIN, VLINK
Text Formatting	<B>, <EM>, <FONT>, <I>, <CODE> <DFN>, <KBD>, <STRONG>, <TITLE>
Lists	<LI>, <DL> (<DT>, <DD>), <DIR>, <MENU>, <OL>, <UL>, VALUE
Tables	<CAPTION>, <TABLE>, <TH>, <TD>, <TR>, CELLPADDING, CELLSPACING, NOWRAP
Forms	<FORM>, <SELECT>, INPUT, METHOD
Frames	<FRAME>, <FRAMESET>, <FRAMESET ROWS>, NAME, SRC
Links	<A>, HREF, <IMG>, ALIGN, ISMAP, MAP, NAME, SRC, USEMAP

The HREF or hypertext reference can be to a URL on the world wide web, or to other possible sources, as listed in Table C.2, Hypertext Links. You use a URL (Universal Resource Locator) to reference or link to files on the Internet. A URL is typically in the form http://www.location.htm. For example, http://www.digital.com or http://www.sgmlopen.org.

Table C.2
Hypertext Links

Reference...	Links to this Location...
HREF="HTTP://...*htm*"	To a specific URL.
HREF=NEWS:NEWSGROUP	To a news group.
HREF="GOPHER://..."	To a Gopher server.
HREF="FTP://..."	To an FTP (File Transfer Protocol) site.
HREF="MAILTO:*mail_address*//..." " TITLE="subject"	To a mail program.
HREF="NEWSRC://..."	To a news source.
HREF="NNTP://..."	To a non-default news server.
HREF="TELNET://..."	To a TELNET site.
HREF="WAIS://..."	To a WAIS index server.

In Table C.3, syntax is as follows:

- vertical lines (|)indicate that you choose from the list of entries
- *color* = a name or hexadecimal number used to specify a color
- [...] indicates optional entries, entries you can omit
- an entry in italics indicates that you supply the specific item such as a name or a URL
- ... between tags indicates where to place text.

Table C.3
HTML Tags

Tag or Element	Attribute	Use
<! *Comment*>		Adds a comment to your file. Can contain the word DOCTYPE.
<A *attribute*>...</A>		Specifies an anchor to a hypertext link.
	BORDER=*n*	Draws a border n pixels wide around the image.
	HREF=" ... "	Gives a specific link location.
	NAME=*name*	Names the anchor for a hypertext link.
	TITLE=*title*	Specifies a title for your link.
	URL=" *url*"	Specifies URL.
<ADDRESS> ... </ADDRESS>		Specifies author addresses. Use with tags to format address.
<APPLET *attribute* >...</APPLET>		Introduces a Java applet, a mini-application.
	ALIGN=left|right|center|top|bottom|middle|texttop|justify	Aligns text.
	ALT=" *filename*"	Specifies alternate file to display, if browser cannot display applet.
	CODEBASE	Specifies a compiled Java file.
	CODE=" *filename*.class"	Specifies height of display area for applet.
	HEIGHT=*n*	Specifies horizontal space around applet.
	HSPACE=*n*	Labels applet for reference.
	NAME=*name*	Specifies labeled file name.
	PARAM NAME=" *name*"	Specifies URL.
	VALUE=" *url*"	Specifies vertical space around applet.
	VSPACE=*n*	Specifies width of display area for applet.
	WIDTH=*n*	Specifies shape of client-side hotspot. See <MAP>
<AREA SHAPE=*shape*>		Adds author names.
<AU> ... </AU>		Bolds text.
<B> ... </B>		
<BASE *attribute*>		Specifies basis for data, typically the base URL.
	HREF=" *url*"	References a file or link to document home page.
	TARGET=" ... "	References a named window.
<BASEFONT *attribute*>		Sets font for all text that follows.
	SIZE=*n*	Changes size on a scale from 1 to 7, or -2 to +4. Default is 3.
	FACE	Changes type face.
<BDO> ... </BDO>		Specifies bi-directional override.
<BGSOUND SRC=*"file"* *attribute*>		Plays a sound file (WAV, AU, MID).
	LOOP=*n*|INFINITE	Plays sound *n* times, or repeatedly.
	DELAY=*n*	Plays sound after n second delay.
<BIG>...</BIG>		Makes enclosed text 1 font size bigger.

Table C.3
HTML Tags (continued)

Tag or Element	Attribute	Use
<BLINK>...</BLINK>		Flashes enclosed text.
<BLOCKQUOTE>...		Displays text as a block, enclosed in quotation marks.
</BLOCKQUOTE>		Encloses your document.
<BODY attribute>...</BODY>		Provides a link with color.
	ALINK=color	
	BACKGROUND="filename.jpg"	Sets the displayed background of your document.
	BGCOLOR=color	Sets background color.
	BGPROPERTIES="file"	Sets a watermark-like background with the supplied image.
	LEFTMARGIN=n	Sets left margin, in pixels.
	LINK="file"	Provides a link.
	TEXT="file"	Inserts text from file.
	TOPMARGIN=n	Sets top margin, in pixels.
	VLINK=color	Sets color for visited link.
<BR [attribute CLEAR[=ALL]]>		Inserts line break. Can center text below image with CLEAR.
<BQ>...</BQ>		Same as <BLOCKQUOTE>.
<CAPTION attribute> ...</CAPTION>		Inserts a caption.
	ALIGN=top|bottom	Aligns caption.
	VALIGN=top|middle|bottom	Displays caption at specified location in table.
<CENTER>...</CENTER>		Centers enclosed text.
<CITE>...</CITE>		Marks text as a citation in italics.
<CODE>...</CODE>		Marks text as code in monospaced type.
<COL attribute>		Specifies columns in table.
	SPAN=n	Spans n columns.
	ALIGN (see <APPLET>)	
<COLGROUP>... </COLGROUP>		Specifies a group of columns.
	SPAN=n	Spans n columns.
	ALIGN (see <APPLET>)	
	VALIGN	Aligns vertically.
<COMMENT>...</COMMENT>		Adds a comment to your file.
<CREDIT>...</CREDIT>		Used to give credit to sources.
<DD>		See <DL>.
<DEL>...</DEL>		Omits specified text from display.
<DFN>...</DFN>		Inserts a definition in dictionary-like format.
<DIR>...</DIR>		Provides a compact directory list, each item up to 20 characters long.

Table C.3
HTML Tags (continued)

Tag or Element	Attribute	Use
<DIV attribute>…</DIV>	ALIGN=left|right|center	Provides a division of the document. Aligns document division.
<DL> <DT>term [</DT>]<DD definition attribute> [</DD>]</DL>		Defines terms, as in a glossary.
<EM>…</EM>	COMPACT	Takes minimum space. Emphasizes text.
<EMBED SRC= "file.gif" WIDTH=n HEIGHT=m		Enables user to edit copy of source file locally. WIDTH, HEIGHT given in pixels.
<FIGURE>…</FIGURE>		Displays image specified.
<FONT attribute>…</FONT>		Changes font.
	COLOR=color	Changes color of font.
	FACE= "face[,face]"	Changes face of font; can give up to three fonts.
	SIZE=n	Changes relative font size, on a scale from 1 to 7, or -2 to +4.
<FORM attribute>…</FORM>		Specifies a form for accepting user input. Uses most formatting and structural tags.
	ACTION= "file.btm"	Specifies file.
	ENCTYPE	Uploads a file to server based on user input.
	<INPUT>	See <INPUT>.
	METHOD= "file.btm"	Specifies method to carry out when user clicks SUBMIT button.
	SRC= "url"	Specifies content of frame.
	CELLPADDING=n	See <TABLE>.
	CELLSPACING=n	See <TABLE>.
<FRAME attribute>	FRAMEBORDER	
	FRAMESPACING	
	MARGINHEIGHT=n	Specifies vertical space between image and frame.
	MARGINWIDTH=n	Specifies horizontal space between image and frame.
	NAME= "name"	Names frame window for reference.
	NORESIZE	Specifies that user cannot resize window.
	SCROLLING=yes|no|auto	Specifies that the user can scroll or not scroll. AUTO is the default.
<FRAMESET attribute>… </FRAMESET>		Defines screen region where browser constructs a frame.
	COLS=n" n%" " *"	Defines height of each frame in pixels, as a percent of available space, or (*) lets the browser determine height.
	ROWS=n" n%" " *"	Defines width of each frame in pixels, as a percent of available space, or (*) lets the browser determine width.

Table C.3
HTML Tags *(continued)*

Tag or Element	Attribute	Use
<H ALIGN= *attribute*>	centerlrightlleftl	
<H1>...</H1>		Specifies heading level 1 (largest).
<H2>...</H2>		Specifies heading level 2.
<H3>...</H3>		Specifies heading level 3.
<H4>...</H4>		Specifies heading level 4.
<H5>...</H5>		Specifies heading level 5.
<H6>...</H6>		Specifies heading level 6 (smallest).
<HEAD>...</HEAD>		Specifies top level head.
<HR *attribute*>		Draws a horizontal rule.
	ALIGN=leftlrightlcenter	Aligns rule on page.
	COLOR=*color*	Specifies rule color.
	NOSHADE	Omits shadow on rule.
	SIZE=*n*	Specifies rule width in pixels.
	WIDTH=*n*	Specifies exact width in pixels or percent of document width.
<HTML> ... </HTML>		Specifies a document encoded with HTML tags.
<I>...</I>		Italicizes text.
<IFRAME>		Specifies floating frame.
<IMG *attribute*>		Inserts an image file.
	ALIGN=absbottomlbottoml leftlmiddlelrightltop	Aligns images.
	ALT=" ... "	Specifies text to show if image cannot be shown.
	BORDER=*n*	Draws a border n pixels wide.
	CONTROLS	Displays panel of buttons below AVI or video clip display for user control.
	DYNSRC="file.src"	Specifies video, AVI clip, or VRML world to run in window.
	HEIGHT=*n*	Specifies image height in pixels.
	HSPACE=*n*	Adds horizontal space.
	ISMAP	Specifies a clickable map.
	LOOP=*n*lINFINITE	
	LOWSRC=" ... "	Specifies a low resolution image to load first, replaced by SRC image.
	SRC="*file or URL*"	Inserts an image from the named file.
	USEMAP="NAME"	
	VRML	
	VSPACE=*n*	Adds vertical space.
	WIDTH=*n*	Specifies image width in pixels.

Table C.3
HTML Tags (continued)

Tag or Element	Attribute	Use
<INPUT attribute>		Accepts user input.
	ALIGN (see <APPLET>)	
	CHECKED	Sets default for check box or radio button as on or checked.
	MAXLENGTH	
	NAME	
	SIZE	
	SRC	
	TYPE	
	VALUE	
<ISINDEX attribute>		Displays default search index text and text box only. A small form.
	ACTION="program name"	Sends user-entered text to specific program.
	PROMPT="text"	Displays customized text with text box.
<ISMAP>		
<KBD>...</KBD>		Displays text as keyboard input.
<KEYGEN>		Generate encrypted key.
<LI>...[</LI>]		Inserts a list element, one entry in a list.
	TYPE=DISC|CIRCLE| SQUARE	Specifies form of list bullet.
<LINK attribute>		Inserts a link to a file, local or external. Can be used with <HEAD>, HREF, METHOD, <TITLE>.
<LISTING>...</LISTING>		Shows text as computer listing, in monospaced font.
<MAP attribute>...</MAP>		Specifies an image map containing user clickable hot spots.
	AREA	Use with SHAPE and COORDS to specify area of hotspot.
	COORDS="x1,y1,x2,y2..."	Specifies coordinates in pixels defining shape of hot spot.
	left|top|right|bottom	
	HREF="URL"	
	NAME="name"	Labels map for later reference.
	SHAPE=RECT(angle)|	Specifies shape of hotspot.
CIRCLE|POLYGON		
<MARQUEE attribute>... </MARQUEE>		Inserts active marquee text.
	ALIGN=top|middle|bottom	Specifies how text is aligned to marquee.
	BEHAVIOR=slide|alternate|scroll	Specifies behavior of text in marquee.
	BGCOLOR=color	Specifies background color.
	DIRECTION=left|right	Specifies direction of scrolling action.

Table C.3
HTML Tags (continued)

Tag or Element	Attribute	Use
	HEIGHT=n	Specifies height of marquee in pixels.
	HSPACE=n	Specifies clear space adjoining marquee in pixels.
	LOOP=n|INFINITE	Specifies how many times to replay a video clip.
	SCROLLAMOUNT=n	Specifies space between scrolled text in pixels.
	SCROLLDELAY=n	Specifies time between scrolls in milliseconds.
	VSPACE=n	Specifies clear space around marquee in pixels.
	WIDTH=n	Specifies width of marquee in pixels or percent of page.
<MENU>...</MENU>		Lists a menu.
	COMPACT	Minimizes space in list.
<META attribute>		Specifies meta-data for document.
	CONTENT=n	Specifies number of seconds between refreshing of URL content. Used with HTTP-EQUIV tag.
	HTTP-EQUIV= "REFRESH"	Used with CONTENT attribute.
	NAME="name"	Labels text for later release.
<NEXTID N= name>		Label added for reference by some HTML editors.
<NOBR>...</NOBR>		Prevents line breaks.
<NOEMBED>...</NOEMBED>		Specifies alternative to <EMBED> text.
<NOFRAMES>... </NOFRAMES>		Provides text to use when browser cannot display specified frame.
<NOSCRIPT>...</NOSCRIPT>		Specifies alternative to <SCRIPT> text.
<NOTE CLASS=NOTE| CAUTION|WARNING>... </NOTE>		Displays text as note, caution, or warning.
<OBJECT>...</OBJECT>		Includes data or applet.
	<PARAM>	Parameter for object.
<OL attribute>...</OL>		Starts an ordered or numbered list.
	START=n	Specifies starting number for list.
	TYPE=A|a|I|i|1	Specifies list style: A = capitals, a = lowercase, I = uppercase Roman numerals, i = lowercase Roman numerals, 1 = numbers.
	VALUE=n	Changes count of lists in a sequence.
<OPTION VALUE="n" >text [</OPTION>]		Specifies text to display nth in a list box. Use with <SELECT> tag.

Table C.3
HTML Tags *(continued)*

Tag or Element	Attribute	Use
<P [*attribute*]>[</P>]	ALIGN=left|right|center	Starts a paragraph. Aligns text in paragraph. Can also use other formatting attributes such as <EM>, <B>, and so on.
<PARAM>		Specifies applet parameter.
<PLAINTEXT>...		Displays text in monospaced type.
</PLAINTEXT>		
<PRE>...</PRE>		Displays pre-formatted text as entered, including line breaks.
<Q>...</Q>		Encloses text in quotation marks.
<S>...</S>		Strikes through text.
<SAMP>...</SAMP>		Shows text as literals or sample, in smaller font.
<SCRIPT *attribute*>...</SCRIPT>	LANGUAGE SRC	Includes a script program. Specifies language. Specifies source file.
<SELECT NAME="*name*" *attribute*>...</SELECT>		Displays drop-down list box. Use with <OPTION VALUE> tag.
<SERVER>...</SERVER>		Specifies program to execute on server.
<SMALL>...</SMALL>		Makes text smaller by one unit.
<SOUND *attribute*>	DELAY SRC	Plays sound.
<SPACER>		Inserts horizontal or vertical space.
<SPAN>...</SPAN>		Spans columns.
<STRIKE>...</STRIKE>		Strikes through text.
<STRONG>...</STRONG>		Shows text with strong or bold emphasis.
<STYLE>...</STYLE>		Provides stylesheet specifications.
_{...}		Shows text as subscript.
^{...}		Shows text as superscript.
<TABLE *attribute*>...</TABLE>	ALIGN=above|below BACKGROUND (see <BODY>) BGCOLOR="*color*" BORDER=*n* BORDERCOLOR="*color*"	Inserts a table. Aligns table. Sets watermark in background. Sets background color. Draws cell borders *n* pixels thick. Used with BORDER attribute, specifies border color.

Table C.3
HTML Tags *(continued)*

Tag or Element	Attribute	Use
	BORDERCOLORLIGHT= "color"	Use with BORDER attribute; sets one of 3D colors.
	BORDERCOLORDARK="color"	Use with BORDER attribute; sets one of 3D colors.
	CELLPADDING=n	Draws white space between cell border and cell contents, n pixels thick.
	CELLSPACING=n	Draws white space between cells, n pixels thick.
	FRAME	
	HEIGHT=n	
	RULES	
	VALIGN	
	WIDTH=n	Specifies table width in pixels or percent of document width.
<TBODY>...[</TBODY>]		Specifies group table body.
<TD attribute>...[</TD>]		Specifies table data.
	ROWSPAN	
	ALIGN=left|right|center	Aligns data in display area.
	BACKGROUND (see <BODY>)	
	BGCOLOR="color"	Specifies background color.
	BORDERCOLOR="color"	Specifies border color.
	BORDERCOLORLIGHT	Use with BORDER attribute; sets one of 3D colors.
	BORDERCOLORDARK	Use with BORDER attribute; sets one of 3D colors.
	COLSPAN=n	Specifies number of columns to span.
	HEIGHT=n	Specifies height of table row in pixels or percent of table (%).
	NOWRAP	Prevents wrapping of text in a cell.
	ROWSPAN=n	Specifies number of rows to span.
	VALIGN=top|middle|bottom	Aligns table vertically.
	WIDTH=n	Specifies width of table cell in pixels or percent of table (%).
<TEXTAREA attribute>... </TEXTAREA>	NAME="areaname"	Specifies text area.
	ROWS=rows	
	COLS=cols	
	WRAP="OFF|VIRTUAL| PHYSICAL"	
<TFOOT>...[</TFOOT>]		Specifies group table footer.
<TH attribute>...[</TH>]		Specifies table heading.
	ALIGN=left|right|center	Aligns heading in cell.

Table C.3
HTML Tags *(continued)*

Tag or Element	Attribute	Use
	BACKGROUND (see <BODY>)	
	BGCOLOR="*color*"	Specifies background color.
	BORDERCOLOR="*color*"	Specifies border color.
	BORDERCOLORLIGHT	Use with BORDER attribute; sets one of 3D colors.
	BORDERCOLORDARK	Use with BORDER attribute; sets one of 3D colors.
	COLSPAN=*n*	
	HEIGHT=*n*	Specifies height of table row in pixels or percent of table (%).
	NOWRAP	Prevents wrapping of text in a cell.
	ROWSPAN=*n*	Specifies number of rows to span.
	WIDTH=*n*	Specifies width of table cell in pixels or percent of table (%).
<THEAD>...[</THEAD>]		Specifies group table head.
<TITLE>...</TITLE>		Specifies a title for your document. Displays title on browser title bar.
<TR *attribute*>...[</TR>]		Specifies data in a single table row.
	ALIGN=left|right|center	Aligns text in cell.
	VALIGN=top|middle|bottom	Aligns text in cell.
	BGCOLOR="*color*"	Specifies background color.
	BORDERCOLOR="*color*"	Specifies border color.
	BORDERCOLORLIGHT	Use with BORDER attribute; sets one of 3D colors.
	BORDERCOLORDARK	Use with BORDER attribute; sets one of 3D colors.
<TT>...</TT>		Shows text in monospaced font.
<U>...</U>		Underlines text.
<UL>...</UL>		Starts a bulleted or unnumbered list.
<VAR>...</VAR>		Shows a variable name, perhaps in italics or monospaced.
<WBR>...</WBR>		Inserts manual line break if needed.
<XMP>		

Table C.4
Colors You can Specify

Color Name	Hexadecimal Value
red	#FF0000
orange	#FF7F00
yellow	#FFFF00
green	#00FF00
blue	#0000FF
violet	#4F2F4F
navy blue	#23238E
white	#FFFFFF
black	#000000
gray	#C0C0C0
light gray	#A8A8A8
dim gray	#545454
very light gray	#CDCDCD
brown	#A62A2A
dark brown	#5C4033
corn flower blue	#42426F
sky blue	#3299CC
summer sky	#38B0DE
slate blue	#007FFF

Table C.4 provides some colors you can use with HTML. You can give the name of a color, or specify it as a hexadecimal value. To specify a color as a hexadecimal value, precede the value with #, for example #FFFFFF is white and

Table C.5
Special Characters

Character	Value	Description	Character	Value	Description
	&#32	space	>>	&#187	Right angle quote
"	&#34	quotation mark, &quot	<<	&#171	Left angle quote
&	&#38	ampersand, &amp	¶	&#182	paragraph sign
<	&#60	less than, &lt	¥	&#165	Yen sign
>	&#62	greater than, &gt	§	&#167	section sign
i	&#161	inverted exclamation	¨	&#168	umlaut, dieresis
¢	&#162	cent sign	©	&#169	copyright
£	&#163	pound sterling	°	&#176	degree sign
¤	&#164	general currency sign	®	&#174	Registered trademark

#000000 is black. The hexadecimal value provides a way to change the color by the addition of more red, green or blue, in the order *rrggbb*. Actual values of these colors are not yet final, so this is a representative sample. Some browsers and screens may not display all colors you can specify.

You can insert special characters (see Table C.5) using the syntax &*value*, where value is a hexadecimal number, for example, &#34 is the same as &quot and produces a double quotation mark ("). Use the hexadecimal value for the double quotation mark inside an attribute.

Standard Generalized Markup Language (SGML) D

The Standard Generalized Markup Language (SGML), adopted as standard ISO 8879 of the International Organization for Standardization in 1986, was originally developed to assist the standardization of publications, their preparation and production. The basic premise of the standard was to separate format and content; format is applied based on output context. SGML, as its name implies, is a markup language that contains tags you add to a text file to identify its structural elements. The convention adopted is to enclose tags in angle brackets (<>) and, with a few exceptions, to enclose text relating to a tag between an opening tag (<*tag*>) and a closing tag (</*tag*>). If you have coded anything in HTML, you are already familiar with this kind of markup.

Initially SGML was designed for the publication of books; it has evolved to support the publication of technical documents and today is used in many industries: financial, defense, automotive, commercial aerospace, pharmaceutical, electronics, telecommunications, transportation, news services, and by the government.

In practice, you use SGML with an overall document management system, illustrated in Figure D.1, An SGML Publishing System. You use the SGML tags in some form with the authoring tool; that tool or another does page composition and prepares the document for delivery. A component management system keeps track of document modules.

The SGML definition is like a large dictionary: it defines the terms but does not tell you how to use them. When an organization decides to use SGML to establish standards or exchange information, it adopts a Document Type Definition (DTD)

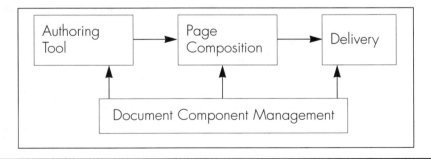

Figure D.1
An SGML Publishing System

based on an analysis of documents that the organization prepares. A DTD is similar to a template used in a text processing system but is more detailed and contains more specific structural elements than the typical template. When establishing a DTD, for example, the DTD definition will probably include tags such as <Chapter> and <Title>. Elements valid for use in chapters will include paragraphs <para>, lists, procedures, tables, and so on. These are called block-oriented elements. In-line elements include subscripts, superscripts, emphasis (italics, bold), and so on.

A Format Output Specification Instance (FOSI) defines the layout and presentation of material. The Document Style Semantics and Specification Language (DSSSL — rhymes with whistle) is a generic language for writing style sheets and formatting instructions. DSSSL, defined in ISO/IEC standard 10179, is a possible extension to SGML. DSSSL's query language has been adopted by HyTime, which applies SGML to hypertext and multimedia. A current effort is to specify XML, which would be a simplified version of SGML intended to be useful to people wanting to prepare material for web browsing.

When an organization develops its own DTD, it selects those terms from the SGML standard that it expects to use and encodes them in its own DTD. The DTD is used with an authoring tool that the organization selects. Authoring tools include ArborText ADEPT Series Publisher, Frame + SGML, WordPerfect SGML, and SGML Tag Wizard (Nice Technologies), an SGML authoring tool for use with Word for Windows. These tools are WYSIWYG systems that do not require the author to explicitly enter tags, but provide menu picks for tag-connected styles, and include page layout software.

Other authoring tools do not include full publishing capabilities; they must be tied into a publishing engine to produce printed or online output suitable for the reader. Publishing engines can be connected to a document or database management system that deals with document components and manipulates those components. One such document management system that has been successful in the pharmaceuticals industry is Documentum's Enterprise; another used in commercial and corporate publishing is Xyvision's Parlance.

A document and its DTD are inseparable. When moving a document from one organization to another, one company to another, or one tool to another, you must always include the DTD to be able to use, publish, convert, or edit the document.

Some vertical industries have adopted industry-specific DTDs. For example, in the defense industry, a military DTD was developed as part of the Computer-aided Acquisition and Logistic Support (CALS) initiative. CALS tables are often used in DTDs for other industries. A DTD used in the software publications industry is the DocBook DTD, developed by the Davenport Group, a group of corporations that produce software documentation.

For more detailed information on the DocBook DTD and other SGML topics, look at the SGMLOpen web site www.sgmlopen.org or www.sil.org/sgml/sgml.html. You can also find information about SGML on the Exoterica and ArborText web sites, www.exoterica.com and www.arbortext.com. A tool summary is available on www.falch.no/~pepper/sgmltool.

Structure of the DocBook DTD

The DocBook DTD contains several structural elements:

- document set
- book
- book elements

A document set is a collection of related documents or books; information for a document set is called metainformation in the DTD. A book contains components. These are shown in the following hierarchy.

```
Set
    set metainformation
    Book
    Book
      .
      .
      .


Book
        Front Matter
    Part
    Part
      .
      .
      .
    Back Matter
Book
        Table of Contents
    List of Tables
    Preface
    [Part]
    Chapter
        Title, Title Abbreviation
        Section
            Para(graph)
            Para(graph)
                Block Element
                    List
                    Cross References
                    Index Terms
                    Links
        Chapter
```

```
            .
            .
            .
      Reference
      Reference
            .
            .
            .
      Appendix
            .
            .
      Glossary
      Bibliography
      Index
```

The full DTD contains all the elements for the complete structure, perhaps several hundred elements.

The greatest difficulty with SGML has been lack of robust and full function tools for authors and publishers. The advantage of using a DTD that guides the author and enables reuse of some material is that a publisher can more quickly and with greater consistency produce reference documents on which every page contains the same structural information, for example, catalogs of drug information from a pharmaceutical company, or data from a mutual fund company on all its basic portfolios. For these uses, a DTD designed specifically with the end object in mind, and an authoring tool that lets data be entered in a standard order without regard to format is a great time saver. Once the data has been entered, then another tool prepares pages for printing or online viewing. The separation of these tasks is possible because of the standard content of the information, and the well defined output formats.

For some other materials, where authors need greater flexibility of structure, and need to rework material significantly, tools that do not require SGML are easier to use. A DTD with several hundred elements to remember and use is harder for the author to manage than a template in a text processing system with a couple of dozen basic styles (the equivalent of SGML tags). Thus SGML has great value in some parts of the publishing industry, but won't be adopted in others quickly.

There is a growing body of literature about SGML, including *Practical SGML* (van Herwijnen, 1996), with a programming focus, extensively reviewed in the *Journal of Computer Documentation,* May 1996, pp. 30-43, *Developing SGML DTDs: From Text to Markup* (Maler, Andaloussi, 1996), probably the best text to use to understand DTD development, and *ABCD...SGML: A User's Guide to Structured Information* (Alschuler, 1995), an excellent guide that clearly explains how SGML relates to and can be used to solve everyday publishing problems. Others less useful for the practitioner are *The SGML Handbook* (Goldfarb, 1990) and *README.1st: A Writer's Guide to SGML* (Turner and others, 1996).

Glossary

This glossary contains terms used in the text. For additional book construction and publishing terms, see *The Chicago Manual of Style* and *Words into Type*.

acronym
A word formed from selected letters of a title or name. For example, the acronym for Beginner's All-Purpose Symbolic Instruction Code, a programming language for beginners, is BASIC.

address
The identification of a location in computer memory. Locations hold the bits and bytes of programs and data.

algorithm
A sequence of instructions that solve a specific problem.

alphabet
The letters of a given language, in an order established by custom. Modern alphabets include Roman (Latin), Greek, Russian, Hebrew, Arabic, and Korean. English, like most European languages, is written in the Roman alphabet. Devanagari, though sometimes called an alphabet, is more correctly a *script* used for writing the Hindi syllabary. Languages not normally written with an alphabet, such as Japanese and Chinese, are sometimes "Romanized" (transliterated in Roman characters) for use with Western printing techniques. Linguists define an alphabet as writing in which a sign normally stands for one or more phonemes of the language. For example, in English the letter *b* stands for the phoneme *b*, but the letter *a* can stand for one of several phonemes, as used in the words "say," "Sam," or "saw."

alphanumeric characters
The characters available on your keyboard, display, or printer. The *alphabetic* characters, in English, are the uppercase and lowercase letters *A* to *Z* and *a* to *z*. The *numeric* characters are the digits 0 to 9. Punctuation marks and other nonalphabetic, nonnumeric characters are called *special*. These include the *national* symbols, such as $, #, @, which may differ in different countries. For example, $ is the United States' symbol of its basic monetary unit, but £ is the United Kingdom's.

ANSI
American National Standards Institute.

antialiasing
A method for removing the "jaggies" from characters represented in bit-mapped forms. The technique adds gray pixels to the edges of each letter to smooth its contours.

application
A software system dedicated to a specific purpose, for example, page layout or database management.

ascender
The part of the lowercase letters *b, d, h, k, l, t* that extends above the top, or x-height, of lowercase letters without ascenders. See **descender** for the diagram illustrating an ascender.

ASCII
American Standard Code for Information Interchange, a standard extensively used in the United States for representing characters in 8-bit bytes. For example, uppercase *A* is ASCII 65 (decimal), while lowercase *a* is ASCII 97.

Backus-Naur form
A notation used to describe computer language syntax. The notation was devised by J. Backus and Peter Naur for Algol 60. Sometimes called *Backus normal form*.

batch processing
Processing on a computer that is not interactive but under the system's control. In batch processing, you give a command to have a job executed, and the system controls all subsequent actions.

baud rate
Commonly used to mean bit rate, or number of bits transmitted per second (bps). Kbps = kilobits per second.

beta test
The second stage of product testing.

bi-directional printer
A printer that prints both forward and backward, eliminating the return of the print head to the left margin at the start of each line. Usually a dot-matrix printer.

bit
A binary digit, either 0 or 1.

bit-mapping
A way to store and display pictures on a computer. A picture or letter is treated as an array of picture elements, or *pixels;* each pixel is stored and displayed separately and can be independently manipulated.

bleed
Print that extends outside the image area of your page, to the edge of the paper.

brightness
The luminous aspect of a color (as distinct from its hue) by which it approaches maximum luminosity of white or the complete lack of luminosity of pure black.

buffer
An area in computer memory where you store data temporarily. Every computer has several buffers. For example, a terminal may have one buffer to communicate with the host computer or processor, one to hold the characters displayed on the screen, and one to hold characters you type on your keyboard. A printer also has buffers it uses to handle the data sent to it for printing.

button
In a windowing system, the small circle within a window that represents a choice. You make a choice by moving your mouse pointer to the particular button and clicking on it.

byte
The amount of space in memory or on disk occupied by a single character. Depending on the convention used on, and the architecture of your computer, a byte can be 6, 8, or 9 bits. The ASCII code uses 8 bits for each character.

CAD
The acronym for Computer-Aided Design, a set of software tools that you can use to prepare engineering designs or drawings.

camera-ready copy
Pages or artwork ready to be photographed and printed in quantity. Camera-ready copy must be totally free of smudges, dust, and stray marks. The camera sees only black and white; light blue pencil marks, for example, are invisible to it.

CD-ROM
Compact-disk read-only memory. A user cannot write on a CD-ROM but only read what is placed there by the manufacturer.

chunking
Presenting material in small, short segments.

clip art
Preprepared libraries of artwork available on some systems.

Clipboard
In Microsoft Windows on the Apple Macintosh, an area where you place text or graphics for transfer between applications. For example, you use the Clipboard to transfer a drawing to a word processing application.

collating sequence
The order of characters recognized by a given computer system, used in sorting with that system. For example, the ASCII standard defines the collating sequence for systems that use that standard.

colophon
Most commonly, the device placed on the spine or title page of a book, or on both, identifying the publisher. A graphic is sometimes used as a colophon, such as Penguin Books' penguin, Houghton Mifflin's dolphin, or Alfred A. Knopf's borzoi dog. The term also refers to information about the printing of a book placed on the last page. The graphic is sometimes called a logo.

color
The sensation caused by stimulation of the retina of the eye by light waves of a particular wave length, or the property of reflecting light waves of a particular wave length. Color is what we perceive. The primary colors are red, yellow, and blue; their combination produces other colors such as orange, green, and violet. Reds are often called warm, and blues cool.

color palette
The range of colors available on a graphics display system.

concordance
An alphabetical list of words in a text or corpus of texts showing every occurrence of a word. The list can contain all the words or only the principal words.

context-sensitive system

A software system that responds to user inquiry or command differently, depending on the context — that is, where the user is in the application.

control character

A character generally invisible to the user that has an effect on how text is processed. For example, the form-feed character in a body of text forces a page-eject at the right moment during printing. Most software inserts control characters where needed, but some allow the user to do so. Some video terminals can display control characters on demand.

dash

See **en dash, em dash.**

data compression

A technique for recording large amounts of data in a small space, typically by replacing long strings of the same character or word with a code that states how many times the character or word is repeated. The many spaces at the end of lines of text are good candidates for such coding. Text files can often be compressed to half their original size, and digitized image files to about one-tenth their size.

default

What the software gives you (for a parameter, setting, file extension) if you don't choose otherwise. For example, a word processing program may give you defaults for page length and line length. You can change these, but if you do nothing, the default is what you get.

degauss

To remove magnetic properties; to demagnetize.

descender

The part of the lowercase letters *g, j, p, q, y,* and, in some typefaces, *f,* that extends below the baseline, that is, the bottom of lowercase letters with no descenders.

desktop publishing

The use of computers to design and prepare camera-ready, professional-quality typeset documents. Desktop publishing is more involved than word processing, as you need to understand typography, graphic design, and page layout to develop publishable material.

discrimination

The ability of the human eye to distinguish between different colors. Studies show that humans can discriminate between several thousand colors.

disk

A device used to store your text and graphics files. Can be magnetic or optical.

display face, display type

Large-size type used, for example, in chapter titles and headings. Sometimes display type is of a design not normally used for regular text.

doctype

A definition of the form a document will take. Specifies format and page size in DEC document.

dot-matrix printer

A printer that forms characters as patterns of dots. Speedy and less expensive than some other printers, but does not produce the highest quality. Used for draft-quality printing.

dots per inch

See **resolution.**

download

Or *downline load.* To transmit a file or data from a main computer system to a smaller system connected by direct wiring or a network.

drop-down menu

A menu display when you click your mouse cursor on a menu bar name or symbol.

editor

Computer software enabling the user to create and edit text in an electronic medium.

electronic mail
Mail exchanged between computers and users over a network, not as paper.

elite
The size of type used in an elite typewriter — 12 characters per inch.

ellipsis
Horizontal or vertical dots that show where words or lines have been omitted.

em
A typesetting measurement equivalent in width to the point size of the type being used. Thus a 1-em space in 10-point type is 10 points wide.

em dash
A dash the width of an em, which is approximately the width of the uppercase *M* in the typeface being used.

en
Half an em.

en dash
A dash the width of an en, or approximately the width of the uppercase *N* in the typeface being used.

EPS
Encapsulated PostScript, a file format used to exchange graphics files between, for example, Aldus and Adobe applications.

escape sequence
A set of codes that control what is displayed on a video screen. The U.S. standard that defines this sequence is the ANSI Screen Control Sequence. All character strings in this standard begin with the Escape character ASCII 27.

floating illustration
An illustration that page layout software can place anywhere on a page.

flush left
Text with an even left margin.

flush right
Text with an even right margin.

foldout

A page so large you must fold it to fit within your book.

font

A complete set of typeforms of one size, style, and face — for example, the 10-point Times Roman italic font. A complete font consists of ABCDE-FGHIJKLMNOPQRSTUVWXYZ abcdefghijklmnopqrstuvwxyz 0123456789 .,;:"'!() [] {}! @ # $ % ^ & * _ – + = | \ /? plus superscripts and subscripts.

footer

In desktop publishing, a line of text running at the foot of a page. Like a running foot in traditional typesetting.

G

Giga, or 1 billion (10^9). One gigabyte of disk storage can hold one billion characters.

graphics terminal

A high-resolution video display capable of reproducing the fine detail of graphics created with specialized graphics editors. A graphics terminal can have a resolution of 1024 by 864 raster points or better. Some such terminals have resolution of 1000 to 5000 scan lines per inch, whereas the usual household television screen has about 200.

greeking

The use of random letters or marks to show the appearance of a printed page on-screen without showing the actual text. Used when the text on the page displayed is too small to be readable.

hot spots

Regions on a graphics screen that you use to access further information not visible but available. You can view the additional information by clicking your mouse button with the cursor on the hot spot. Hot spots are links to additional information.

hue

A particular variety of a color, a shade or tint; sometimes considered the same color.

HyperCard

A programming environment for data management on the Apple Macintosh. Information is arranged in stacks, or collections of cards. As you display each card, you can see its parts. You can also connect data items on one card to data items on other cards, and you can create your own cards.

hypertext
A nonhierarchical system for storing text in chunks and providing multiple reading paths for the reader. Requires a computer for storage and display.

icon
A graphic symbol usually representing a word, for example, the fuel pump icon on an automobile dashboard that stands for "fuel." The experience of the Sumerians and the Chinese, who developed hundreds of pictograms and struggled for millenia to use them unambiguously, shows that you should always accompany an icon with a word.

ideogram
A sign representing a concept or idea. Single, wordless cartoons are common ideograms. The term is sometimes but inaccurately used as a synonym for *logogram*.

impact printer
A dot-matrix, typewriter-like, or daisy-wheel printer. Used for letter-quality printing.

ISO
International Organization for Standardization. This body creates international standards for many industries. ISO, not an acronym, stands for iso, equal, as in isobar, isometric.

italic
A style of type having letters slanting to the right; so called because it is patterned after a fifteenth-century Italian calligraphic style.

justification
Inserting extra space between words or letters in a line so one or both margins are straight, not ragged.

K
Kilo, or 1000 (10^3). Used to describe the number of bytes available on a system. A kilobyte is 2^{10} or 1024 bytes. This is because addressable computer memory increases in powers of two, not ten.

kerning
Typographer's term for space between characters and the adjustment of that space. Donald Knuth used the term *glue* for the space between the *boxes* he defined as the locus of points in which a character was formed; he used his glue for kerning. Not all text processing systems use kerning.

keyboard

The device containing lettered, numbered, and other keys for special symbols and control characters, used by humans for interacting with computer systems and preparing information for electronic storage.

landscape

Page orientation, wider than it is high. A page printed with landscape orientation is called a *turnpage*.

language

(a) Any method of communicating ideas, as by a system of signs, symbols, gestures, or the like. (b) Any method of communicating, as by characters in a defined syntax, used by a human to communicate with a computer. (c) The special vocabulary and usages of a scientific, professional, or other group. (d) Language as a subject of study (linguistics).

laser

A device that converts radiation of mixed frequencies to discrete, amplified, and coherent visible radiation. Acronym for Light Amplification by Stimulated Emission of Radiation.

laser printer

A printing device that uses a laser beam to form an image of an entire page on an electrostatic surface, then transfers the image to paper. A laser printer is more versatile and more expensive than an impact or dot-matrix printer. Laser printers with sufficient resolution (600 to 1200 dpi) can produce high-quality output for printing masters.

leading

(Rhymes with "heading.") Spacing between lines of text, measured from the bottom of the line above to the bottom of the line below. So called by extension from the thin strips of metal used to separate lines of handset type.

legend

Explanation of symbols on a map or graphic.

letter-quality printer

A device such as an ink-jet or laser printer that can produce printing of acceptable quality for correspondence or manuscript submission. In general, more expensive than a dot-matrix printer.

lexical

Of or relating to the vocabulary, words, or morphemes of a language.

ligatures
Characters linked together as a single unit — for example, fl or ff.

line weight
The thickness of lines in letters in a font. The relative thickness or heaviness of a line. For example, line weight in the regular style is thinner than the line weight in the bold style for the same font.

linguistics
The science of language; the study of the nature and structure of human speech. Sometimes extended to include writing.

logogram
A word sign. In English, for example, $ (dollar) and 2 (two) are common logograms. Chinese characters and Japanese *kanji* characters are logograms.

M
Mega, or 1 million (10^6). A computer with a memory of 1 million bytes is called a 1-megabyte computer.

microspacing
Spacing in printed text that is smaller than most characters.

mnemonic
A device that helps you remember. Also called an *aide-memoire*. Pronounced "ne-mon-ik."

morpheme
A linguistic unit of relatively stable meaning that cannot be divided into smaller meaningful parts — for example, words such as *man, most,* and word elements such as *ly* and *al* (manly, almost).

morphology
The study of word formation, including the origin and function of inflections and derivations.

mouse
An input device for a computer with a rolling ball underneath and up to three buttons you "click" to execute an action on the computer.

near-letter quality
Printing quality that is better than draft quality but not as good as letter quality. Some dot-matrix printers can produce near-letter-quality printing.

operating system
The software on every computer system that manages all the system's hardware and software resources. Operating systems for personal computers include Windows, MS-DOS and OS/2; for minicomputers, VMS, ULTRIX, UNIX, MVS.

optical center
A point on a page or screen slightly above the true center. Used for placement of graphics.

optical disk
A storage medium where data are stored optically, not magnetically.

orphan
In desktop publishing, a header or first line of a paragraph left at the bottom of a page.

Orphan Head

orthography
The art or study of correct spelling according to established usage.

overlapping windows
Windows, or display areas, on a graphics screen that hide parts of other windows when displayed.

PageMaker
A software program developed by Aldus Corporation for page layout of text and graphics. Not a word processing program.

page
A single face of a sheet in a book.

page break

Special control characters or start-page tags that specify where the software is to begin a new page.

paste up

The manual arrangement of page elements (graphics, text, heads) to form a page for printing.

PDL

Page Description Language; a computer language like PostScript with which you specify your page format and layout.

personal computer

A small, single-user computer system such as the IBM PC and the Apple Macintosh.

phoneme

A phonetic unit of a language; for example, the letter *a* in English represents several phonemes, as used in "man," "hay," and "saw."

pica

A printer's unit of measure equal to 12 points or about 1/6 inch, commonly used to measure larger increments of space, particularly the width of a text line. There are about 6 picas to the inch.

pitch

The distance between lines on a typewriter, usually either 10 or 12 points.

pixel

A picture element. On a terminal screen, individual pixels are lit to display characters and shapes. A typical screen might contain 800 by 240 pixels. The more pixels on your screen, the higher its resolution.

point

A unit of type size equal to 0.01384 inch or approximately 1/72 inch. Leading and small increments of space are also measured in points.

pop-up windows

Display areas on a computer screen that appear when you click a mouse button. Generally overlapping.

portrait
The usual orientation of a printed page, which is higher than it is wide.

PostScript
A page description language (PDL) created by Adobe Systems, Inc., used to send page formatting instructions to certain laser printers such as the Apple Laserwriter and the DEC LN03R. A PostScript-capable printer can print characters, many font sizes, and graphics.

printer
An electromechanical device for placing text and illustrations on paper.

publication-quality printer
A printing device that can prepare material of high enough quality to be used as printing masters for multiple copies.

pull-down menu
A menu you display on your screen by placing your mouse cursor on the menu name or symbol and moving the cursor down. This "pulls down" the menu.

punctuation
(a) The use of standard marks and signs in writing and printing to separate words into sentences, clauses, and phrases to clarify meaning. (b) The marks themselves.

ragged right
Text in which the right margin has a ragged or uneven appearance.

raster
The pattern of rows and columns that form the image on a cathode-ray tube such as a video display terminal or television set. A raster is sometimes described as being made of pixels.

redlining
Crossing out text graphically without deleting it from your file.

regressions
Backtracking motions of the eyes in reading.

resolution
The ability of an electronic device or the human eye to distinguish between the parts of an object or of adjacent optical images. Usually measured in dots per inch (dpi). Most video screens have a resolution of about 72 dpi; a laser printer can be 300 dpi or more.

rhetoric
The study of certain elements of communication including content, structure, cadence, and style.

river of white
A distracting series of gaps between words on successive lines of a printed page, giving the impression of continuous white "rivers" running straight or at an angle down the page.

roman
The most common style of printed script for many European languages. This typeform has upright letters with serifs and vertical lines that are thicker than their horizontal lines; so-called because the style is taken from that used in ancient Roman inscriptions and manuscripts. Roman script uses the Latin alphabet. The term roman also means non-italic.

saccades
Eye motions during reading, typified by movements forward and short fixations.

sans serif
A typeface without serifs, that is, having no fine stroke-ending lines characteristic of serif typefaces. In this book, all the display type is in a sans serif typeface, but the text itself is in a serif typeface.

saturation
The degree of purity of a color; chroma. For example, a fully saturated blue contains no additives of other colors.

script
An alphabet or syllabary.

serif
A fine line finishing off the main strokes at the ends of lines in a character, as shown, for example, in the *E*.

set width
In computer typography, the unit width of the most common lowercase letters in a given typeface.

sheet
Paper at a specified size. You can print on both sides of a sheet. Also called a *leaf.*

sidenotes
Notes along the side of a page.

spelling
See **orthography**.

style
A specific size and form of a typeface, for example, boldface, italic, or plain. Also "house style," the typographical and phraseological conventions used by a group or corporation to make their work reasonably uniform.

syllabary
A system of writing in which a sign normally stands for one or more syllables of the language. Thus in Devanagari, for example, one sign has the syllabic value "ba." Modern syllabaries include the Japanese romanization syllabaries *Hebonshiki* (Hepburn), *Kunrei-shiki* (official), and *Nihon-shiki* (Japanese). Japanese syllabaries include *hiragana,* used for prefixes and suffixes to Chinese characters *(kanji),* and *katakana.*

syntax
In computer languages, constructs using conventional symbols ([], {}) that show how commands or elements of the languages are put together to form software commands or statements.

T$_E$X
Donald Knuth's text and page formatting software.

tiled windows
Windows — display areas on a computer screen — that don't overlap.

title page
The page of a book bearing the title of the document, the name of the author, the publisher, the date, and the cities where the publisher is located. In technical documentation, the title page typically carries an abstract, a software name, and a software version number, if the publication describes software.

translation
To express in another language, retaining the original sense. For example, to translate the Greek word "ti" into the English word "what."

transliteration
To represent letters or words in the corresponding characters of another writing system. For example, to write Greek words in roman characters, such as the word "τι" as "ti."

turnpage
A page turned 90 degrees from the normal. Used when you must present information in many columns. Also called landscape orientation.

type
(a) (archaic) A small block of metal or wood bearing a raised letter or character on the upper end. When inked and pressed upon paper, the block leaves a printed impression. (b) The modern, computer-created equivalent prepared electronically by a printing or display device; also called *typeform.*

typeface
A particular style or design of type, such as Baskerville or Times Roman, usually produced as a complete font. Also called a "typeform" or "face." A complete typeface of one design includes roman, italic, boldface, small capitals, and all symbols required for specialized needs such as mathematics or scientific texts. See **descender,** figure of typeform.

typeform
See **typeface, descender.**

typesetting
The act of setting type; formerly done manually with metal types; now done by computer with electronic typeforms.

typography
The art and technique of designing typeforms for printing or video display.

video display
An electronic display used to view text and pictures, typically 80 or 132 characters wide and 24 lines long. Some video displays are larger, others smaller.

widow
A word or short phrase left by itself at the top of a page or column, separated awkwardly from its associated text, as shown in the following illustration.

word processor
An electronic machine on which text can be created using a keyboard, examined and edited on a video display, and recorded on a magnetic medium such as tape, disk, or diskette. A word processor is a single-purpose machine dedicated to word processing.

workplan
The sequence you follow to complete a writing project and deliver your result.

workstation
A computer system used with a wide variety of user applications, including text processing, scientific applications, graphics display, and so on.

WORM
Write-Once-Read-Many device for storing data. A type of optical disk.

writing
(a) Written form. (b) Language symbols or characters written, imprinted on a surface, or displayed; readable matter. (c) Any written work. (d) The act of creating written material.

writing direction
The direction normally used when writing in a given language, established by custom. Writing is always from top to bottom of a page. English is normally written from left to right, as are all Indo-European languages. Arabic and Hebrew are prominent examples of right-to-left scripts. Japanese and Chinese, in their more traditional forms, are written in vertical columns from right to left. Modern Japanese texts are, however, often written in horizontal lines from left to right.

WYSIWYG

What You See Is What You Get: a descriptive acronym applied to certain software tools that display text and graphics on your computer terminal. What you see on your screen is a close approximation of what your text and graphics will look like when you print it. No WYSIWYG system provides a view of your material that is exactly like what it will look like when you print it, but some come close.

xerography

A dry process with which an image, formed with a powder on an electrically charged plate, is transferred electrically to and fixed by heat on paper.

x-height

The height of lowercase characters excluding ascenders and descenders, so-called because the size of the lowercase letter x is taken as the unit height for the typeface. See **descender** for the diagram illustrating x-height.

Select Bibliography

This appendix lists selected books and papers in the field, as well as all publications cited in the text. The order is alphabetical by author, except for reference works such as dictionaries or works without a named author which are alphabetized by title. When I order documents by title, I ignore initial articles such as "a" or "the." For example, to find papers by Jan Walker, look under "Walker," and to find the *American Heritage Dictionary,* look under "American." A number in Arabic numerals following a journal title is the volume number of a periodical. I omit place of publication because if you know the publisher, which is given, the place is redundant.

You should be able to find these books and articles in a local public or institutional library. If not, consult *Books in Print* at a local bookstore or library for ordering information. All the publications in this list are worth examination, but if a book or paper is particularly good, I give it two checks (✓✓). Excellent books that are getting out of date have one check (✓).

Adobe Systems, Inc. *PostScript Language Tutorial and Cookbook.* Addison-Wesley, 1985.

> Start with this one if you want to learn PostScript.

———. *PostScript Language Reference Manual.* Addison-Wesley, 1985.

> Use this for reference once you know PostScript.

Albers, Josef. *Interaction of Color.* Yale University Press, 1975.

> A classic: describes and illustrates how colors work together.

Alley, Michael. *The Craft of Scientific Writing.* 3rd ed. Springer, 1996.

> A quick guide with advice on writing for scientists. Major confusion in presenting bibliographical information, however.

Alschuler, Liora. *ABCD...SGML: A User's Guide to Structured Information.* Thomson Computer Press, 1995.

> Well written, informative; contains a wealth of information on how structure adds value to information. Clearly explains how SGML relates to everyday publishing problems. An excellent guide on how to strike a balance between SGML and non-SGML implementations and tools. Discusses cost justification, document architectures, system design, data conversion, SGML-based production in depth.

Altick, Richard D. *The English Common Reader: A Social History of the Mass Reading Public 1880–1900.* University of Chicago Press, 1957.

Provides a brief background for the period 1477 to 1800, with information on early printing; estimates of literacy; cost of books and magazines; numbers printed; and the rise of the bookshop and public library, the book trade, and circulating libraries (book rentals). Gives unique statistics on early bestsellers. Data confined almost exclusively to England.

Alvarez, Joseph A. *The Elements of Technical Writing.* Harcourt Brace Jovanovich, 1980.

AMA. *American Medical Association Encyclopedia,* 1989.

Shows how a large mass of information is presented.

✓✓ *American Heritage Dictionary.* Houghton Mifflin, 1976.

Includes special articles on the history of the English language, usage, dialects, grammar and meaning, and Indo-European origins and roots.

Anderson, M. D. *Book Indexing.* Cambridge University Press, 1971.

Good, brief guide to preparing an index by manual methods.

Anderson, P. V. *Technical Writing: A Reader-Centered Approach.* Harcourt Brace Jovanovich, 1987.

——— . Carolyn R. Miller, John Brockman. *New Essays in Technical and Scientific Communication.* Baywood, 1985.

Andrews, Clarence A. *Technical and Business Writing.* Houghton Mifflin, 1975.

Andrews, Deborah C., Margaret D. Blickle. *Technical Writing: Principles and Forms.* Collier Macmillan International, 1982.

Addresses engineering students, scientists, business people, and professionals. Discusses audience profiling, organizing information and writing. Shows sample texts to illustrate forms. Stresses visual forms. Incorporates some research findings in technical rhetoric. A bit general (engineers to home economics).

——— . W. D. Andrews. *Business Communication.* Macmillan, 1988.

Andrews, William D., Deborah C. Andrews. *Write for Results: How to Write Successful Memos, Letters, Summaries, Abstracts, Proposals, Reports, and Articles.* Little, Brown, 1982.

Brief. Provides guidelines for planning and presenting information and for writing sentences. Shows the forms listed in the title with guidelines for each. Includes brief examples of rewritten texts to illustrate the guidelines.

ANSI Z39. "American National Standards Institute Standard for the Preparation of Scientific Papers for Written or Oral Presentation." *ANSI Z39.16-1979.* Gives sound advice on preparing papers for publication. Well written.

Bailey, Peter. "Speech Communication: The Problem and Some Solutions," *Fundamentals of Human-Computer Interaction.* Edited by Andrew Monk. Academic Press, 1985.

Excellent perspective on the elements that make up speech.

Barrett, E., ed. *Text, ConText, and HyperText: Writing with and for the Computer.* MIT Press, 1988.

———. *The Society of Text.* MIT Press, 1989

A collection of papers written by practitioners in the field. A bit uneven.

Barrett, Leslie. "Choosing the Right Graphic Tool," 1995, private communication.

Batho, Robert Lloyd. *A Practical Guide to Technical Illustration.* Muller, 1968.

A bit out of date, but provides a good framework for understanding how to do this work.

Beakley, George C., Donald D. Autore. *Introduction to Scientific Illustration.* Macmillan, 1983.

Bell, Paula, Charlotte Evans. *Mastering Documentation.* John Wiley & Sons, 1989.

Describes the use of document masters or templates to develop technical documentation for systems development, control, and delivery.

Beniger, James R., D. Eleanor Westney. "Japanese and U.S. Media: Graphics as a Reflection of a Newspaper's Social Role," *Journal of Communication* 31 (2) (Spring 1981): 14–27.

Excellent and insightful comparison of how Japanese and U.S. newspapers do and do not use graphics. The authors conclude that Japanese newspapers use more graphics, in more meaningful ways, than U.S. newspapers do. However, the article does not consider *USA TODAY,* a newspaper that has excellent graphics.

Bernstein, Mark. "The Shape of Hypertext Documents," *Proceedings of the 36th International Technical Communications Conference* May 1989, RT-173-RT-175.

Bernstein, Theodore. *The Careful Writer: A Modern Guide to English Usage.* Atheneum, 1965.

Bertin, Jaques. *Graphics and Graphic Information-processing*. Walter de Gruyter, 1981.

Shows many examples, some extremely complex, of converting numerical data to meaningful graphics.

——— . *Semiology of Graphics*. University of Wisconsin Press, 1983.

Bethune, James D. *Technical Illustration*. John Wiley & Sons, 1983.

Birnes, William J., ed. *McGraw-Hill Personal Computer Programming Encyclopedia*. McGraw-Hill, 1989.

Definitions of commands, statements, and source code in high-level programming languages and in personal computer operating systems such as OS/2. Tells you what they are but not how to use them.

Blair, David C., M. E. Maron. "An Evaluation of Retrieval Effectiveness for a Full-text Document Retrieval System," *Communications of the ACM 28*, no. 3 (1985): 289–299.

Blicq, Ron S. *Technically-Write!* Prentice-Hall, 1981.

Bly, Robert, Gary Blake. *Technical Writing: Structures, Standards, and Style*. McGraw-Hill, 1982.

Combines writing guidelines with a smattering of theory.

Bookstein, A. "Probability and Fuzzy-Set Applications to Information Retrieval," *Annual Review of Information Science Technology* 20 (1983): 117–151.

Borko, Harold, Charles L. Bernier. *Indexing Concepts and Methods*. Academic Press, 1978.

Brehmar, Berndt. "Systems Design and the Psychology of Complex Systems," *Empirical Foundations of Information and Software Science III*. Edited by Jens Rasmussen and Pranas Zunde. Plenum, 1987.

Brinegar, B., C. Skates. *Technical Writing: A Guide with Models*. Scott, Foresman, 1983.

Brockman, R. John. *Writing Better Computer User Documentation*. John Wiley & Sons, 1990.

Describes common problems of user documentation, outlines the author's solution — the Standard Documentation Process — to help you set standards in your workplace.

✓✓ Brogan, John A. *Clear Technical Writing.* McGraw-Hill, 1973.

> An outstanding workbook with numerous examples from which every writer can benefit. You can use the workbook to help improve the clarity of your writing style.

Browning, Christine. *Guide to Effective Software Technical Writing.* Prentice-Hall, 1984.

Brunner, Ingrid, J. C. Mathes, Dwight W. Stevenson. *The Technician as Writer: Preparing Technical Reports.* Bobbs-Merrill, 1980.

Brusaw, Charles T., et al. *Handbook of Technical Writing.* St. Martin's, 1987.

Bullinger, H. J., R. Gunsenhauser. *Software Ergonomics: Advances and Applications.* John Wiley & Sons, 1988 (translated from 1986 German edition).

> Gives principles of dialog and screen designs with some practical applications. Covers several input devices such as the mouse, joystick, and light pen. A bit too short to be really useful.

Burke, James. *The Day the Universe Changed.* Little, Brown, 1985.

> Discusses the route by which typography reached Europe. Companion to PBS television series.

Caernarven-Smith, Patricia. *Audience Analysis and Response.* Firman, 1983.

Calishain, Tara. *Official Netscape Guide to Internet Research.* Ventana, 1997.

> Well written source book for learning about how to use the internet to find information. Includes advice on how to make web citations.

Carlson, Patricia A. "Cognitive Tools and Computer-Aided Writing," *AI Expert* (October 1990): 48–55.

> An interesting description of computer tools that can aid the writing process.

Carosso, R. B. *Technical Communication.* Wadsworth, 1987.

Carroll, John M. "Minimalist Training," *Datamation,* November 1, 1984, 125–136.

> Describes how you can minimize the amount of text you provide.

——. *The Nurnberg Funnel: Designing Minimalist Instruction for Practical Computer Skill.* MIT Press, 1990.

> Addresses learning, study, and teaching.

——. *Interfacing Thought: Cognitive Aspects of Human–Computer–Interaction.* MIT Press, 1987.

> Discussion of user interfaces, interactive systems, cognitive psychology, system design, human factor engineering.

————. *Scenario-based Design: Envisioning Work and Technology in Systems Development.* Wiley, 1995.

Covers UI interfaces and system design, with bibliography.

Chambers Dictionary of Science and Technology. Barnes & Noble, 1972.

The Chicago Guide to Preparing Electronic Manuscripts. University of Chicago Press, 1987.

Advice for preparation of documents with some new tools. Already out of date.

✓ *The Chicago Manual of Style.* University of Chicago, 1982.

Sound advice for preparation and copyediting of documents. Well organized and comprehensive. A standard.

Christ, R. E. "The Effects of Extended Practice on the Evaluation of Visual Display Codes," *Human Factors* 25 (1983): 71–84.

Cleveland, Donald, Ana D. Cleveland. *Introduction to Indexing and Abstraction.* Libraries Unlimited, 1990.

Clifton, Chris, Hector Garcia-Molina. *Indexing in a Hypertext Database.* Princeton University, Dept. of Computer Science, 1989.

Describes considerations for working in a hypertext environment.

Comeau, J., G. Diehn. *Communication on the Job: A Practical Approach.* Prentice-Hall, 1987.

Concise Science Dictionary. Oxford University Press, 1980.

Sound dictionary of British, not American, usage.

Conway, Richard, David Gries. *An Introduction to Programming.* Winthrop Publishers, 1979.

Presents a structured approach using the computer languages PL/I and PL/C. Outstandingly clear presentation, although the printing is typewriter style.

Cornsweet, Tom. *Visual Perception.* Academic Press, 1970.

Provides research results in visual perception. Quite detailed, supplements the work of Tinker and Marr.

Crispin, F. S. *Dictionary of Technical Terms.* Bruce, 1970.

Crowder, R. G. *The Psychology of Reading.* Oxford University Press, 1982.

Cunningham, Donald H., Gerald Cohen. *Creating Technical Manuals: A Step-by-Step Approach to Writing User-Friendly Instructions.* McGraw-Hill, 1984.

Cypert, Samuel A. *Writing Effective Business Letters, Memos, Proposals and Reports.* Contemporary Books, 1983.

Dagher, Joseph P. *Technical Communication: A Practical Guide.* Prentice-Hall, 1987.

DeGennaro, Richard. *Libraries, Technology, and the Information Marketplace.* G. K. Hall, 1987.

DeMorgan, R. M., I. D. Hill, B. A. Wichman. "A Supplement to the ALGOL 60 Revised Report," *The Computer Journal* 19, no. 3 (1976): 276–288.

Where to find information on BNF, the Backus-Naur Form.

Denton, Lynn, Jody Kelly, *Designing, Writing, and Producing Computer Documentation.* McGraw-Hill, 1993.

Prescriptive but without any support from research for recommendations. Based on experience at IBM. Lots of publishing jargon, better dealt with in documents such as the Chicago Manual of Style.

✓✓ *Dictionary of Computing: Data Communications, Hardware and Software Basics, Digital Electronics.* Datology Press, 1982.

Small, selective, excellent.

The Digital Dictionary. DECbooks, 1986.

Good coverage of Digital Equipment Corporation terminology. A bit out of date.

Diringer, David. *The Book Before Printing.* Dover, 1982.

Good, if you are interested in the history of writing.

Dobrin, David N. "What's Wrong with the Mathematical Theory of Communication," *Proceedings of the 29th International Technical Communication Conference,* 1982, E-37-E-40.

Asserts that technical writers translate one practice into another, going from engineer to user; that technical writers are not agents of information transfer in the literal, data communication sense.

Dodd, Janet S., ed. *The ACS Style Guide.* American Chemical Society, 1986.

Defines the house style of the American Chemical Society. Gives advice on how to prepare a paper for publication; addresses grammar, hyphenation, names, usage, reference style, and illustrations. Brief advice on writing style.

Doheny-Farina, Stephen, ed. *Effective Documentation: What We Have Learned from Research.* MIT Press, 1988.

——. "Writing in an Emergent Business Organization: An Ethnographic Study," *Written Communication* 3, no. 2 (1985): 158–185.

——, William Karis. "A Comparative Case Study of Technical Environmental Communication in Canada and the U.S.," *Technical Communication* (Fourth Quarter 1990): 454–456.

Dowlin, Kenneth E. *The Electronic Library.* Neal-Schuman, 1984.

A case study of putting a library catalog online.

Downing, Mildred Harlow. *Introduction to Cataloging and Classification.* McFarland, 1981.

Basic information on how libraries classify information.

Driver, G. R. *Semitic Writing from Pictograph to Alphabet.* Oxford University Press, 1976.

Historical background of writing. An example of book design dictated by a need to minimize typesetting in a new edition.

Durrett, H. John, ed. *Color and the Computer.* Academic Press, 1987.

Provides data on the use of color and its effectiveness, in studies from industry and academia. A good source for data on this topic.

Earle, James H. *Technical Illustration.* Creative Publishing, 1978.

An early work by this author, with excellent advice.

——. *Drafting Technology.* Addison-Wesley, 1983.

A more up-to-date version of the previous, profusely illustrated. Eisenberg, Anne. *Effective Technical Communication.* McGraw-Hill, 1982.

Englebart, Douglas. "A Conceptual Framework for the Augmentation of Man's Intellect," *Vistas in Information Handling.* Spartan Books, 1963.

Describes the symbiotic relationship between human and computer in which "the symbols with which the human represents the concepts he is manipulating can be arranged before his eyes . . ." This synergy between machine, mental structures, and symbolic manipulation is the essence of cognitive tools.

Falcione, Raymond. *The Guide to Better Communication in Government Service.* Scott, Foresman, 1984.

Fear, David. *Technical Communication.* Scott, Foresman, 1981.

✓✓ Flesch, R. *The ABC of Style: A Guide to Plain English.* Harper & Row, 1980.

A classic work that stresses the readability of prose.

Forth-83 Standard. Forth Standards Team, Mountain View, CA 1983.

Fowler, H. W. *A Dictionary of Modern English Usage.* Oxford University Press, 1987.

Another classic.

Fox, Edward A. "The Coming Revolution in Interactive Digital Video," *Communications of the ACM* 32, no. 7 (July 1989): 795–801.

Shows how video disks can help the scholar.

Freed, Richard C., David D. Roberts. "The Nature, Classification, and Generic Structure of Proposals," *Journal of Technical Writing and Communication* 19, no. 4 (1989): 317–351.

Summarizes the generic structures of proposal writing.

Freedman, Alan. *The Computer Glossary: The Complete Illustrated Desk Reference.* AMACOM, 1991.

Frenkel, Karen A. "The Next Generation of Interactive Technologies," *Communications of the ACM* 31, no. 7 (July 1989): 872–881.

Gagné, Robert M., Leslie J. Briggs, Walter W. Wager. *Principles of Instructional Design.* Holt, Reinhart and Winston, 1988. 3rd ed.

A classic, used often for teaching the discipline.

Gelb, I. J. *A Study of Writing.* University of Chicago Press, 1963.

A brief description of writing from the time of its invention in Sumer.

Gery, Gloria J. *Electronic Performance Support Systems.* Weingarten Publications, 1991.

Many case studies.

Gibson, Walker. *Tough, Sweet, and Stuffy: An Essay on Modern American Prose Style.* Indiana University Press, 1966.

Examines the style and voice of prose. Identifies sixteen factors of discourse with a rating scale.

Gilliland, J. *Readability.* Unibooks, 1972.

Girill, T. R., Joanne J. Perra. *Guidelines for Preparing Computer Reports.* Lawrence Livermore, 1982.

Glass, Arnold Lewis, Keith James Holyoak, John Lester Santa. *Cognition.* Addison-Wesley, 1979.

An excellent textbook, still valid.

Goldfarb, Charles. *The SGML Handbook.* Oxford, 1990.

The standard text, more for SGML developers than for people who use a DTD to tag and process documents.

✓ Goodman, Danny. *The Complete HyperCard 2.0 Handbook.* Bantam, 1990.

Describes the HyperCard programming environment for the novice.

Gosney, Michael, Linnea Dayton. *Making Art on the Macintosh.* Scott, Foresman, 1989.

Graham, Ian S. *HTML Sourcebook Third Edition, A complete guide to HTML 3.2 and HTML Extensions.* Wiley, 1997.

Graves, Robert, Alan Hodge. *The Reader over Your Shoulder.* Macmillan, 1964.

Discusses the properties of English, provides twenty-five principles of clear statement and sixteen graces of prose, and analyzes many prose texts; provides rewrites. Good for helping you reexamine what you write.

Gray, Henry. *Anatomy, Descriptive and Surgical.* Classic Edition. Bounty Books, 1977.

A classic medical reference work, often called "Gray's Anatomy." Shows an excellent combination of technical diagrams and text.

Gribbons, William, "Color as Communication: Human Factors Theory and Practice." Private communication.

Griffin, C. W. *Writing: A Guide for Business Professionals.* Harcourt Brace Jovanovich, 1988.

Grimm, Susan J. *How to Write Computer Manuals for Users.* Lifetime Learning Publications, 1982.

Gross, Alan G. "Extending the Expressive Power of Language: Tables, Graphs, and Diagrams," *Technical Writing and Communication* 20, no. 3 (1990): 221–235.

Suggests that tables, graphs, and diagrams are not language but visual displays.

Haag, Dietrich E. "Guidelines for the Identification and Formatting of Technical Periodicals," *Technical Communication* (First Quarter 1989).

Shows how to format, or not format, your texts.

Hackos, JoAnn. *Managing Your Documentation Projects.* Wiley, 1994.

A full discussion of how to manage documentation projects from planning and design to implementation, production, and evaluation. Provides a dependencies calculator to help estimate project scope, a four phase process, and a publications process maturity model against which to compare your organization, from oblivious to optimizing.

Haramundanis, Kathy. "Author/Publisher/Reader of the Future," *Abridged Proceedings, HCI International '89,* 1989, 38.

Stresses the move from paper to electrons.

——— . "On-line vs. Manual." *Journal of Information Science* 3, no. 4 (September 1981): 198–199.

Suggests that online texts should include bibliographic references that can also be retrieved online.

——— . "Documentation Project Management" ACM SIGDOC, 1995.

Provides tips and methods for managing documentation projects.

——— . "Writing the Scientific Review Article" STC Interchange Conference, 1995.

Advises on how to collect and distill information in a review article.

——— . "Why Icons Cannot Stand Alone." * *The Journal of Computer Documentation* 20, no. 2 (May 1996): 1-8.

Hastings, G. Prentice, Kathryn J. King. *Creating Effective Documentation for Computer Programs.* Prentice-Hall, 1986.

✓ Hayakawa, S. I. *Language in Action.* Harcourt, Brace, 1941.

Classic work on the value, significance, and importance of the words we use. Required reading for any writer.

——— . *Language in Thought and Action.* Harcourt Brace Jovanovich, 1978.

Heines, J. M. *Screen Design Strategies for Computer-Assisted Instruction.* Digital Press, 1984.

Herwijnen, Van. *Practical SGML.* Kluwer, 1994.

Attempts to explain SGML in practical terms.

Hirschhorn, Howard. *Writing for Science, Industry, and Technology.* Krieger, 1980. Hoadley, Ellen D. "Investigating the Effects of Color," *Communications of the ACM* 33, no. 2 (1990): 120–125.

Hochheiser, R. M. *Don't State It ... Communicate It!* Barron's Educational Series, 1985.

Hodges, John C., Mary E. Whitten. *Harbrace College Handbook.* Harcourt, Brace & World, 1990.

A standard reference for questions on grammar and orthography. My favorite because of its content and format. Later editions use too much color.

Holmes, Nigel. *Designer's Guide to Creating Charts and Diagrams.* Watson-Guptill, 1984.

Based on manual work by an artist; designs for newspaper and magazine layouts.

Holtz, Herman. *The Complete Guide to Writing Readable User Manuals*. Dow Jones-Irwin, 1988.

Horn, Robert E. *Mapping Hypertext*. Lexington Institute, 1989.

"The analysis, organization, and display of knowledge for the next generation of on-line text and graphics." Discursive presentation, heavily annotated with graphics, about the basis for the Information Mapping methodology. Includes a cursory description of argumentation analysis, a method sometimes used in artificial intelligence prototypes.

Hoover, Hardy. *Essentials for the Scientific and Technical Writer*. Dover, 1981.

Horton, William. *Designing and Writing Online Documentation: Help Files to Hypertext*. John Wiley & Sons, 1990.

A practical approach to designing and writing online texts; experience backed by academic research. Good perspective, though sometimes hard to follow all the advice given by the author. Nice discussion of how to use animation.

Houp, Kenneth W., Thomas E. Pearsall. *Reporting Technical Information*. Macmillan, 1988.

Hubbard, Stuart W. *The Computer Graphics Glossary*. Oryx, 1983. Colloquial, dated.

Huckin, Thomas N. "A Cognitive Approach to Readability," *New Essays in Technical and Scientific Communication*. Baywood, 1985, 90–108.

Suggests that experts read differently than novices; readers assume that highlighted or underlined text is more important, and they remember things mentioned first and last better than those mentioned in the middle.

Hulbury, Allen. *Layout*. Watson-Guptill, 1989.

Hulme, Charles. "Extracting Information from Printed and Electronically Presented Text," *Fundamentals of Human-Computer Interaction*. Edited by Andrew Monk. Academic Press, 1985, 35–47.

Excellent collection of papers with research results.

Jacobs, Lisa Ann. *Guide to Microsoft Word for the Apple Macintosh*. Microsoft Press, 1989.

Handy pocket guide to Word.

James, Geoffrey. *Document Databases*. Van Nostrand Reinhold, 1985.

The author's thesis is that it is easier to prepare documents with computers. Techniques do not use structured databases; they are mainly files on a computer.

"JASA Style Sheet," *Journal of the American Statistical Society* (March 1976): 257–261.

> Provides advice on the use of graphics and tables in documents. A little dated.

✓✓ Jastrzebski, Zbigniew J. *Scientific Illustration.* Prentice-Hall, 1985.

> Excellent advice and examples of how to lay out illustrations on a page. Contains beautiful scientific drawings from nature not yet achievable with computer software.

Jonassen, D. H., ed. *The Technology of Text: Principles for Structuring, Designing, and Displaying Text.* Educational Technology Publications, 1982.

——, Wallace H. Hannum, Martin Tessmer. *Handbook of Task Analysis Procedures.* Praeger, 1989.

> Often referenced.

Keene, M. L. *Effective Professional Writing.* D. C. Heath, 1987.

Killingsworth, M. Jimmie, Michael K. Gilbertson, Joe Chew. "Amplification in Technical Manuals: Theory and Practice," *Journal of Technical Writing and Communication* 19, no. 1 (1989): 13–29.

> Shows that amplification (use of rhetorical techniques to elaborate discourse) in computer manuals can improve them.

Knuth, Donald E. T_EX and METAFONT. Digital Press, 1979.

> Seminal work on using computers to create typeforms and do page layout.

——, T. Larrabee, P.M. Roberts. "Mathematical Writing." Dept. of Computer Science, Stanford University. Report no. STAN-CS-88-1193, 1988.

> Charmingly written; notes for a computer science course of the same name. Includes vignettes from and about Leslie Lamport, Paul Halmos.

Kohonen, T. *Self-Organization and Associative Memory.* Springer-Verlag, 1988.

> Describes principles of distributed associative memory and how an adaptive physical system can encode information.

Kramer, S. *The Sumerians.* University of Chicago Press, 1963.

> Describes the invention and early use of writing.

Krull, R. "Communicative Functions of Icons as Computer Commands," *Proceedings of the IEEE Communication Society,* October 1985.

> Discusses the suitability of icons for representing various computer concepts.

——, ed. *Word Processing for Technical Writers.* Baywood, 1988. Three volumes.

———, Philip Rubens. "Graphics in Computer Documentation: A Meta-analysis," *IEEE* (1982): 100–103.

Lang, Kathy. *The Writer's Guide to Desktop Publishing.* Academic Press, 1987.

Lannon, John. *Technical Writing.* Scott, Foresman, 1988.

LaTorra, Michael. "Standard Text Markup: What SGML Means for Technical Writers," *Technical Communication* (Fourth Quarter 1989): 382–384.

Lay, Mary M. *Strategies for Technical Writing: A Rhetoric with Readings.* Holt, Rinehart, and Winston, 1982.

Lee, Marshall, ed. *Bookmaking: The Illustrated Guide to Design, Production, Editing.* R. R. Bowker, 1980.

LeMay, Laura. *Teach Yourself Web Publishing with HTML 3.2 in a Week.* Sams, 1996.

Levine, Norman. *Technical Writing.* Harper & Row, 1978.

Lyons, John, ed. *New Horizons in Linguistics.* Penguin, 1970.
    Overview of the field: natural and artificial languages, linguistic analysis, generational and transformational grammars.

MacKenzie, R., W. Evans. *Technical Writing: Forms and Formats.* Kendall Hunt, 1982.

Maggio, Rosalie. *The Nonsexist Word Finder: A Dictionary of Gender-free Usage.* Oryx, 1987.

Maler, Eve, Andaloussi, J.E. *Developing SGML DTDs: From Text to Markup.* Prentice-Hall, 1996. The best text to use to understand DTD development and implementation.

Mañas, José A. "Word Division in Spanish," *Communications of the ACM* 30, no. 7 (July 1987): 612–619.
    Describes how a text and page formatting software tool must take into account the needs of different languages.

Mancuso, Joseph. *Mastering Technical Writing.* Addison-Wesley, 1990.

Mandel, Carol A. *Multiple Thesauri in Online Library Bibliographic Systems, A Report Prepared for the Library of Congress Processing Services.* Library of Congress Cataloging Distribution Service, 1987.

Markel, Michael. *Technical Writing: Situations and Strategies.* St. Martin's, 1988.

✓✓ Marr, D. *Vision*. W. H. Freeman, 1982.

> A modern analytical study of human vision. Contains instructive examples of visual effects.

Martin, M. "The Semiology of Documents," *IEEE Transactions on Professional Communications* 32, no. 3 (September 1989): 171–177.

> Emphasizes how information processing, graphics, and reading styles interact during reading.

——. "The Visual Development of Documents," *IPCC 1988 Conference Record, On the Edge: A Pacific Rim Conference on Professional Technical Communication,* 1988, 7–10.

> Uses information processing theory to analyze how a reader visually processes a page.

Mathes, J. C., Dwight Stevenson. *Designing Technical Reports*. Bobbs-Merrill, 1976.

McArdle, Geri E.H. *Developing Instructional Design*. Crisp, 1991.

> Part of a 50-minute series. Includes sample lesson plan and checklist for instructional designer.

McGraw-Hill Concise Encyclopedia of Science and Technoloy. McGraw-Hill, 1984.

> A single volume, designed for ease of use.

McGraw-Hill Dictionary of Science and Engineering. McGraw-Hill, 1984. *McGraw-Hill Encyclopedia of Science and Technology.* McGraw-Hill, 1987.

> Excellent, extensive.

McGraw-Hill Personal Computer Programming Encyclopedia. See Birnes.

McGrew, P. C., W. D. McDaniel. *On-line Text Management*. McGraw-Hill, 1984.

> How to select and use online text, including hypertext.

McKerrow, Ronald B. *An Introduction to Bibliography for Literary Students*. Oxford University Press, 1965.

> Provides information on the construction of the printed book and its early history, including sources for early printing in the Far East. Gives instructions on how to prepare a complete bibliographical description of a book.

McNeill, Dan. *Quick & Easy Guide to Desktop Publishing*. Compute! Publications, 1987.

> A short, encouraging text for those who want to publish their own books.

Mencken, H. L. *The American Language* (with Supplements One and Two). Alfred A. Knopf, 1978.

A discussion of new words introduced into English by American usage and exposure to indigenous tongues.

The Merck Index: An Encyclopedia of Chemicals, Drugs, and Biologicals. Merck, 1983.

An encyclopedia of biologicals, chemicals, and drugs. An example of the presentation of a large amount of information.

Miles, J., D. Bush, A. Kaplan. *Technical Writing: Principles and Practice.* SRA, 1982.

Miller, Carolyn. "A Humanistic Rationale for Technical Writing," *College English* 40 (February 1979): 610–617.

——. "Invention in Technical and Scientific Discourse: A Prospective Survey," *Research in Technical Communication,* edited by Michael G. Moran and Debra Journet. Greenwood Press, 1985, 117–162.

Miller, Casey, Kate Swift. *The Handbook of Nonsexist Writing.* Harper & Row, 1988.

Miller, Diane. *Guide for Preparing Software User Documentation.* Society for Technical Communication, 1988.

✓✓ Miller, George A. "The Magical Number Seven, Plus or Minus Two: Some Limits on Our Capacity for Processing Information," *The Psychological Review* 63, no. 2 (March 1956): 81–97.

A classic work, somewhat superseded by later work, that describes the limitations of human processing capacities (vision, hearing, and so on), based on experiments.

Mills, Gordon, John Walter. *Technical Writing.* Holt, Rinehart, and Winston, 1986.

Monk, Andrew, ed. *Fundamentals of Human–Computer Interaction.* Academic Press, 1985.

An excellent collection of papers on how humans interact with computers.

Moxley, Joseph M. "Commentary: The Myth of the Technical Audience," *Journal of Technical Writing and Communication* 18, no. 2 (1988): 107–109.

Mracek, Jan. *Technical Illustration & Graphics.* Prentice-Hall, 1983.

National Information Standards Series. *Basic Criteria for Indexes.* Transaction Publications, 1984.

Nelson, Robin. "Wurd Processing," *Personal Computing,* August 1990, 49.

Cites a university study that compared students who use character-based text-processing programs and those who use the Mac with pull-down menus. Students using character-cell programs wrote at a higher grade level (twelfth instead of eighth), made fewer grammar and spelling errors, and chose weightier subjects. The study did not examine how the students did their work.

Nelson, Roy P. *Publication Design.* Wm. C. Brown, 1987.

Newell, A., D. L. McCracken, G. G. Robertson, R. M. Akscyn. "ZOG and USS Carl Vinson," *Computer Science Research Review,* Carnegie-Mellon University (1980–81): 95–118.

Describes ZOG, an early hypertext-like system.

Nielsen, Jakob. *Hypertext and Hypermedia.* Academic Press, 1990.

Describes the development of several existing hypertext systems. Illustrates several, including Guide, Intermedia, and others. Outstanding annotated bibliography.

Oliu, Walter, Charles Brusaw, Gerald Alred. *The Business Writer's Handbook.* St. Martin's, 1987.

——, Charles Brusaw. *Handbook of Technical Writing.* St. Martin's, 1987.

A practical desktop reference organized alphabetically by topic.

Olsen, Leslie. "Computer-Based Writing and Communication: Some Implications for Technical Communication Activities," *Journal of Technical Writing and Communication* 19, no. 2 (1989): 97–118.

——, T. Huckin. *Technical Writing and Professional Communication.* McGraw-Hill, 1991.

Good advice, good examples, excellent use of color and illustrations. Not so strong as other texts on how to perform tasks.

——, T. Huckin. *Principles of Communication for Science and Technology.* McGraw-Hill, 1983.

Ong, Walter J. *Orality and Literacy: The Technologizing of the Word.* Methuen, 1982.

Describes the author's thesis that modern prose comes from an oral tradition that writers are currently moving to eradicate.

The Oxford English Dictionary (and its supplement). Oxford University Press, 1933, 1970.

Multivolume, comprehensive.

Parker, Roger C. "The 25 Worst Desktop Publishing Mistakes (and How to Avoid Them)," *PC Computing*, May 1989, 87–91.

Pauley, Steven. *Technical Report Writing Today.* Houghton Mifflin, 1979.

Pearsall, Thomas, Donald Cunningham. *How to Write for the World of Work.* Holt, Rinehart, and Winston, 1986.

Pfaffenberger, Bryan. *Using Microsoft Word 4, Macintosh.* Que Corp., 1989.
A clearly written tutorial on this word processing software.

Pickett, Nell Ann, Ann Laster. *Technical English: Writing, Reading, and Speaking.* Harper & Row, 1988.

✓✓ Postman, Neil. *Amusing Ourselves to Death: Public Discourse in the Age of Show Business.* Penguin, 1988.
Author's thesis is that Huxley, not Orwell, was right. Of course, good technical documentation may show them both to be wrong.

Prentice-Hall Encyclopedia of Information Technology. Prentice-Hall, 1987.

Random House Dictionary of the English Language, The Unabridged Edition. Random House, 1987.

Raymond, J., C. Yee. "The Collaborative Process and Professional Ethics," *IEEE Transactions on Professional Communications* 33, no. 2 (June 1990): 77–81.
Shows that before people can work together as a group, they must resolve issues of collaboration and professional ethics.

Rayner, K., ed. *Eye Movements in Reading: Perceptual and Language Processes.* Academic Press, 1983.

Reform of the Chinese Written Language. Foreign Languages Press, Beijing, China, 1958.
For those with an interest in the development of Chinese characters; describes the methods used to simplify the written language.

Rew, L. J. *Introduction to Technical Writing: Process and Practice.* St. Martin's, 1989.

Richardson, Graham T. *Illustrations.* Humana Press, 1985.
An excellent guide to creating high-quality scientific illustrations by hand. Contains many format and page design guidelines.

Riney, Larry A. *Technical Writing for Industry: An Operations Manual for the Technical Writer.* Prentice-Hall, 1989.
A good process book — develops the process from setting goals and identifying readers to writing style, knowing concepts, and presenting information.

Robertson, C. K., D. McCracken, A. Newell. "The ZOG Approach to Man-Machine Communication," *International Journal of Man-Machine Studies* 14 (1981): 461–488.

Robinson, Patricia. *Fundamentals of Technical Writing.* Houghton Mifflin, 1985.

Rogers, David F., Rae A. Earnshaw, eds. *Techniques for Computer Graphics.* Springer-Verlag, 1987.

Collection of papers from a summer institute on computer graphics. Includes several papers on human factors, user interface design, and online documentation. Describes ODA (Office Document Architecture), which is becoming popular in Europe for presenting online integrated text and graphics.

Roget's International Thesaurus. Crowell, 1962.

The early standard for English synonyms.

Roundy, N., with D. Mair. *Strategies for Technical Communication.* Little, Brown, 1985.

Rowley, Jenifer E. *Abstracting and Indexing.* Clive Bingley, 1982.

Rubens, P., R. Krull. "Application of Research on Document Design to Online Displays," *Technical Communication* (Fourth Quarter 1985): 29–34.

Received award for outstanding article of the year at the International Technical Communication Conference, Detroit, Michigan, May 1986.

Rubinstein, Dick, Harry M. Hersch. *The Human Factor: Designing Computer Systems for People.* Digital Press, 1984.

An early work on the need to understand how humans interact with computers.

Rubinstein, Richard. *Digital Typography: An Introduction to Type and Composition for Computer System Design.* Addison-Wesley, 1988.

An excellent book on typography done with computers. Printed in a typeface hard to read for some.

Salton, Gerard. *Automatic Text Processing.* Addison-Wesley, 1989.

Advocates use of mainframe computers for writing and maintaining technical documents. Describes SCRIPT, T_EX, Scribe, and automatic indexing.

✓✓ Samuels, Marilyn Schauer. *The Technical Writing Process.* Oxford University Press, 1989.

An excellent book, highly recommended. Overview of contemporary research (writing, rhetoric, cognitive science, collaborative learning), understanding the reader, problem solving, revisions, and examples.

Sandman, P., C. Klompus, B. Yarrison. *Scientific and Technical Writing*. Holt, Rinehart, and Winston, 1985.

Schell, John, John Stratton. *Writing On the Job: A Handbook for Business and Government*. Plume, 1984.

Schmid, C. F. *Statistical Graphics Design Principles and Practices*. John Wiley & Sons, 1983.

Schoff, Gretchen H., Patricia A. Robinson. *Writing and Developing Operator Manuals*. Lifetime Learning Publications, 1984.

Schriver, Karen A. "Document Design from 1980 to 1989: Challenges that Remain," *Technical Communication* (Fourth Quarter 1989): 316–331.

A very full account of the problems and challenges of designing technical documents. Thorough bibliography.

———. *Dynamics in Document Design*. Wiley, 1997.

A full account of how document design has changed over the years; interesting timeline of design and technology. Extensive bibliography.

Shaw, Harry. *The Harper Handbook of College Composition*. Harper & Row, 1981.

Sherlock, James. *A Guide to Technical Communication*. Allyn & Bacon, 1985.

Sherman, Theodore, S. Johnson. *Modern Technical Writing*. Prentice-Hall, 1983.

✓ Shneiderman, Ben. *Designing the User Interface: Strategies for Effective Human–Computer Interaction*. 2nd ed. Addison-Wesley, 1992.

———. "Future Directions for Human–Computer Interaction," *Designing and Using Human–Computer Interfaces and Knowledge Based Systems*. Edited by G. Salvendy and M. J. Smith. Elsevier Science Publishing, 1989.

———, Greg Kearsley. *Hypertext Hands-on!* Addison-Wesley, 1989.

More from this experienced author on the use of hypertext. A nice feature is the software that comes with the book. The authors interestingly simulated hypertext links in the printed book, which, though brief, contains useful information.

Sides, Charles H. *How to Write Papers and Reports about Computer Technology*. Professional Writing Series, ISI Press, 1984.

Silver, Gerald A. *Graphic Layout and Design*. Van Nostrand Reinhold, 1981.

A good basic introduction to layout of commercial pieces such as posters, brochures, pamphlets, books, and business cards.

Simpson, Henry, Steven M. Casey. *Developing Effective User Documentation: A Human Factors Approach*. McGraw-Hill, 1988.

Advice on evaluating and debugging your user documentation.

Sippl, C. J., R. J. Sippl. *Computer Dictionary*. Howard W. Sams, 1982.

One of many computer dictionaries by C. J. Sippl. Strong on older terms. Skees, William D. *Writing Handbook for Computer Professionals*. Lifetime Learning Publications, 1982.

Skillen, M., R. Gay. *Words into Type*. Prentice-Hall, 1974.

Excellent reference for fine points of grammar, usage, style, and production methods. A classic aid for the copyeditor, well organized, indexed, and formatted.

Slocum, Jonathan, ed. *Machine Translation Systems*. Cambridge University Press, 1988.

Describes the current state of machine translation systems.

Smith, Leila R. *English for Careers: Business, Professional, and Technical*. John Wiley & Sons, 1985.

Smith, Ross. *Learning PostScript: A Visual Approach*. Peachpit Press, 1990.

SoftQuad Inc. *The SGML Primer*. SoftQuad Inc., 1991.

SoftQuad's quick reference guide to the essentials of the standard. Describes SGML needed to read a DTD, documents tagged or marked with SGML, and discuss them.

Souther, James, Myron White. *Technical Report Writing*. John Wiley & Sons, 1984.

Spencer, Donald D. *The Illustrated Computer Dictionary*. Merrill, 1980.

For the novice.

Stanek, William R. *Web Publishing Unleashed: HTML, CGI, SGML, VRML Java*, Sams, 1996.

Stibic, V. *Tools of the Mind: Techniques and Methods for Intellectual Work*. North-Holland, 1982.

Stone, Eric M., Chris Doner. *The WordPerfect Question and Answer Book*. Sybex, Inc., 1989.

An excellent practical book on this software.

Stratton, Charles. *Technical Writing: Process and Product*. Holt, Rinehart, and Winston, 1984.

——. "Anatomy of a Style Analyzer," *Technical Writing and Communication* 19, no. 2 (1989): 119–134.

Compares several style or readability computer tools. Useful.

✓ Strunk, W. E. B. White. *The Elements of Style.* 3rd ed. Macmillan, 1979.

The classic containing advice for the writer of prose. Pleasantly brief. Required reading for any technical writer.

Stuart, A. *The Technical Writer.* Henry Holt, 1988.

Sullivan, Frances J., ed. *Basic Technical Writing.* Society for Technical Communication, Anthology Series No. 7, 1987.

A collection of papers from STC conferences for beginning technical writers.

Sullivan, Patricia. "Visual Markers for Navigating Instructional Texts," *Technical Writing and Communication* 20, no. 3 (1990): 255–267.

Analyzes how people use texts with the visual markers authors place in such texts.

Taylor, John. *The New Physics.* Basic Books, 1972.

Good example of a basic, popular book that covers a complex subject well. Clearly written.

Tevis, Jim J. *Desktop Publishing with WordPerfect 5.0.* John Wiley & Sons, 1989.

Includes document composition and printing exercises you can do with this software.

Thomas, T. A. *Technical Illustration.* McGraw-Hill, 1978.

Thorell, L. G. *Using Computer Color Effectively: An Illustrated Reference.* Prentice-Hall, 1990.

Tinkel, Kathleen. "Dingbats and Doodads," *Personal Publishing,* March 1991, 42–44.

One of many excellent articles on typography by this author, which appear monthly in this magazine.

Tinker, Miles A. "Prolonged Reading Tasks in Visual Search," *Journal of Applied Psychology* 39 (1955): 444–446.

——. *Legibility of Print.* Iowa State University Press, 1963.

——. *Bases for Effective Reading.* University of Minnesota Press, 1965.

Tinker spent his working lifetime testing the factors that influence our ability to read. A useful source for real data on this subject.

Travis, Brian E., Dale C. Waldt. *The SGML Implementation Guide: A Blueprint for SGML Migration.* Springer, 1995.

✓✓ Tufte, Edward R. *The Visual Display of Quantitative Information.* Graphics Press, 1983.

The view of a practitioner who has studied this area in great detail: how to present statistical data effectively; "pictures of numbers."

——— . *Envisioning Information.* Graphics Press, 1990.

Emphasis on the use of color in graphics; includes many interesting anecdotes; "pictures of nouns."

——— . *Visual Explanations.* Graphics Press, 1997. Eminently readable, effectively illustrated, even to little fold-outs to show the 'before' and 'after' of some pictures. Extensive discussion of Challenger data and its presentation; "pictures of verbs," sort of. Excellent discussion of the problems of constructing certain types of charts, and a six-step recommendation on how best to present information, based on the performance of magicians, those experts at disinformation.

Turner, Maxine. *Technical Writing: A Practical Approach.* Reston, 1984.

✓ *U.S. Government Printing Office Style Manual.* Government Printing Office, 1973.

Provides a succinct summary of the practices of the U.S. Government in preparing documents for printing. Includes extensive tables on the transcription of many modern western languages.

van Herwijnen, Eric. *Practical SGML.* Kluwer, 1994.

Programming and implementor focus on how to use SGML. Extensively reviewed in commentaries in the *Journal of Computer Documentation*, May 1996, pp. 40–43.

Venit, Sharyn. "Add Color Impact to PC Publishing," *PC Computing,* December 1990, 114–122.

Useful article on how to cut costs and maintain control of a print job when working with vendors; provides information on spot and process color and on use of a color style sheet.

Venolia, Jan. *Write Right! A Desktop Digest of Punctuation, Grammar, and Style.* Ten Speed/Periwinkle Press, 1988.

Handy, compact. Good for the novice writer.

Walker, Janet H. "The Role of Modularity in Document Authoring Systems," *Proceedings of the ACM Conference on Document Authoring Systems,* December 1988.

———. "Authoring Tools for Complex Document Sets," *The Society of Text*. MIT Press, 1989a.

———. "Hypertext and Technical Writers," *Proceedings of the 36th International Technical Communication Conference,* 1989b.

Lots of information on developing and using an early hypertext system, with the writer's tool Document Examiner, on a Symbolics workstation.

Walton, Thomas F. *Technical Manual Writing and Administration.* McGraw-Hill, 1968.

Warren, Thomas. *Technical Communication: An Outline.* Littlefield, Adams, 1978.

———. *Technical Writing: Purpose, Process, and Form.* Wadsworth, 1985.

Watkins, Floyd C. *Practical English Handbook.* Houghton Mifflin, 1986.

Webster's Collegiate Thesaurus. Merriam-Webster, 1976.

✓✓ *Webster's New Collegiate Dictionary.* Merriam-Webster, 1987.

Webster's New Twentieth Century Dictionary, Unabridged. World, 1970.

Good, but not a true Merriam-Webster dictionary.

✓✓ *Webster's Third New International Dictionary Unabridged.* G. & C. Merriam, 1966.

Weinberg, Bella H., ed. *Indexing: The State of Our Knowledge and the State of Our Ignorance.* Learned Information, 1989.

Weisman, Herman. *Basic Technical Writing.* Merrill, 1985.

———. *Technical Report Writing.* Merrill, 1980.

Abridged version of *Basic Technical Writing.*

Weiss, Edmond. *The Writing System for Engineers and Scientists.* Prentice-Hall, 1982. Good advice for the engineer or scientist who wants to improve writing style and write effectively. States that the greatest single waste of a writer's time and the cause of weak, unclear, ineffective communication is writing without planning.

———. *How to Write a Usable User Manual.* ISI Press, 1985.

———. "Visualizing a Procedure with Nassi-Shneiderman Charts," *Journal of Technical Writing and Communication* 20, no. 3 (1990): 237–254.

Shows how to use N-S decision graphics to verify or correct a written procedure.

Whidden, Samuel B. "T$_E$X: Typesetting for Almost Everybody," *Proceedings of the Digital Equipment Users Society,* December 1984, 287–308.

White, Alex. *How to Spec Type*. Watson-Guptill, 1987.

> For computer typography.

✓ White, Jan V. *Color for the Electronic Age*. Watson-Guptill, 1990.

> Good description with illustrations of the use of color. Contains many examples. Appendices define the standard color systems: Munsell, Pantone, Natural (Swedish color notation), and CIE (Commission Internationale de l'Eclairage or International Commission on Illumination).

—— . *Graphic Design for the Electronic Age, the manual for traditional and desktop publishing.*. Watson-Guptill, 1988.

—— . *Using Charts and Graphs*. R.R. Bowker, 1984.

> Represents many ways to enliven charts and graphs with added embellishments, in direct contrast to Tufte's recommendations to avoid "chart junk."

Wileman, Ralph. *Exercises in Visual Thinking*. Hastings House, 1980.

Williamson, Hugh. *Methods of Book Design*. Yale University Press, 1983.

Winograd, Terry. *Language as a Cognitive Process*. Addison-Wesley, 1983.

> Excellent basic introduction to the fields of both language and cognition.

WordPerfect 5.0 On-Screen Help Book. Geyser Publishing, 1990.

> Both electronic and printed materials, including a reference manual and a command dictionary. Packaged as a "book," but as light as a CDROM.

Wixon, Dennis, Judith Ramey, eds. *Field Methods Casebook for Software Design*. Wiley, 1996.

WordPerfect 5.1 "On-Line Advisor." SYBAR, 1990.

> Includes on-screen software, smart index, flash lookup, and 1400 prelinked references.

Wright, Patricia. "Can Research Assist Technical Communication?" *Proceedings of the International Technical Communications Conference,* May 1989, RT-3-RT-6.

Yankelovich, Nicole, Bernard J. Haan, Norman K. Meyrowitz, Steven M. Drucker. "Intermedia: The Concept and the Construction of a Seamless Information Environment," *Computer,* January 1988, 81–96.

> Clear and factual description of the development and use of this online, multimedia teaching tool.

Yee, C. "Technical and Ethical Professional Preparation for Technical Communication Students," *IEEE Transactions on Professional Communications* 31, no. 4 (December 1988): 191–194.

Zimmerman, Carolyn M., John J. Campbell. *Fundamentals of Procedure Writing*. GP Publications, 1987.

Zimmerman, D. E., D. G. Clark. *The Random House Guide to Technical and Scientific Communication*. Random House, 1987.

Zinsser, William. *Writing with a Word Processor*. Harper & Row, 1983.

———. *On Writing Well: An Informal Guide to Writing Nonfiction*. 3rd ed. Harper & Row, 1990.

Good advice for the nonfiction writer, from how to gather facts and interview people to watching your words.

———. *Writing to Learn: How to Write and Think Clearly about any Subject at All*. Harper & Row, 1989.

Zuboff, Shoshana. *In the Age of the Smart Machine*. Basic Books, 1988.

Describes a new view of the computer, that it both automates and "informates."

Zusne, Leonard. *Visual Perception of Form*. L. Erlbaum, 1970.

Summarizes literature on visual perception. No longer up to date, but a good place to start.

Index

Entries found in tables are indicated with
a "t" after the page number.

firmware, 82
hardware, 82
marketing representative input, 82–83
software, 82
Proficiency, in writing documents, 93
Programmer, writing for, 31–32
Programmer manual, 45
Project, description of, 81–82
Project leader, 17, 20–21, 87, 90
Project team
consulting writer as part of, 15–16
documentation supervisor as part of, 14–15
example of, 14–16
Proofreading, 107
Proportional spacing, 137–138
Prototypes, 78
Proxies, 80
Pull-down menus, 166
Punctuation
apostrophe, 151
backslash, 151–152
braces, 152
brackets, 152
colon, 152–153
comma, 153
dash, 153–154
description of, 150–151
ellipsis, 154
exclamation point, 154–155
hyphen, 155–156
parentheses, 156
period, 156
question mark, 156
quotation marks, 156–157
semicolon, 157
slash, 157
spaces, 157
underlines, 157–158

Q

Quality, elements of
accuracy, 4
appeal of package, 8
appropriate content and scope, 8
clarity, 5–6
completeness, 4
conciseness, 6–7
grammaticality, 7
language appropriateness, 7
logical progression, 6
readability, 6

usability, 5
Quality documentation process
books about, 115–116
elements of, 79–80
planning phase, 87–92
research phase, 80–81
reworking phase
description of, 95
reviewing, 95–96
team work, 100
technical editing, 97–100
testing, 100–106
testing phase, 95
understanding phase
conceptual techniques
brainstorming, 83–84
decomposition, 84
mapping, 86
metaphor, 84–86
modeling, 86
description of, 81–82
writing phase, 92–95
Question mark, 156
Questionnaire, 102
Quick-start guide, 47–48
Quotation marks, 156–157

R

Ragged margin, 135
Railroad diagrams, 159
Raster graphics, 184
Readability, 6
information presentation and, 141–150
tests for
Clear River, 142
Fog index, 142
Read and locate test, 102–103
Readers
classification of, 26
of computer industry, 32t
computer operator, 30
computer software, 27
experienced, 29–30
hardware engineering, 27–28
information presentation based on level of, 140–141
information systems manager, 31
novice, 28–29
programmers, 31–32
system manager/administrator, 30
Reading path diagram, 43
Read-only memory. *See* ROM

Recto page, 161
Redundancy, elimination of, 64
Reference cards, 45, 47
Reference manual
description of, 31–32
organization of, 39
Regressions, 137
Reporting pieces, 2
Reports, sources for preparing, 115
Requirements analysis, 35
Research, in quality documentation process, 80–81
Resolution, 188
Retrieval, of information
classification of, 168
definition of, 167
hardcopy, 168
human-computer interfaces, 170–172
human memory and, 170–171
human sight and, 171–172
hypertext systems, 169
importance of, 167–168
modern systems, 168
softcopy, 168
Review
proofreading, 107
verification, 98
Reviewing, of documents
comments necessary for, 96
description of, 95–96
peer, 96–97
Review meeting, 99
Reworking phase, of quality documentation process
description of, 95
reviewing, 95–96
team work, 100
technical editing, 97–100
testing, 100–106
Robohelp, 101
ROM, 82

S

Saccades, 137
Salary range, 17
Sample application, 93
San serif fonts, 38
Saturated color, 121
Schedule
graphing of, 91
milestone setting, 91

3140